TOM PETERS AND MANAGEMENT

Tom Peters is the management guru's management guru. His is the story that launched a thousand management stories. This new book offers a critical assessment of Tom Peters' contribution to management thought and practice.

The author, a globally recognized expert on management gurus, places Tom Peters at the forefront of the narrative turn in management. Charting and accounting for Tom Peters' contributions to management, the book analyses the practices that Peters has used to shape our appreciation of the business of excellence and in so doing probes and accounts for the preferences of the excellence project.

An accessible and illuminating work, the book will appeal to students and scholars as well as thoughtful managers and leaders.

David Collins is Professor in Management at Newcastle Business School, Northumbria University, UK, and Visiting Professor in Management at the University of the Faroe Islands, Denmark.

Routledge Key Thinkers in Business and Management
Series Editor: **David Collins**, *Northumbria University, UK*

Students of business often emerge from their years of business school training without having had the benefit of seeing how its ideas have evolved. A black hole is developing in management education, and this intellectual vacuum needs to be addressed. The solution is to look at the major intellectual figures in the development of business, management and organisation thinking and practice. In short, who are the makers of modern management? And why should we care?

This series provides authoritative accounts of the key thinkers across the business disciplines. Critical, contextual and comprehensive, books in the series will include figures who've made significant impacts to management thought and practice.

Tom Peters and Management
A History of Organizational Storytelling
David Collins

For more information on this series please visit: www.routledge.com/Key-Thinkers-in-Business-and-Management/book-series/THINKBUS

TOM PETERS AND MANAGEMENT

A History of Organizational Storytelling

David Collins

Routledge
Taylor & Francis Group

LONDON AND NEW YORK

Cover credit: Getty images

First published 2022
by Routledge
2 Park Square, Milton Park, Abingdon, Oxon OX14 4RN

and by Routledge
605 Third Avenue, New York, NY 10158

Routledge is an imprint of the Taylor & Francis Group, an informa business

British Library Cataloguing-in-Publication Data
A catalogue record for this book is available from the British Library

Library of Congress Cataloging-in-Publication Data
Names: Collins, David, 1966- author.
Title: Tom Peters and management : a history of organizational
storytelling / David Collins.
Description: Abingdon, Oxon ; New York, NY : Routledge, 2022. |
Series: Routledge key thinkers in business and management | Includes
bibliographical references and index.
Identifiers: LCCN 2021037679 (print) | LCCN 2021037680 (ebook) |
ISBN 9781032037776 (hardback) | ISBN 9781032037769 (paperback) |
ISBN 9781003188940 (ebook)
Subjects: LCSH: Communication in management—United States. |
Storytelling—United States. | Industrial management—United States. |
Organizational change—United States. | Business consultants—United
States | Peters, Thomas J.
Classification: LCC HD30.3 .C57 2022 (print) | LCC HD30.3 (ebook) |
DDC 658.4/5—dc23
LC record available at https://lccn.loc.gov/2021037679
LC ebook record available at https://lccn.loc.gov/2021037680

ISBN: 978-1-032-03777-6 (hbk)
ISBN: 978-1-032-03776-9 (pbk)
ISBN: 978-1-003-18894-0 (ebk)

DOI: 10.4324/9781003188940

Typeset in Bembo
by codeMantra

Made in Kilmarnock

CONTENTS

About the author   *ix*

Introduction   1

1   The genesis of the excellence project   23

2   The works of Tom Peters, 1982–1985   50

3   The works of Tom Peters, 1987–2018   84

4   An introduction to organizational storytelling   111

5   Types of organizational stories   138

6   Excellence and the management storyteller   162

7   Hierarchy and anxiety in management stories   191

8   Women in management stories   205

9   Concluding comments   223

Bibliography   *231*
Index   *241*

ABOUT THE AUTHOR

David Collins is Professor in Management at Newcastle Business School, Northumbria University and Visiting Professor in management at the University of the Faroe Islands. David holds advanced degrees from the Universities of Glasgow, Strathclyde and Essex.

In an academic career extending over more than 30 years Professor David Collins has published on matters relating to organizational change; management fads and fashions; management consulting; management gurus; organizational storytelling and financial regulation. This is the eighth book that David has produced for Taylor & Francis, Routledge. Previous works include *Organizational Change*; *Management Fads and Buzzwords*; *Narrating the Management Guru*; *Stories for Management Success*; *The Organizational Storytelling Workbook*; *Management Gurus* and most recently *Rethinking Organizational Culture*.

David is British by birth and Scottish by the Grace of God.

INTRODUCTION

Introduction

In 1981 Tom Peters was unemployed. He was that lonely, awkward thing – a middle-aged, furloughed management consultant and the would-be author of a business book that, frankly, no one expected would sell more than a few thousand copies. Just two years later, however, he was famous across Europe and the United States as the leading writer within a new and fast-developing global market now known as 'popular management'.

Since 1982, when Peters, in partnership with Bob Waterman, published *In Search of Excellence* (Peters and Waterman, 1982) the market for 'popular management' has mushroomed. Most of those active in the arena of 'popular management', we should note, have bloomed briefly and have since faded from public consciousness. Tom Peters is therefore distinctive in this arena for at least two reasons. First, his pioneering work on the business of management and his success as an author effectively seeded what is now a billion-dollar market for management knowledge (Collins, 2021a). Commenting on the spectacular growth of this market segment, Kiechel (2010: 156) confirms Peters' position within this industry. Popular management is, he tells us, 'the house that Tom Peters built'. Second, while others have blossomed briefly and have subsequently fallen from public consciousness,[1] Peters has remained prominent in the field of popular management. Indeed, he continues to reap the harvest that he, in the company of a few others, sowed some 40 years ago (see Peters, 2021 for the most recent bounty).

This book has been designed to explore the development of this market for management knowledge and Tom Peters' place within it. Indeed, this book on 'Tom Peters and Management' has been timed to coincide with the 40th anniversary of the publication of text which launched Peters on to the international

DOI: 10.4324/9781003188940-1

stage. But this book is not just about *In Search of Excellence*; it is, in fact, concerned, more broadly, with 'the excellence project' – the 40-year continuing revolution in thinking and practice that Peters has wrought in the fields of business and management.

In this introductory chapter, I will set the scene for this analysis of Tom Peters and the excellence project. As the title of this work suggests this book is, at one level, an account of the manner in which Tom Peters, as the phrase goes, entered and altered the field of management (see Crainer, 1997; Collins, 2007, 2021a) – changing the ways in which we think about management, talk about management and, indeed, act managerially. A key aim of this book is therefore to allow readers to understand the changes demanded by Peters in the name of 'excellence' *and* the ways in which academics, journalists and practitioners of management have attempted to come to terms with these developments.

I recognize, of course, that Peters has many fans who will regard the year 2022 and the anniversary of the publication of *In Search of Excellence* as a very real cause for celebration. While it is difficult to estimate his sales (partly due to the complexities of licensing agreements and, frankly, counterfeiting (see Collins, 2007)) it would not be unreasonable to suggest that Tom Peters has now sold in excess of ten million books. And he has by his own estimation offered presentations to some five million people. More modern indicators of success and persuasion are, we should note, similarly impressive: Peters has in excess of 168,000 followers on *Twitter* and has logged more than 55 million hits on *Google*. I also recognize however that there are many others who would more happily craft a 'death notice' for a text and project that have been attacked as being, variously, flawed and faddish. Typically I stand somewhere between these positions on the excellence project but my approach is, nonetheless, uncompromising: Tom Peters and what became, in hindsight, his excellence project are, I will argue, hugely important. Indeed, I will demonstrate that the impact of the excellence project is both significant and enduring. Furthermore, I will show that Tom Peters and the excellence project which he, with the help of a few others, spawned merits detailed scrutiny. I will leave it to you, however, to decide whether the excellence project deserves a jamboree or a funeral pyre. Yet, no matter what you decide – whether you cheer or complain, I am very clear in my own mind that this is an anniversary that should be observed, if only, because it offers an opportunity (a) to offer an account of (and an education on) the genesis of the 'excellence project' that might (b) provide a timely assessment of its core concerns – its impact and, crucially, its legacy. There are consequently at least two market segments for this book. For those under the age of, say, 40 this book will offer a critical introduction to a time and to a movement that is fast becoming part of what Thompson and McHugh (1990) would describe as management's pre-history.[2] To those born after 1982 therefore I offer this book as a critical, yet reliable, introduction to an author who has become central to the practice of management and to a movement that has altered, quite fundamentally, the manner in which we think about and talk about management.

All of this surely begs the question: If Peters is so central to modern management practice why is this book necessary? The answer is, I suggest, straightforward: While Peters has (re)shaped the very essence of that we which we, too glibly, reduce to 'management', his preferred representation of the business of management is seldom, fully and properly, scrutinized in those materials that have been designed to provide a formal education on the business of management. Thus, my experience suggests that readers of this book, aged under 40, will know very little of the work of Peters. Indeed, my guess is that this (imagined) constituency will not have studied Peters 'in the original' and if they know of his work will have derived this understanding through second-hand summaries that are, typically, very short and, too often, hagiological in nature (Collins, 2000, 2019, 2021a). Recognizing that the work of Tom Peters

- *will* have shaped the education in management offered to those aged under 40
- and *will* have shaped the manner in which this (loose) grouping thinks about managing and, indeed, acts managerially, this book has been designed to provide the resources necessary to allow (these) readers to locate their own managerial practices, within an account of the key ideas that will have shaped their conduct.

To those over the age of, say, 50^3 – to those who may have read (some of[4]) *In Search of Excellence* and who may well have been introduced to the academic critiques ranged against this text in the 1980s, this book offers both 'a refresher' and a balanced appreciation of the manner in which the excellence project has continued to evolve and change since its inception. While recognizing the essential veracity of those critiques that have questioned (a) the conceptualization of 'excellence' and (b) the methodology that Peters employs to gauge business practice, this text will demonstrate that criticisms constructed in conventional academic terms largely misunderstand the excellence project. Indeed, I will argue that *In Search of Excellence* and the excellence project as a whole are largely immune to conventional forms of academic critique. Thus, I will argue that the excellence project does not seek a correspondence with empirical facts and with *the truth*. Rather 'excellence' is to be read and understood as a narrative projection that in portraying business as a noble endeavour, and management as an heroic calling, seeks to connect with more general and enduring romantic *truths*.

I am of course not the first to highlight this. Boltanski and Chiapello (2007) for example suggest that the primary function of 'popular management' is to persuade those who must deliver on its promise that managerial plans for change are necessary, useful and commendable. In a similar fashion Frank [2000] (2002: 192) notes that the role of popular management texts such as *In Search of Excellence* is,

> not to oversee the change [whether this be downsizing, delayering, out-sourcing or disaggregating] but to legitimize it, to explain why the new "marketized" corporate form [is] in fact, the ideal productive model, the source of efficiency as well as democracy.

Yet I am perhaps the first to locate this appreciation of the excellence project within an empirical analysis of the tools that it has used to advance and to substantiate its core concerns.

In this text I will demonstrate that 'excellence', is a project which calls on the arts of the storyteller to secure its meanings and effects. Furthermore, I will show that we may build on an empirical analysis of Peters' stories and, indeed, his storytelling practice (a) to explore and (b) to reconsider the enduring and underlying priorities that (c) bring shape and meaning to the excellence project. To this end the book as a whole is structured as follows:

In Chapter 1 I will offer an account of the genesis of the excellence project. Textbooks on management generally agree that *In Search of Excellence* builds on what has come to be known as 'The McKinsey 7-S Framework' (which is often reduced to, either, 'the 7-S framework' or, less often, 'the happy atom'). This framework, as we will learn, was developed in the early 1980s and in suggesting that business is built around 'seven hunks of complexity' (Peters and Waterman, 1982: 11) was designed to demonstrate that successful managerial practice depends on securing a balance between the human, or 'soft-s' elements of business and the 'hard-s' factors such as 'strategy' and 'systems'. Most textbooks prepared for students of management observe that in considering the balance between these 'soft' and 'hard' factors, Peters and Waterman argued that their 'excellent' organizations demonstrated eight common attributes, which set them apart from their less successful counterparts and competitors. Yet few textbooks linger over these developments. In Chapter 1, I will remedy this. I will consider the circumstances that brought a key artefact of the excellence project – the 7-S framework – to public notice and in so doing, will take my cue from Bruno Latour (1987).

Ready-made science *versus* science-in-the-making

Latour (1987) complains that the 'lay appreciation' of science is based on a 'ready-made' narrative. This 'ready-made' narrative, he warns us, offers an account of scientific endeavour that is constructed *after* all the controversies have been resolved. In this respect the ready-made narrative of science is a cold dish, served long after the heat has gone out of the debate. Recognizing the manner in which this 'ready-made' appreciation of science limits our understanding of human endeavours, I will offer an account of 'science-in-action' designed to reveal and to explore the controversies that shaped the 'McKinsey 7-S framework'. While reflecting on the development of this framework I will contrast *In Search of Excellence* with a notable contemporary account – *The Art of Japanese Management* (Pascale and Athos, [1981] 1986) which, as we shall see, actually showcased the McKinsey 7-S model. Comparing these texts, and the commercial success enjoyed by Peters, (if not Waterman[5]) in the light of the more modest performance of *The Art of Japanese Management*, I will offer reflections on the relative fortunes of these analyses of the business of management. While rationalizing the success of Peters and Waterman I will, nonetheless, suggest that, in the 1980s, the field of 'management' had a choice to make and selected *In Search of Excellence* as its core guide to the business of management. Yet I will argue that in so doing the field took a wrong turn. Indeed, I will suggest that the fork taken has, for a generation denied, us the opportunity to secure an approach to management, which while based within a market economy, might have been founded on a genuinely reciprocal policy of social enterprise.

In Chapters 2 and 3 I will offer a critical analysis and review of *In Search of Excellence* and of the key works that Tom Peters has published since 1982. Chapter 2 will focus on *In Search of Excellence* and *A Passion for Excellence* (Peters and Austin, 1985) while Chapter 3 will offer an account of the remaining, key texts published between 1987 and 2018.

In other contributions to this debate I have suggested that we may group Tom Peters' works according to their underlying narrative structure (see Collins, 2007). In Chapters 2 and 3, however, I will offer a more conventional, chronological, analysis designed to allow readers (whatever their birth date) to form an appreciation, if you will allow a slightly paradoxical suggestion, of the dynamic stabilities in Peters' work.

In Chapter 4 we will consider core debates on organizational storytelling. In addition I will offer an account of the methodology that underpins the analyses offered in Chapters 5–8. Many practitioners of management, thanks in part to the activities of Tom Peters, will now vouchsafe that management is, at root, a communication process rooted in and dependent on the persuasive arts of the storyteller. And this claim is, of course, broadly truthful. Yet this bald assertion, while accurate at root, remains problematic because it fails to acknowledge (a) the continuing debate as to the essential nature of stories and (b) the efficacy of those approaches, which simply assume that storytelling offers managers a genuinely reliable means of animating and orientating others within organized contexts. In Chapter 4, I will consider these debates while calling on a rich array of narrative and storytelling resources. I will acknowledge that Tom Peters *has* genuinely changed the manner in which we conceptualize the work of 'management', yet I will focus particularly on the contests associated with

- sensemaking and sensegiving,
- narrative and ante-narrative perspectives and
- elaborate stories and terse tales.

I will argue that these (often unacknowledged debates) oblige us to qualify the untested and now commonly held conviction that 'management' is *simply and reliably* a communication process rooted within storytelling.

In Chapters 5–8 I will build on the knowledge of the excellence project (developed in Chapters 1–3) and on our new appreciation of the debates that shape storytelling within an organized context to offer a 're-view' of Peters' core approach and key concerns. Chapter 5, as we shall, see builds on and yet updates an earlier analysis timed to coincide with the 25th anniversary of the excellence project (Collins, 2007, 2008). Chapter 5 will therefore offer an account of Peters' changing storytelling practices and will consider the extent to which Peters' preference for the epic story-form actually facilitates his project.

In Chapter 6, I will consider the key characters featured in Peters' storyworld. Tom Peters' heroes, as we shall see, have changed over time. Yet, as we will learn, the heroics of the excellence project remain largely unchanged. While mapping these heroes and their heroics, this chapter will also observe a shift in Peters' place within the storyworld. Noting the author's transformation from 'narrator' to 'hero', from *guide on the side* to *sage on the stage*, I will argue that Peters' narratives – at least in their written form – often lack the seductive qualities necessary to win converts to his credo.

In Chapter 7 I will offer reflections on Tom Peters' storyworld, which builds on the work of Martin et al. (1983). The work of Martin and her colleagues, as we shall see, was developed around the same time as *In Search of Excellence* and, like the excellence project, focuses on organizational storytelling. Yet, despite these overlaps, Martin and her colleagues essay an approach to storytelling that is quite different to that preferred by Peters. Thus, Martin et al. explore an enduring organizational paradox which may be rendered as follows: Typically, organizations proclaim their uniqueness in cultural terms. Yet when organizational members are invited to justify such claims to uniqueness they tend to render tales of management and organization that are remarkably similar.

Accounting for this paradoxical outcome, Martin and her colleagues assure us that the stories commonly rendered across a range of contexts are developed and maintained within organized settings because they express and account for the enduring anxieties that shape the experience of paid employment. Reviewing Peters' texts in the light of this observation I will argue that his storyworld lacks authenticity insofar as it offers a top-down projection of the world that simply fails to concede the presence of those enduring anxieties, which in being directly associated with the experience of paid employment, shape the storyworld at the bottom of the organizational pyramid. Chapter 8 in contrast will consider the presence/absence of women in the excellence project. I will argue that women are under-represented and under-valued in Tom Peters' storyworld and, despite a very public epiphany, are seldom granted full organizational membership within his accounts of the business of management.

It may be useful to observe that I had planned, initially, to include a chapter offering critical reflections on Peters' seminar performances and on the manner in which Peters uses tales of organizational life within such contexts (a) to substantiate his concerns and (b) to maintain the affiliation of the audience present. I regret that due to limitations of space I have been unable to fulfil this plan. I regret this omission I hasten to add because I accept that any account of the work of Tom Peters that reduces his contribution to 'management' to a consideration of written, textual sources alone is in some sense limiting. Yet having offered this concession I will take this opportunity to remind readers that I have written on this topic only recently *and at length* (see Collins, 2018, 2021a). And since, I have little further to add to the discussion at this point in time, and no space here to rehearse my core concerns, I will politely suggest that those keen to learn more about the performance artistry of Tom Peters might consult my most recent contribution to this debate *Management Gurus: A Research Overview* (Collins, 2021a). This account of Peters is, I will add, distinctive insofar as it offers (a) critical reflections on the extant academic literature within this arena while (b) exploring the similarities evident between Tom Peters' performances and those offered in the context of stand-up comedy!

In our final chapter, Chapter 9, I will build on the critical 're-view' developed throughout this text to offer reflections on the legacy of Tom Peters. While conceding that Peters has genuinely altered the manner in which we think about management, talk about management and act managerially I will, nonetheless, suggest that the impact of Peters' preferred approach and credo is undone by two key limitations, these being first the failure to promote a genuinely social policy of enterprise and second the tendency to render tales of managerial endeavour that lack an authentic connection with the lives and concerns of key organizational stakeholders. But before we get to all of this it will be useful, now, to introduce our subject: Mr Tom Peters.

Introducing Tom Peters

Tom Peters – the man feted world-wide as a, if not *the*, guru of management (see Collins, 2007, 2021a) – was born in Baltimore in 1942. Despite being 'let go', by McKinsey and Co., Peters was, by his forty-third birthday, publicly acknowledged (and celebrated) as, both, a key commentator on 'management' *and* a powerful orator on the contemporary problems of business. Indeed, by the mid-1980s Peters was, to his surprise and, indeed, to the surprise of his publisher, a best-selling author who spent the bulk of each year 'on tour', spreading his distinctive gospel of management on the international lecture circuit that has grown up to educate and to edify managers. When not travelling the world to spread his message Peters, at this point in his life, tended to divide his time between a home in Palo Alto (a legacy of his former employment within the San Francisco office of McKinsey and Co.) and his, 1,600 acre farm in rural Vermont. This farm we would do well to note was purchased with the proceeds of *In Search of Excellence,* which had in the year of its first publication out-sold every other text bar one, that text being a new edition of the Bible.[6] Commenting on the (surprising) success of this text, Kiechel (2010: 147) reminds us that while Bob Waterman had negotiated a very lucrative furlough settlement for his colleague, which afforded Peters the time and space to craft the first draft of *In Search of Excellence,* he himself had no contractual entitlement to the royalties that would flow from this text. Indeed, Kiechel observes adds that McKinsey did little to acknowledge Waterman's role in the birth of the excellence project and, what is worse, did nothing to sustain his commitment to the firm: 'when *Bantam* approached [Bob Waterman] with a lucrative deal for a second or third book and

McKinsey replied, in his words "it all belongs to us," he felt he had to leave the firm' after 21 years of faithful service.

During the last two decades Peters has altered his working practices a little. He has reduced his time on the road (or perhaps more accurately 'in the air') for business and has become a regular visitor to New Zealand, retreating there to escape the harsh winters of the northeastern United States. Peters now holds an adjunct faculty position with the University of Auckland's Business School. Indeed, his most recent major work (Peters, 2018) was developed on the back of the modest teaching commitment that he now fulfils as a condition of his appointment. When in America, Peters and his wife now divide their home-life between their farm in Vermont and an island retreat off the coast of Massachusetts.

Peters has built his career as management guru by lambasting corporations for their (over)dependence on 'hard data' and for the litany of sins consequent on conglomerate ownership and committee decision-making. Given this, his academic and intellectual background may come as a surprise: Peters holds two engineering degrees from Cornell University (BCE, MCE) and two business degrees from Stanford University (MBA, PhD). In addition he holds a number of honorary degrees including a doctorate from the State University of Management in Moscow, which was awarded in 2004. Yet despite this academic pedigree Peters, remains sceptical as regards the relevance and capacity of formal educational qualifications – in the managerial field at least. For example he routinely protests that the internationally recognized qualification in management which has been designed to prepare participants for 'executive' and 'leadership' positions – the master of business administration qualification – should be redesigned as the Master of Business Arts.[7]

In *Re-imagine* (Peters, 2003) Peters offers us a concrete illustration of (a) his misgivings about the nature of management education and (b) his frustrations as regards the conduct of corporate America. He reports that in 2002 he tried (and failed) to return his Stanford MBA following the scandal, which surrounded Enron's collapse. Peters took the decision to return his degree, he tells us, after he had watched Robert Jaedicke – an Enron Board member and chair of the Board's Audit Committee – insist, in a live television broadcast, that he knew nothing of the peculiar transactions and accounting methods that ruined this company (and the pensions of many employees). Explaining his, apparently, extreme reaction to Jaedicke's protestations of innocence Peters observes that, 30 years previously, this man had been the Professor on the 'Advanced Accounting' within his MBA curriculum:

> When a guy who served as Enron's *audit* boss ... the last bastion of bean counting ... invokes the "Clueless" defense, it makes you wonder: Did he have any clue as to the usefulness of the curriculum at the school where he'd been dean? Did he have any clue as to what lessons I'd extract from his "advanced" accounting course?
>
> *Peters (2003: 8 emphasis and ellipses in original)*

Thankfully Peters' knowledge of work, management and, indeed, 'advanced accounting' is not, solely, derived from the tuition he received at Stanford University. Between 1966 and 1970, for example, his knowledge of organized systems was broadened and deepened by his service in the US Navy (see Peters, 2003, 2018). During this time in the navy, Peters made two active service deployments to Vietnam where he served with the Navy's construction battalion (commonly known as the Seabees). In addition Peters spent some time on secondment with Britain's Royal Navy. Pointing to a sense of humour that is not always readily apparent in his early written work this, former sailor, points out that that during his Navy career he also survived a gruelling tour of duty in the Pentagon.

Following his service in the Navy, Peters worked for the consulting firm Peat Marwick Mitchell in its Washington office (Blackhurst, 2003). Following a brief sojourn with this company, Peters took up a post in the White House as a senior drug-abuse advisor. In 1974, however, he left the White House to join the, now, famous consultancy firm McKinsey and Company. Between 1974 and 1976 Peters worked on a variety of consulting projects for this firm. However, his career with McKinsey was interrupted in January 1976 when a kidney complaint forced him to take an extended period of sick leave. During this period of, enforced, absence from work Peters completed the PhD thesis which he had begun while studying for his MBA at Stanford University. This thesis, he tells us, was the first to focus on strategic implementation and in this regard may be considered to be, perhaps, the first stirrings of the discontent that would become the excellence project.

Having completed his, previously, stalled programme of research Peters returned to McKinsey and Company in early 1977 and was made a partner of the company in that same year. During this second period with 'the firm' Peters began work on a project, which in 1982 would propel him to more-or-less instant and, certainly, lasting fame. This programme of work, whose genesis and orientations we will examine in more detail in the chapter that follows, was designed to explore 'organizational effectiveness'.

Peters it seems enjoyed this 18-month assignment but he was becoming increasingly unsettled at McKinsey and Co. In 1981, armed with a modest, advance payment of $5,000 from his publishers, he resigned from McKinsey and settled down to write up the findings of the research that he, with others, had been developing into 'organizational effectiveness'.

Thanks to his senior colleague at McKinsey and Co., Bob Waterman, Peters was granted a severance package of $50,000 from his employer on the understanding that the firm would receive 50% of any royalties on his first 50,000 book sales. This was, frankly, a generous settlement. Given the, then, reading habits of the general public, both, author (Peters only later invited Bob Waterman to become his co-author as he struggled to develop a lucid and compact account of business effectiveness) and publisher were sanguine about the potential of this book. Crainer (1997) for example notes that the publishers estimated that the book which became *In Search of Excellence* might sell somewhere between

10,000 and 20,000 copies nation-wide, and so, commissioned an initial print run of 15,000 books for the US market. Peters (2018: 62) it is worth noting has a different recollection: 'the publisher had low expectations, and the first print run was a meagre five thousand'. This dispute as to the initial print-run, of course, matters little today because to the surprise of all concerned, *In Search of Excellence* quickly became a best seller in the United States. Indeed, in April 1983 this text became the first (non-biographical) book, directly, concerned with the nature and processes of managing to top the prestigious *New York Times* best seller list. Furthermore, it remained atop this list for two years until it was toppled by Peters' next book entitled *A Passion for Excellence* (Peters and Austin, 1985).

It would not be an exaggeration to suggest that *In Search of Excellence* defined and created a new market segment for the publishing industry (Collins, 2021a). The book was, and remains, a world-wide phenomenon. Despite focusing on American companies and on the American economy the book has achieved mass sales in Britain, in Continental Europe and in the Far East (see Lorenz, 1986a; Huczynski, 1993). Indeed, Crainer (1997) reports that when Tom Peters travelled to China, for the first time, in 1988 he was greeted by five publishers each of whom had produced best-selling (and unlicensed!) *ersatz* Chinese editions of *In Search of Excellence!*

Tom Peters has now produced 19 books on management (see Figure I.1). In addition he has written many articles for the popular business press. Indeed, for a time he produced a regular newspaper column that was widely syndicated. Furthermore, he has, as we shall see, inspired many, many more academic and journalistic analyses of his contribution to the business of management.

When not engaged in these writing projects, Peters is often to be found on stage and/or in company boardrooms offering presentations on his core philosophy and current concerns. His consulting/touring schedule is altogether less frenetic now than in the early years of his guru career. Nonetheless, he is, and has for many years been, one of the most highly paid speakers on this very lucrative lecture circuit. Describing his own pricing strategy he offers an insight into the humour that has become a hallmark of his seminars. Thus, he confides that his pricing strategy is really quite simple. He tells us that he endeavours to ascertain what Nobel Prize winner Henry Kissinger (perhaps the leading figure on the international seminar circuit) is currently charging and comes in at a price just below this rate of exchange.

And how much does he charge? Quoting an off-the-record yet, nonetheless, reliable source, Collins (2007) observes that in the early noughties Peters could command a fee of $85,000 for a one hour speech. Recent off-the-record discussions with a similarly reliable source, however, suggest that Peters now demands $101,000 for a similar engagement. This 16% price rise, in the light of the global financial crisis of 2008 and the austerity measures that have gripped so many of us since that date, suggests that the guru business – or at least that segment occupied by Peters – may be pretty much recession-proof!

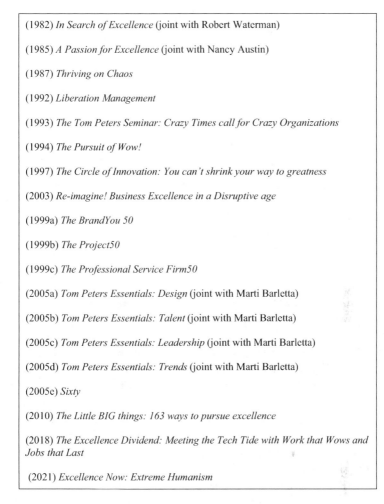

(1982) *In Search of Excellence* (joint with Robert Waterman)

(1985) *A Passion for Excellence* (joint with Nancy Austin)

(1987) *Thriving on Chaos*

(1992) *Liberation Management*

(1993) *The Tom Peters Seminar: Crazy Times call for Crazy Organizations*

(1994) *The Pursuit of Wow!*

(1997) *The Circle of Innovation: You can't shrink your way to greatness*

(2003) *Re-imagine! Business Excellence in a Disruptive age*

(1999a) *The BrandYou 50*

(1999b) *The Project50*

(1999c) *The Professional Service Firm50*

(2005a) *Tom Peters Essentials: Design* (joint with Marti Barletta)

(2005b) *Tom Peters Essentials: Talent* (joint with Marti Barletta)

(2005c) *Tom Peters Essentials: Leadership* (joint with Marti Barletta)

(2005d) *Tom Peters Essentials: Trends* (joint with Marti Barletta)

(2005e) *Sixty*

(2010) *The Little BIG things: 163 ways to pursue excellence*

(2018) *The Excellence Dividend: Meeting the Tech Tide with Work that Wows and Jobs that Last*

(2021) *Excellence Now: Extreme Humanism*

FIGURE I.1 A catalogue of Tom Peters' books on management.

Peters' reputation within the field of management and his notoriety within the popular press has led to the production of three 'professional biographies'. I call these texts 'professional biographies' because they are focused, almost exclusively, on matters that relate, narrowly, to his working life. Accordingly, Tom Peters' private life remains for the most part, just that. Consequently those elements of Peters' life, which may have had an important impact on his work as a writer and commentator – his early days, his three marriages, his time in therapy (Durman, 1997) – remain, for the most part, beyond the purview of the biographers of his career, this one included!

The first of these 'professional biographies' was penned by the British business journalist Stuart Crainer (1997) who, for a time, was a part of a team retained to conduct research and to write field-reports on behalf of Tom Peters. Crainer's often insightful text offers a useful account of the genesis of the excellence project and interesting reflections on the birth of the modern guru that is Tom Peters. Importantly this work also provides occasional glimpses of Peters' complex character.

The second 'professional biography' written some three years later by the British journalist, and founding editor of the journal *Management Today,* Robert Heller (2000) is, for our current purpose, altogether less satisfactory. Reading Crainer's biography of Peters one senses in the author a frustration. I have read this work on numerous occasions and genuinely enjoy the text. Yet I sense that the author was slightly disappointed with his book. It seems to me that, despite Crainer's attempts to find out something about the man behind the myth, the subject of this professional biography chose to remain aloof throughout the production of the text and co-operated with his former employee only to a very limited degree. Consequently Tom Peters appears as a complex, yet elusive and somewhat enigmatic presence throughout what is, actually, a fairly lengthy book (see also Postrel, 1997). When I read Heller's account of Tom Peters I am, likewise, struck by a sense of frustration. Yet in this case the frustration is mine alone. Heller's text is we should note shorter and is, altogether, less substantial than that produced by Crainer. Yet there is nothing in this work to suggest that Heller is less than completely content with a text, which tends to lack, both, critical intent and insight.

The third of the three professional biographies alluded to above was produced by Collins (2007) and was timed to coincide with the 25th anniversary of the publication of *In Search of Excellence* (Peters and Waterman, 1982). The text written by Collins offers an account of Peters' career and critical reflections on the major works produced by this author up to and including the year 2003. The book which you now hold in your hands updates, revises and extends this earlier work. Thus, the contribution to the 'history of organizational storytelling' developed here considers the works published since 2003 (Peters, 2010, 2018) and adds to the earlier analysis (a) sustained, critical reflection on the genesis of the excellence project (b) a consideration of the authenticity of Peters' storyworld and (c) reflections on the place of women within this canon.

It is perhaps worth noting, too, that this book departs from the work produced in 2007 insofar as it offers – meekly and genuinely – an apology. In *Narrating the Management Guru* (Collins, 2007) I offered an account of Tom Peters that was, to be honest, strident and forceful to the very point of rudeness. Despite this and in subsequent exchanges – face-to-face, via e-mail and/or on *Twitter* – Tom Peters has been unfailingly polite. Doubtless Peters will suggest that, together, we owe our experience to his upbringing and to the wise counsel of his mother. Given the tales of Peters' mother that pepper especially his later works, there is every reason to suspect that this is an accurate supposition (see Peters, 2010, 2018). Some years on from my discussion of the excellence project in its silver jubilee year I now realize that I might have done better to reflect on my own mother and on my own upbringing even as I took cheap shots at Peters. In the light of this self-reflection, I hope that this text, and these introductory remarks, will be read (and accepted) as an overdue apology. That said, I must point out that I do continue to believe that my earlier analyses of the work(s) of Tom Peters remain, substantially, correct. I do, however, regret those elements of my analyses that more even-handed commentators would understand to be, strident up to *and beyond* the point of rudeness. In this text, therefore, while offering a re-view and reappraisal of the excellence project that is 'critical', I will work to moderate my expression. While maintaining the energy and the plain speech that I do believe recommends my work to the reader (see Gabriel, 2008 for a review), I will endeavour to keep things 'sporting'[8] (see Collins, 2021b). Yet before we proceed to this analysis of Peters' works, it will be useful to pause in order to consider what I will term 'the guru question'.

Is Tom Peters a guru?

In earlier works (see for example Collins, 2007, 2019, 2021a) I have suggested that Peters should be considered to be not just 'a guru' but *the* guru of management. Indeed, I have suggested that Tom Peters should be considered to be the prototype that became the archetype of the modern management guru. Yet unlike those who have developed hagiological accounts of popular management (see Collins, 2000, 2019, 2021a) I remain mindful of the origins of the term 'guru' and have, consequently, chosen to deploy this term in a manner which invites more careful reflection on what it is that management's gurus would do in our name.

What's in a name?

Tom Peters has been labelled as a guru of management, as the uber-guru of management, as the Ur-guru of management and (of course) as *the* guru of management.[9] Many of the commentators who use this terminology to applaud Tom Peters have suggested that the gurus of management are very special individuals. They are, we are assured, quite unlike lesser commentators in the field of management insofar as they generate ideas and tools that are novel and which offer enduring benefits to organizations. In earlier works (Collins, 2000, 2019, 2021a), however, I have suggested that these claims simply do not bear close scrutiny. Organizations, I have argued, are simply too complex – too pluralistic to allow us to assert that any particular change programme, or innovation, will carry benefit for *the organization* as a whole. For example it is plain that the radical downsizing associated with 'business process reengineering' (Hammer, 1990) placed costs on some components of 'the organization' even while it allowed others to maximize their bonuses and stock options! In addition we should note that innovations such as 'business process reengineering' tend to impose costs on the communities that host those organizations downsized in the name of reengineering (Collins, 2000). We may therefore reject the suggestion that *the* gurus are special because they offer unalloyed benefits to organizations!

Grint (1994) has also considered the merits of the term 'guru'. He offers a simple rebuttal to the suggestion that the gurus generate novel ideas and solutions. Indeed, Grint suggests that the ideas conveyed within popular management texts secure, however fleetingly, a market presence *precisely because they lack novelty.*

I have by my own admission often treated Tom Peters harshly. Indeed, I have suggested that *In Search of Excellence* is a deeply flawed piece of writing (see Collins, 2000[10]). Yet I continue to insist that the term 'guru' is useful in this context. My willingness to acknowledge Peters as a guru is, however, forged within a context which recognizes that there are some, prominent within the field of management studies who continue to doubt his contribution to 'management'. Hindle (2008) notes, for example, that in 2003 *Harvard Business Review* conducted a survey which invited a number of key business thinkers to nominate the leading gurus of management. Peter Drucker, he notes, came first in this listing with James March second. Tom Peters, however, featured not at all!

Yet for every account that would exclude Peters from 'the pantheon' there is at least one alternative source that would place this individual comfortably among a small A-list grouping. Collins (2007) for example notes that the publisher *Bloomsbury* named *In Search of Excellence* the best business book *of all time!* In addition Peters (2018: 30) draws our attention to an additional source that while it does not, quite, place this individual at the summit of Mount Olympus does suggest that the excellence project remains a very important innovation that has had a broad and enduring influence on the business of management. Thus, Peters observes,

> In 1999, a book was published by AMACOM, titled *The 75 Greatest Management Decisions Ever Made,* featuring Julius Caesar, Ted Turner, Henry Ford, Warren Buffett, and others of their ilk. Number forty-eight on the list, to my astonishment. Was the spur-of-the-moment decision by John Larson to ask me to give a presentation to Dart Industries on Good Friday 1978.

We will return to this very important Friday in our next chapter as we consider the genesis of the excellence project. For the moment, however, we must continue to explore 'the guru question' for it is clear that despite the endorsements noted above, many of my contemporaries do continue to dispute the utility of the guru label.

Should we love our gurus?

Jackson and Carter (1998) suggest that anyone with a developed appreciation of etymology *should* choose to oppose the application of the term 'guru' within the field of business and management. They observe:

> The word "guru" means a spiritual leader, and it derives from the Sanskrit word for venerable. "Venerable" means worthy of worship, and its Latin origins are connected with Venus, the goddess of love: we should worship our gurus as fountains of love for us.
>
> *Jackson and Carter (1998: 153–154)*

Pio (2007: 184) offers a similar analysis. She notes,

> The Sanskrit word *guru* is derived from *gu,* meaning darkness, and *ru,* meaning light or the removal of the darkness of ignorance through enlightenment. The guru is expected to live up to what he or she preaches. The guru is also seen as the bridge between the individual and god and a channel for divine grace.

Plainly the spiritual origin of the term 'guru' presents difficulties for Jackson and Carter. Indeed, they simply refuse to countenance the suggestion that those who have, in recent years, acted to reshape the business of management actually spread enlightenment, and so, deserve our veneration. Pattison (1997) recognizes the power of this sentiment. Yet he suggests that the term 'management guru' has utility in this context because it offers insights into the ways in which these actors secure and solidify their representations of the world. Thus, Pattison argues that the label – management guru – might be retained even by archly critical scholars because it highlights the manner in which those commentators who form the leading edge of popular management are able to shape how we think, feel and act. Expanding on this point, Pattison suggests that the gurus of management acquire and sustain followers in a fashion that is similar to that commonly employed by religious leaders and scholars. Thus, he argues that gurus (secular and otherwise) act to threaten our sense of self and in so doing promise to provide – if not redemption – then at least a release from our more pressing problems and dilemmas (see also Jackson, 1996, 2004). Offering a concrete example of this more general process, Pattison suggests that Tom Peters' second work, produced in concert with Nancy Austin (Peters and Austin, 1985) amounts to a secular re-telling of the story of Noah and the flood and, like this biblical tale, promises salvation to those who are prepared to embrace what we might now term *the rapture of business excellence.*

Greatbatch and Clark (2005), however, dispute the suggestion that the leading edge of 'popular management' is actually populated by individuals who deserve to be known as 'gurus'. They do concede of course that the guru label enjoys common currency and has been deployed within academia to focus attention on the representations that 'gurus' use to substantiate their core concerns. And yet they insist that the label is inappropriate in this context. In an attempt to substantiate this complaint[11] they insist that there is, in fact, no evidence to suggest that those who read guru texts, or who listen to what these individuals have to say about the business of management, actually undergo a conversion experience.

Yet we must wonder what it is that Greatbatch and Clark (2005) actually expect of *the* gurus! To suggest, for example, that practitioners of management have simply failed 'to convert' to the philosophies of management's gurus is surely to overlook the extent to which managers and politicians of all hues do, now, think and speak about 'culture change', 'customers', 'quality', 'TQM' and 'BPR'! Indeed, the fact that so many managers now speak of their work in terms of narratives, symbolism and storytelling is largely down to the influence exerted by Peters and just a few others (see for example Deal and Kennedy, 1982; Kanter, 1989). But these facts do not seem to be enough for Greatbatch and Clark (2005). Indeed, it would appear that the authors are willing to acknowledge as gurus only those who could pass 'the Kool-Aid test'.

The Kool-Aid test

In the 1970s the Reverend James Jones and around 1,000 followers established a utopian commune in a settlement named, modestly enough, Jonestown in the Guyanese jungle. In 1978 a delegation of five individuals led by US Congressman Leo Ryan travelled to the commune to investigate claims of abuse. The members of this delegation were murdered, however, on November 18, 1978. In the aftermath of this crime Jones, flanked by armed guards, ordered his congregation to consume *Kool-Aid* that had been laced with cyanide and sedatives. Most did as they were instructed. Nine hundred died.

Reviewing the appeal and legacy of those dubbed management's gurus, Greatbatch and Clark (2005), as we have seen, complain that these individuals simply do not deserve this accolade. Management gurus, they assert, are unworthy of the term because they have failed to manufacture converts to their cause. We have already suggested that, the gurus of management (with Peters prominent in this loose collective) have genuinely *converted* the corporate world to a new (albeit loose) credo that is built around a commitment to, customers, culture and change that depends on symbolism and storytelling. But do we need really to find evidence of zealous converts fired with new managerial passions in order to apply the term guru in this context?

To portray Peters as a guru is it, truly, necessary to assume that his followers would, as the phrase has it, 'drink the Kool-Aid'?

The Scots journalist Kenneth Roy (2013) offers us useful guidance on the nature of the religious conversion and renewal experience. Roy's reflections, as we shall see, suggest that Greatbatch and Clark simply expect too much of management's gurus.

Reflecting on Billy Graham's evangelical mission to Scotland in the mid-1950s, Roy (2013: 180) readily affirms his subject's oratorical and persuasive powers: two-and-a-half million people (one half of Scotland's population), he tells us, attended Graham's events in Glasgow or watched the proceedings on relayed broadcasts. Yet despite this quite staggering level of engagement, Roy notes the general absence of converts moved to a new life in Christ. Indeed, Roy notes that, despite Graham's Scottish mission of 1955, and despite a subsequent visit in the late 1980s, membership of the Church of Scotland has continued to decline from its mid-1950s peak of 37% of the adult Scottish population to its present-day standing of less than 9%. Furthermore, Roy observes that the reaction of Scotland's 500,000 Roman Catholics to Graham's mission of 1955 (and to subsequent visitations) was 'negligible'.

Given Scotland's experience of Graham's evangelism and given that Peters' interventions *have* truly changed the manner in which we conceive of management as a social practice it seems sensible to suggest that, in opposing the guru label, Greatbatch and Clark (2005) actually

* *misrepresent* the reach and appeal of management's gurus and in so doing
* *misunderstand* the nature of religious evangelism.

In short, the opposition of Greatbatch and Clark (2005) to the guru label seems to be based on an abstract and idealized account of the religious conversion experience. And this benchmark, we should note, sets the bar too high – even for Billy Graham!

I submit therefore that while Peters would plainly (and thankfully) flunk 'the Kool-Aid test', any analysis of his texts and any well-grounded analysis of his *modus operandi* (see Collins, 2021a[12]) demonstrates the utility of the guru labelling device insofar as it reminds us that Peters, *the* guru of management trades in *fear* and *hope* as he works to secure converts (*yes* converts) to his agenda for change.

My position on Peters' status as a/*the* guru of management therefore resolves in opposition to that suggested by Greatbatch and Clark (2005). Thus, I suggest that most mature and sensible commentators would concede that Peters (in the company of a few others) has changed quite fundamentally the manner in which we think about management, talk about management and act managerially. Indeed, I am prepared to concede the existence of a small A-list of managerial commentators who have (a) enjoyed popular acclaim and (b) volume sales because they have, (c) through writing and public speaking (d) constructed an account of the business of management that (e) threatens and redeems managerial identities. The contents of this A-list will vary geographically and, I suspect, with your date of birth (see Collins, 2021a). Nonetheless, it seems sensible to suggest that Tom Peters (despite the misgivings of Greatbatch and Clark and despite the prejudices of those who read the *Harvard Business Review*) would make the list. And beyond this observation, frankly, I have no real or sustained interest in debating who is and who is not 'a guru'. Nor do I wish to debate which individuals would occupy a 'top 10', 'top 50' or even a 'top 100' collection of gurus. Such activity is to my mind a toxic distraction – a form of *listeria* if you will. Yet we do not need to conclude our discussion on this downbeat because Huczynski's (1993) account of 'guru theory' offers crucial insights on the nature and appeal of popular management.

Guru theory

Huczynski (1993) observes that managers have been able to purchase books designed to revolutionize the practice of management since at least the 1900s. Nevertheless, Huczynski reminds us that the growth of a mass market in 'popular management', and the related rise of management's gurus are very much products of the 1980s. Yet unlike others who have sought to personify the gurus of management (see Collins, 2021a), Huczynski warns us against any attempt to reduce *the* gurus to a compact or regimented collective. Indeed, he argues that when we make reference to *the* gurus we are actually highlighting the existence of a diverse grouping and the presence of a rather loose bundle of ideas. Nonetheless, Huczynski does suggest that those who have been labelled as management's gurus tend to belong to one of three broad classes of commentator, these being the academic guru, the consultant guru and the hero-manager. Reflecting on the ways in which these classes of individuals derive their authority and appeal, Huczynski argues that the academic and consultant gurus tend to highlight their education and training whereas the hero-managers trade more on their experience. Suddaby and Greenwood (2001), however, question this categorization. They suggest that this categorization fails to capture the complexity of the CVs which these actors possess. At one level, of course, this is fair criticism. Tom Peters, who remains, I insist, among the leading 'consultant gurus' holds advanced degrees in civil engineering and in management. He is, consequently, *at least* as qualified as his academic counterparts. Likewise the modern executives who run our corporations and who are, from time-to-time, celebrated as 'hero-managers' are, thanks to a revolution in management education (see for example Khurana, 2007), often qualified to a very high standard nowadays. Yet, despite this Huczynski is, I believe, correct in his assertion that the gurus tend to speak in different registers. Thus, the consultant and academic gurus *do* generally play on their training, whereas the 'hero-managers' prefer to trade on their experience and on their intrinsic leadership capabilities.

Reflecting on the marketability of the gurus of management, Hindle (2008) reminds us that the career prospects of these commentators are far from assured. Thus, Hindle observes that, aside from a 'famous five' (Peter Drucker, Douglas McGregor, Michael Porter, Alfred Sloan and FW Taylor) who have sustained prominent positions in the market for management knowledge (and in the listings of 'top gurus'), most of those who have been dubbed 'management gurus' flourish briefly and then fade (sometimes ignominiously) from public life (see Collins, 2021a for a discussion of Al Dunlap). Huczynski (1993) however adds an important caveat to this discussion: while *gurus* come and go, *guru theory* endures.

Outlining the nature and character of 'guru theory', Huczynski (1993: 38) concedes that

> the term "guru theory" is used as a convenient label to refer to [the] different contributions that have been so influential [since the 1980s]. The label encompasses a rag-bag of prescriptions which include the importance of innovation, more teamwork, more empowerment of the individual, more employee participation, fewer levels of hierarchy and less bureaucratization (38).

Huczynski insists, however, that there is a deeper structure of orientations and representations which, if you will allow, draws the strings of this 'rag-bag' together. Indeed, he suggests that modern guru theory develops and retains an audience by focusing on presentation and by cultivating an ideological focus which serves to enhance the rights and privileges of management. Fleshing out this point Huczynski suggests that what is often reduced to 'guru theory' might more usefully be conceived as a broad family of ideas. Tracing the genealogy of this family Huczynski suggests that it exhibits three, common, core traits and, within these traits, twelve interdependent, complementary and overlapping features.

Guru theory therefore articulates an understanding of the world of work which is:

1 Readily communicable through acronyms, alliteration or slogans. For example the 3Cs of Business Process Reengineering (Hammer, 1990) and the McKinsey 7-S framework which underpins, both, *In Search of Excellence* (Peters and Waterman, 1982) and *The Art of Japanese Management* (Pascale and Athos, [1981] 1986) spring readily to mind.
2 Focused on the presumed capacity which leaders have to change the conduct of others.
3 Happy to assert that human thoughts and feelings are malleable in the hands of the skilled leaders lauded at point two.

Exploring the second trait said to typify guru theorizing, Huczynski suggests that successful representations of managerial work have been designed to enhance the status of the intended purchaser. Marketable representations of managerial work he suggests:

4 Provide legitimation and self-affirmation for those engaged in this endeavour.
5 Build on a unitary account of managerial work (see Fox, 1985; Collins, 1998) which suggests that there is no room for meaningful dissent with respect to organizational ends or, indeed, the means used to secure these goals.
6 Allow local modifications which enable managers (a) to tailor the model to local problems and contingencies and in so doing allow practitioners (b) to voice the suggestion that they have usefully and meaningfully acted on their own initiative.
7 Focus on 'leadership' and in so doing suggest that colleagues will volunteer their support even to the point of altruism (see Pettigrew, 1985).

Examining the third trait, Huczynski focuses, unsurprisingly, on practical application. Thus, he argues that successful forms of guru theory:

8 Promise control over market conditions otherwise notable for their volatility.
9 Outline a limited number of steps that, in execution, will deliver useful, planned, change (see Collins, 1998).

10 Suggest that the idea, tool, or initiative enjoys universal applicability.

11 Carry authorization or proof but not in the traditional academic or empirical sense. Commenting on this Lischinsky (2008) observes that popular management ideas rarely build on original empirical research but depend instead on 'persuasive examples'.

12 Has ready applicability and can be utilized without special tools or knowledge. Commenting on this dimension, Grint (1994) suggests that guru theory is appealing to users because it implies that, while others must change (and are, in fact, defined as being 'other' precisely because they are in need of change) the conduct, preferences and predilections of the prime users may proceed unchallenged.

As this text will make plain Peters is, in the terms outlined above, fully deserving of the management guru label. He has

a sustained a prominent position in the competitive market for management knowledge over four decades and has

b brought to prominence the understanding that business success is, to a considerable extent, derived from the ability to manage the ways in which people feel about their work.

I will, of course, leave it to you to decide whether Peters' influence in this arena is truly a cause for celebration but will add this warning: No matter whether you come to praise or to bury Peters he cannot be ignored and it is simply wrong to suggest – as the contributors to the *HBR* survey have done – that he is not a leading shaper of the social principles and practices of that complex endeavour that we, too readily, reduce to the noun 'management'.

And on that bombshell … I will conclude these introductory remarks with a few final reflections on the manner in which the work of Tom Peters has been handled by those who have attempted, in any sense, to come to terms with 'the gurus of management'.

★ ★ ★ ★ ★

By my own admission I have, in the past, been (unnecessarily) rude in my treatment of Peters and his work. I do now regret these comments and now willingly reiterate my apology. Yet as we shall see my commentary while muscular is notable in one additional respect beyond its testiness, and is different to that which has been developed by at least some of my peers. Thus, while I may have been overly harsh in my comments, my words and opinions have been based, always, on a reading of Tom Peters that develops from primary sources. Glaring errors and omissions in the works of others who have written on Tom Peters, however, suggest that many contemporary critiques do not proceed from such a careful reading. Indeed, the sheer quantity of these errors and omissions, as we shall see in Chapter 2, suggests that Peters belongs to that category of writers who *must be criticized but need not be read.*

In what follows therefore I offer you, this reassurance. While attempting to moderate my tone, I will continue to offer an account of 'Tom Peters and Management', which while it is certainly critical is, nonetheless, based on knowledge of the man and his work that has been developed over 30 years of sustained personal research and careful scholarship!

Concluding comments

This introductory chapter has been designed to offer a map of the book and to establish Peters' position within the pantheon of popular management. I have acknowledged that Peters has often been unnecessarily abused and/or impugned, sometimes by me, but more often by those who have simply chosen to write about this guru without, first, reading his work. With this issue to the forefront our next chapter will take time reflect on the very foundations of Tom Peters' guru career. Thus, Chapter 1 will consider the genesis of the excellence project – the birth of the idea that propelled Peters to guru status, to riches and to international stardom. As we shall see, the excellence project and the McKinsey 7-S framework, which provides its foundation, have become key components of the modern management curriculum. Students are, of course, typically introduced to these ideas at an early stage of their studies and are expected – however half-heartedly – to apply these tools in their assessments. Yet the textbooks developed for our students seldom offer any discussion of the context within which these tools and ideas were developed. In our next chapter we will remedy this as we consider the birth-pangs of the excellence project. The genesis of the excellence project is, I will demonstrate, an engaging tale that really is worth telling, in part, because it has rather a lot to teach us about economics, about politics – in short about all those things that shape the managerial world but which seldom feature in the textbooks!

Notes

1 I have borrowed this allusion from Robert Burns. In the song Willie Stewart, written as a birthday gift and tribute to his friend, Burns writes (beautifully),

> *The flower it graws; it fades it fa's*
> *And nature cannot renew it*
> *But worth and truth, eternal youth*
> *We'll gie tae Willie Stewart*

2 When Thompson and McHugh first employed this phrase they used it to refer to a pre-Taylorist period. The processes of modern education and the reading habits of both students and instructors I fear have moved this 'pre-historical' period to a point in the calendar that I continue to regard as pretty contemporary!

3 I am aware that there is a gap of some ten years in my account of the book's key constituencies. I am, however, trying to be fair. Some of those aged 40 and over,

I accept, may well have encountered the work of Tom Peters. My experience, however, suggests that this will be a small grouping. Likewise some of those aged over 50 may have passed a managerial career in ignorance of Tom Peters. Yet, again, my experience suggests that this will also be a small grouping. For good or ill, therefore, I have chosen to assume that my main constituencies are aged under 40 and 50 and over. If you are aged between these limits please do not feel slighted: you should, of course, feel free to read on!

4 There is some evidence to suggest that many practitioners have not, in fact, read any of the guru texts they own and there is, in addition, good reason to suspect that among those who have actually opened their copies, most have merely 'dipped into' these texts.

5 As we shall see Bob Waterman had no contractual rights to the royalties earned by *In Search of Excellence.*

6 John Lennon it has been suggested once observed that The Beatles were bigger than God. That was, for some, an inflammatory comment. Peters' sales figures do not suggest that he is bigger than God. They do suggest, however, that Peters ran Her a close second.

   And that's how you make an inflammatory comment.

7 As Peters voices this complaint he makes common purpose (a) with Peter Drucker who, in the 1950s (see Whyte [1956] 1961: 95) suggested that a vocational education in management would be one that involved 'the writing of poetry or short stories' and (b) with Wright-Mills (1978) who suggested that sociologists of organization had much to learn from novelists. Collins (2021c) has recently produced a short monograph which builds on this advice in an attempt to redeem culture through stories and storytelling.

8 To employ a footballing analogy I will play the ball and not the man.

9 Peters has, I believe, always been slightly uncomfortable with the guru moniker, preferring instead to be labelled as 'curmudgeon' or, more positively, 'gad fly'. Nowadays he is often introduced as (and seems to take pride in being known as) 'the Red Bull' of management. This term of course signals the extent to which Peters is, through his writing and seminar presentations, considered to be an organizational stimulant and catalyst for business change. Stewart [2009] (2010: 279) takes this a step further but suggests a more guarded position as to the influence of Peters: Tom Peters he suggests is a corporate 'amphetamine'.

10 In this text, for example, I quip (unkindly) that the public claims which Peters makes of/for his work represent a breach of the Sale of Goods Act (1979).

11 The complaint is not robust and is, indeed, later openly contradicted by Clark. Working with others, for example (see Groβ et al., 2015) Clark not only applies the guru label to a group of speakers on the management lecture circuit but does so in a fashion that could be seen as casual. In short, and despite his earlier comments concerning the utility of the term, Clark now seems content to use the guru label.

12 In this text I argue that the work of Greatbatch and Clark (2005) is undermined by problems conceptual, methodological and empirical.

1

THE GENESIS OF THE EXCELLENCE PROJECT

Introduction

This chapter will offer an account of the genesis of the excellence project. In our next chapter we will offer an analysis of *In Search of Excellence* (Peters and Waterman, 1982) and of *A Passion for Excellence* (Peters and Austin, 1985). Chapter 2 will therefore build on the analysis developed here and will consider the constitution of the eight organizational attributes said to be necessary to secure the business processes required to change organizations and, indeed, to revitalize the US economy. In addition Chapter 2 will offer reflections on the manner in which the excellence project has developed since the mid-1980s. In this chapter however we will move 'upstream' (Latour, 1987) to offer an account of the genesis of the excellence project. Surveying this admittedly protracted moment of creation[1] we will focus on the development of the 'McKinsey 7-S framework', which, as we shall see, constitutes the very foundations of the excellence project.

★ ★ ★ ★ ★

Textbook accounts of business excellence, developed for students of management tend to be built on, what Latour (1987) would call, a ready-made account of scientific endeavour. Latour employs this culinary metaphor, as we have seen, to suggest that the textbooks, which we use to induct our students in the business of management, are based on a pedagogy that accounts for ideas from a vantage point that, in being informed by hindsight, is blissfully free from controversy. Noting the manner in which this pedagogy acts to obscure or to elide the very real and active controversies that shape human endeavour, Latour invites us to consider ideas as they are constructed. Thus, Latour insists that our pedagogy should explore and account for concepts at the point in time at which they remain

DOI: 10.4324/9781003188940-2

contested and indeed contestable. Accepting the essential truthfulness of Latour's analysis, this chapter will offer an account of the genesis of the excellence project, which considers the human contests and controversies that shaped its formulation and development. To this end we will consider the network of associations that, in effect, built the McKinsey 7-S framework.

★ ★ ★ ★ ★

The McKinsey 7-S framework is routinely taught to students and is offered, more generally, as a heuristic, which usefully captures the socio-technical totality of the organized world. The framework is, of course, now known globally and has been summarized in countless textbooks and student essays. Yet the 'ready-made' science offered by these textbooks simply invites students (a) to recount the fact of the framework's existence while (b) considering its implications for structure and conduct within business organizations. This 'cold' account of the birth of the excellence project however simply fails to acknowledge that '7-S' model, emerged as a collaborative endeavour and as an expedient response to a competitive crisis that had developed within McKinsey and Co. This chapter will explore the development and emergence of this framework within this context. I will show that while the McKinsey 7-S framework is, now, very closely associated with Peters and Waterman, the framework actually developed as a collaborative arrangement between a number of key individuals and was, in fact, first showcased not by Peters, but by his contemporaries, Pascale and Athos [1981] (1986) in *The Art of Japanese Management*.

Compared to the commercial success enjoyed by *In Search of Excellence,* the work of Pascale and Athos is generally taken to be, frankly, something of a failure (see Collins, 2018, 2021a). Noting core similarities between *The Art of Japanese Management* and *In Search of Excellence*, Crainer (1997: 41) observes that the differing fortunes of these texts resolves to the question of tone. He suggests that Peters and Waterman (1982) offer an endorsement of American values and business practices (*mom and apple pie*) whereas Pascale and Athos ([1981] 1986) offered only 'humble pie'.

There is, as we shall see, much to recommend Crainer's summary position. Yet as we approach the 40th anniversary of the publication of *In Search of Excellence,* there is an opportunity to pause and to reflect more fully on these consanguine texts. Indeed, as we observe the 40th anniversary of the excellence project we have an opportunity to reflect on what *might* have happened had the public chosen Pascale and Athos (over Peters and Waterman) as their gurus of business excellence!

Counter-factual history is, of course, a potentially fraught and contested endeavour. Indeed, some historians would suggest that counter-factual history is little more than a parlour game that tends to indulge idle and, often, ill-informed speculation (see Ferguson, 1997). This may well be an accurate summary of much counter-factual history. Nonetheless, it will be useful for our purposes to highlight the ways in which *In Search of Excellence* and *The Art of Japanese Management* offered contrasting accounts of the essence of management. Building on this reflection I will suggest that in pursuing the search of excellence over the art of (Japanese) management American business chose an easy path and over the long term, *the wrong route* out of the crisis. Indeed, I will argue that a change project launched from the foundations established by Pascale and Athos *would* have enabled a qualitatively different appreciation of 'management' and, *might* have prompted a strategic reformulation founded on a genuinely social policy of enterprise, informed by and sensitive to ideas of plurality.

Accordingly, our chapter is structured as follows: We begin with an account of the development of the 7-S framework. Tracing the networked associations that enabled and enacted this formulation we will reveal the many hands that formed this now familiar heuristic. While noting that the 'happy atom' has become known (and applied) worldwide as a tool, which captures and expresses the social-technical totality of the organizational world, I will highlight Atkinson's (1997) attempt to extend this framework. Atkinson's suggested extension is, I will argue, frankly, unnecessary and unhelpful. Yet I will argue that this flawed modification is, nonetheless, useful for our purposes because it serves to demonstrate both the core wisdom of the 7-S framework and the extent to which this device has become foundational (a) to the teaching of management and (b) an important constituent of its routine practice.

The work of Pascale and Athos [1981] (1986) builds and depends on the heuristic that Atkinson would have us develop and extend. And yet, the work of Pascale and Athos has often been ignored by the public or, worse, has been derided by the managerial elite that was active in business and hence prominent in the United States during the 1970s. While accounting for the contrasting fortunes of these texts I will suggest that *The Art of Japanese Management* like its cousin *In Search of Excellence* was (and remains) an important work on management. Yet I will argue that *The Art of Japanese Management* has a significance beyond that accorded to *In Search of Excellence*. Thus, I will argue that the work of Pascale and Athos offers a qualitatively different account of business in its social context that, in application *just might have* enabled an approach to management that was truly deserving of the 'hands-on, values driven' endorsement that Peters and Waterman (1982) suggest is a key component of business excellence.

The constitution of the McKinsey 7-S framework

Tom Peters dates the birth of the excellent project quite precisely. The problem being that he does this twice and each time suggests a different point on the calendar.

In 1982 (Peters and Waterman, 1982: 12) Peters suggested that July 4, 1979 represents the birth date of his research on excellence. It was, he tells us, on this date that a successful presentation to Royal Dutch Shell offered feedback that was sufficient to convince those who had been developing reflections on 'organizational effectiveness' to continue with their work. More recently however Peters (2018: 30) has offered an alternative birth date, which suggests that the excellence project is just a little older than previously acknowledged, this date being 'Good Friday 1978'.

Elaborating on this moment in time Peters tells us,

It was Easter week 1978. The main computer in the San Francisco office of McKinsey & Co., where I worked as a consultant, chose to crash thirty-six hours before our managing director was scheduled to give a report on an important project to the top team at Dart Industries in Los Angeles.

> With the computer down, his team was unable to prepare the sort of pres-
> entation he wished to make. I, meanwhile, was working frantically and
> independently on a project commissioned by the powers that be in the
> firm's New York headquarters. Though I was psyched by the project, it had
> the uninspiring title of "Improving Organizational Effectiveness." John
> Larson (the S. F. McKinsey boss) came to me in desperation (Dart was a
> core client) and said, in effect, *"Can you put something short but somewhat sweet
> together and fob it off on Dart and save my ass?"*
>
> "Sure," I said in a flash; one dreams of saving one's boss's ass, right? ... I
> got home about 10:30 pm and, in a daze, dutifully went to my home office
> and started pulling material together for Dart. I honestly have no idea what
> next transpired, but I do know, Bic pen in hand ... I crafted a draft cover
> page with but one word, in all capital letters: EXCELLENCE.
>
> *28 (original emphasis, capitalization, parentheses and ellipses)*

Later we will return to the moment of clarity that saw Peters render, in all capital letters, 'excellence' on the draft cover of his rushed presentation. For the moment however we must continue to trace the now contested timeline and the network of associations that led to the development and public articulation of the 7-S framework.

The account of the genesis of the excellence project that is offered by Pascale and Athos [1981] (1986: ix) confirms much of the narrative offered, above, by Peters. It acknowledges, for example, that Peters was truly instrumental to the development of the 7-S framework: 'Peters pointed out in a working paper on "excellent companies" that firms so designated explicitly managed a wider range of variables than other companies'.

Yet in offering this endorsement, Pascale and Athos also remind us that Peters' working paper was actually developed to support a programme of applied research that McKinsey instituted around 1978. Pascale and Athos do concede however that Tom Peters, partnered by his McKinsey colleague Jim Bennett had been active in this corporate research project from the outset.

Commenting on the aims and scope of the research project instituted by McKinsey, Pascale and Athos ([1981] 1986: viii–ix) note that together Peters and Bennett,

> set out to review the entire literature and current thought about effective-
> ness. They concluded that the emphasis upon strategy and structure had
> gone beyond the point of diminishing returns, and that other factors were
> also critically important and deserved more attention.

Following the publication of Peters' working paper on 'excellence', Bob Waterman was drafted to the project by more senior operators within McKinsey, Pascale and Athos ([1981] 1986: ix) observe that Waterman accepted the core concerns articulated by Peters but feared that these would be 'very difficult to convey persuasively to a wider audience of consultants and executives steeped in the strategy-structure emphasis.' Mindful of this issue, Waterman, we are told, invited Athos (who had combined consultancy, research and graduate school teaching) to join the research project as a consultant. Soon afterwards, it seems, Waterman tendered a similar invitation to Pascale, whose cross-comparative work, we are told, made him amenable to what we might term Peters' 'additional variables hypothesis'. Accounting for this enlargement of the team, Pascale and Athos, tell us that Bob Waterman anticipated that their involvement would add conceptual sophistication and communicability to the outline prospectus that Peters and Bennett had begun to craft.

In June 1978, just as Waterman had hoped, Athos made a suggestion to this small collective that we might now view as highly significant. Athos suggested the need for a conceptual schema designed to organize the core variables identified by Peters and Bennett 'so that their interrelationships might be emphasized, and so that "fit" among the variables might be better understood' (Pascale and Athos [1981] 1986: ix). Arguing that an alliterative approach would improve memorability, and thus, learning and acceptance within a population that had been schooled in a fundamentally different (and 'hard') way of thinking, Athos (a) proposed a 5-S framework and (b) persuaded Peters and Waterman to embrace this schema.

Substituting what had previously been labelled 'guiding concepts' for 'superordinate goals', the collective agreed, initially, on three 'hard s' factors (strategy, structure and systems) and two 'soft s' factors, namely, 'style' and 'superordinate goals'. Almost immediately however Peters and Pascale, together, suggested the need to add an additional 's-factor' which they labelled 'sequencing'. By 1978, therefore, McKinsey and Co. had the bones of a 'six-s' framework.

Pascale and Athos concede that it was Bob Waterman who carried the torch for this six-s framework within McKinsey, in part through the publication of a paper entitled 'Structure is not Organization'. Building on the account of 'organizational capability' that Waterman had developed within this paper, Peters soon began to lobby the team for two changes within the developing framework. He argued (a) for the inclusion of 'skill' and (b) for the removal of 'sequencing', which it was suggested was a poor fit with the remaining 's' variables.

At this stage Pascale and Athos, tell us that they began to use the outline model in their teaching. Around this time McKinsey and Co. also began to offer workshops on what was, at that point a 'six-s' model. Pascale attended these early McKinsey workshops and was then invited to host subsequent iterations. Julian Phillips of McKinsey who had also contributed to these workshops added his voice to those suggesting that 'sequencing' should be dropped from the model in favour of 'staff'. Commenting on this development, Pascale and Athos ([1981]

1986: x) observe that not one of those who had worked to develop the emerging and still, skeletal, model was truly comfortable with 'sequencing'. Consequently this factor was soon dropped from the emerging framework by common consent.

> And since Peters was proposing that "people" and "power" needed somehow to be included (Athos was adding "aggregates of people" [to his teaching] at Harvard), it was also possible to agree that Staff was an addition which resolved various concerns.

Thus, the now familiar McKinsey 7-S framework came to be:

- Strategy
- Structure
- Systems
- Staff
- Style
- Skills
- Superordinate Goals (Shared Values)

Atkinson (1997), perhaps better known for his work on Total Quality Management (TQM), acknowledges the vision of his contemporaries. Indeed, he concedes that the McKinsey framework offers a very useful heuristic by which (a) to understand the problems of business and (b) to secure necessary change in the structure and function of organizations. Yet Atkinson argues that this framework needs to be extended (in part) to accommodate the requirements of TQM. Thus, Atkinson suggests that the 7-S framework should be revised to accommodate a '9-S' model, which adds 'synergy' and 'symbols' to the framework whose development we outlined above. I am, however, unconvinced by this suggested extension. Indeed, I believe that it is (a) unhelpful (b) unnecessary and in (c) demonstrating redundancy demonstrates the essential wisdom of the consultative/peer review process that led to the formation of the original '7-S framework'. Thus, it is worth observing that Atkinson's eighth s-factor, 'synergy', might be taken to be a component of 'strategy' or, indeed, a strategic aspiration, which (ironically) adds nothing to our understanding of the social-technical totality of organizational life. Furthermore, we might suggest that a modicum of teamwork and consultation would have revealed this to Atkinson! Similarly, we should note that Atkinson's ninth s-factor, 'symbols', is plainly implicit within 'shared values' and might more usefully be taken to be but one of a number of conduits for the development and transmission of such cultural aspirations. Indeed, we might ask, why did Atkinson choose to focus on 'symbols' rather than, say, 'storytelling'? After all, Peters and Waterman (1982) are clear that the excellence project builds and depends on persuasive forms of communication – principally storytelling! Recognizing these problems and limitations I suggest that Atkinson's proposed extension to the '7-S' model is unnecessary and frankly unhelpful. Indeed, it is, surely, surprising that Atkinson's, proposed extension failed to highlight what the excellence project has made plain over some 40 years: that managers are at root world-builders (Latour, 1987) who depend on storytelling to secure their strategic aspirations!

Acknowledging the competitive context

Crainer (1997) does not seek to extend or to revise the McKinsey 7-S model. He does, however, offer an account of the genesis of the excellence project that, while somewhat slimmer, is similar to that offered by Pascale and Athos.

In keeping with our Latourian appreciation of the genesis of the excellence project it is important to acknowledge that Crainer, in common with Pascale and Athos, documents the contests, controversies and false-starts associated with the constitution and crystallization of the, now, familiar 'happy atom' that is reproduced below (see Figure 1.1). Yet Crainer (1997) adds a competitive dynamic that is under-played in the account developed by Pascale and Athos. Thus, Crainer suggests that the excellence project developed as Tom Peters', then, employers the consulting firm, McKinsey and Co. sought to defend their company's market position and reputation against two key competitors, namely, the Boston Consulting Group and Bain and Co.

Crainer's account of the genesis of the excellence project, in common with that recently rendered by Peters (2018), focuses, in particular, on the activities of the Boston Consulting Group (BCG). Both Crainer and Peters note that in the early 1970s the Boston Consulting Group had developed and, successfully,

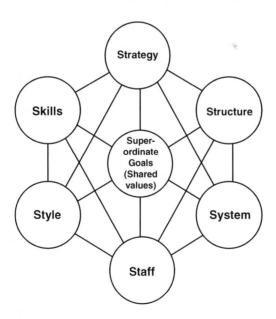

FIGURE 1.1   The McKinsey 7-S Framework.

marketed two management tools, 'The Experience Curve' (which suggested that those companies which have accumulated significant experience in the production of particular goods and services would reap the benefits of reduced unit costs) and the 'Boston Matrix' (which offered the managers of conglomerate organizations a tool that, it was claimed, would measure market growth potential across its portfolio).

Within McKinsey there were fears that market developments of this sort were raising the reputation and profile of competitors at the expense of 'the firm'.[2] In an attempt to reverse this process the senior management of McKinsey cast around for a tool, idea or technique that might serve to rebuild their reputation in the marketplace as, truly, leading-edge strategic thinkers (McDonald [2013] 2020).

In 1977[3] following this period of reflection, McKinsey launched three new practices configured around 'Strategy', 'Organization' and 'Operations'. Together, these practices had a brief to consider the relationship between strategy, structure and effectiveness and in so doing were expected to rejuvenate and rekindle the reputation of the firm. Tom Peters who had recently returned to McKinsey and Company following a period of leave due to illness (which had afforded him time to complete his PhD) was recruited to the 'Organization Practice' and was dispatched on an eight-week trip to gather knowledge and information on the practices of 'effective organizations'. This trip, Peters and Waterman (1982: 4) tell us, involved extensive discussions with key business executives and, later, visits to 'a dozen business schools in the United States and Europe' (5). On the strength of this and other such knowledge gathering activities (including a review of the published literature on 'effectiveness'), the 'Organization Practice' soon began to develop, what was for McKinsey and its clientele a, rather, radical proposal. Thus, the members of the 'Organization Practice' came to understand that focusing on 'strategy' and 'structure' was unproductive in the absence of a more detailed appreciation of the organizational processes that put structures to work and strategies into action.

Defining the problem in such negative terms was, of course, relatively easy for the 'Organization Practice'. Stating a positive solution to the problem identified, however, proved to be more problematic both for clients and for colleagues. Indeed, Crainer (1997) notes that early reaction to the stirrings of the Peters, and his collaborators, was muted within McKinsey and among its clientele. Elaborating on this point, Crainer (1997) observes that between 1978 and 1979 Peters and his colleagues pitched their reflections on 'organizational effectiveness' to *DART*, to *Royal Dutch Shell*, to *PepsiCo* and to *Siemens* but were unable to secure any clients for the effectiveness practice.[4] These organizations were it seems, amenable to the broad thrust of the analysis but doubted that this might be codified and applied to produce tangible business outcomes.

Hewlett-Packard in the shape of John Young (who would later be lauded as the inspiration for MBWA – Management by Wandering Around), however, was persuaded by the outline analysis developed by Peters and chose to offer his support and the collaboration of his organization. Furthermore, *Business Horizons* was sufficiently intrigued to invite the main project partners to publish an account of the project and its core concerns (Waterman, Peters and Phillips, 1980). This article seems to have been instrumental to the launch of the excellence project for in the 18 months following its publication, Peters responded to invitations which saw him give 200 speeches and 50 workshops on 'excellence'. It is worth noting, too that following the publication of the *Business Horizons* article Peters secured a book deal which would allow him to carry his developing reflections on the managerial process to a larger public. Within McKinsey and Co., however, not all were supportive.

McKinsey's internal machinations

Peters (2018) offers a broad endorsement of the (genesis) narratives developed by Crainer (1997) and by Pascale and Athos [1981] (1986) but is careful to remind us of the on-going political machinations within McKinsey which, as he sees it, hampered the development of the excellence project. Thus, Peters' (2018) recent reflections on the genesis of the project remind us that there were those within McKinsey and Co. who sought to undermine the excellence project and in so doing persuaded both Peters and Waterman that their futures would not be with 'the firm'.

Peters' (2018: 60) preferred genesis narrative gives a starring to Ron Daniel, then, the Managing Director of the firm. Daniel he tells us 'had noticed … that McKinsey provided sound advice to its clients, but far too often the grand plans failed the implementation test'. To remedy this failing, Peters tells us that Daniel chose to launch 'mostly beneath the radar' (60) an 'organizational effectiveness' practice in parallel to the 'strategy' and 'operations' practices that had, in contrast, been introduced to the public with some fanfare. Recognizing that Tom Peters had recently completed a PhD, focused on 'implementation', Ron Daniel secured Peters' appointment to the organizational effectiveness practice.

Thanks to Daniel, Peters (2018: 60) spent six months voyaging 'on an unlimited travel budget … in pursuit of the best and most progressive and provocative thinking'. These progressives and provocateurs (located within corporations and within academic institutions), Peters (2018: 61 ellipses in original) tells us led him to the conclusion 'that what makes an organization soar was … "the soft stuff" … the nonlinear "people stuff"'. Yet he complains that the presentations around these themes that were offered 'to McKinsey grandees were met mostly with indifference' (61).

Aware that within McKinsey and Co. there were those who offered outright opposition to that which resisted quantification, Peters (2018: 61) tells us that he embarked on an insurgency designed to enrol like-minded 'renegades' who understood instinctively 'what McKinsey-ites considered secondary – the messy "implementation bit" was indeed the difference between winning and losing'. This insurgency however did not go unnoticed:

> As I gained traction, McKinsey traditionalists fought back. Through my network, I managed to get an op-ed published in *The Wall Street Journal* that was all about the impact of corporate culture on business results and implicitly (pretty explicitly, to be honest) downgraded the role of strategy. I was told that the head of the New York Office actually went to Daniel in an effort to get me fired. But Daniel remained steadfast; in fact such controversy and publicity around "McKinsey ideas" was just what he had been looking for.
>
> *Peters (2018: 61)*

Peters (2018: 61) acknowledges that it was Herb Henzler, a 'renegade' located within the German office who persuaded *Siemens* to fund another round-the-world, fact-finding trip for the Organization Practice. This trip we should note was unlike that previously undertaken. Thus, while the first phase of research had been content to quiz academics and leading executives, the *Siemens* funded trip was designed to review practices within 'the world's top companies'. The findings of these research trips, Peters observes, were published in an internal, company, paper in 1979. This paper once again highlighted the importance of people, of soft stuff – in short 'culture'. Yet many within McKinsey remained openly hostile to the suggestion that the firm might usefully concern itself with 'people stuff'. 'No one at McKinsey' Peters tells us 'was more dismissive of the "soft stuff" I was championing than senior partner Lou Gerstner' (Peters, 2018: 62).

Having, in effect, been pushed out of McKinsey and Co. in the early 1980s, Peters now seems to take pleasure from the fact that opponents and detractors within his Palo Alto office were, soon enough, called together to witness the success of his implementation credo. Noting the slow conversion of those who had chosen to act as his blockers, tormentors and detractors, Peters (2018) gleefully observes Gerstner's belated cultural epiphany. Gerstner who had left McKinsey for top jobs at American Express and RJR Nabisco, Peters tells us, had taken the top job at IBM in the early 1990s and had been charged with its turnaround. In a book published some two decades after *In Search of Excellence*, Peters points out that IBM's chief executive (see Gerstner, 2002) finally, publicly acknowledged, what Peters had known since 1977 *and what Gerstner had sought to refute*, namely that his company's problems were made of the soft stuff and were, at root, cultural.[5]

Peters' reflections on the genesis of the excellence project, suggest that its success as both a practical and a commercial endeavour turns on three factors. First, it was self-evidently truthful insofar as businesses do need the 'soft' stuff and the 'hard' stuff to work together! Second, it built its narrative not on cold, facts but on storytelling (Kiechel, 2010: 156). And third, the core of the argument was novel in presentation and in substance. Combining these elements Peters has, in fact, suggested that the excellence project was successful because he and Bob Waterman were pioneers, the first to suggest that the leaders of business organizations might seek and demand 'excellence'.

It would, I think, be fair to suggest that Peters and Waterman were, perhaps, the first to use this expression, systematically, to explain managerial conduct and to advance an agenda for change.[6] Yet it would be misleading to suggest that Peters and Waterman were simply, and plainly, the first to speak of business excellence.[7] In 1970, for example, Townsend [1970] (1971), former chairman of Avis Rent-a-Car, published what amounts to 'a devil's dictionary' of management designed as its sub-title suggests 'to stop the corporation from stifling people and strangling profits'. On page 56 of this text there is, we should note, an entry framed as a question which, like the draft cover page of Peters' Easter presentation of 1978, is rendered in 'all capitals':

EXCELLENCE: OR WHAT THE HELL ARE YOU DOING HERE?

Townsend, we should note, provides an answer to this inquiry, which resolves to another more rhetorical question:

> If you can't do it excellently, don't do it at all. Because if it's not excellent it won't be profitable or fun, and if you're not in business for fun or profit, what the hell are you doing here?
>
> *Townsend ([1970] 1971: 56)*

Given this, I suggest that if anyone deserves to be recognized as the first person to speak of excellence in a business context it is, surely, Townsend.

Does this really matter? Yes, but perhaps not in the manner that you imagine.

* * * * *

Readers may protest that my digression to highlight the, now, contested origins of 'business excellence' is a distraction. If my digression constituted a simple exercise in etymology this criticism would probably be legitimate. Yet my intention in discussing the origins of the term 'excellence' within the business arena is not, simply, to suggest that Townsend was the *real* pioneer and that Peters and Waterman were late to the party. Rather, my concern is to highlight resonances common to the analysis of Peters and Waterman and the more comical and ironic account developed by Townsend.

And why does this matter? What difference does this make? My suggestion is that it is important to understand these resonances because they can help us to understand just why it was that *In Search of Excellence* bucked the trend and became a best-seller.

A little context on the market for business books before *In Search of Excellence* may help.

The market for management knowledge

Between 1960 and 1980, McKinsey and Co. published just two books on management (see McDonald, [2013] 2020: 156) and as Collins (2021a: 39) observes 'neither of [these] could be considered to be inviting prospects'. Since the 1980s, however, McKinsey and Co. have published in excess of 100 books on the business of management that have been authored by its partners and associates (McDonald, [2013] 2020: 156). As we explore the origins of the excellence project, it is important that we understand this context and it is important that we recognize that *In Search of Excellence* is significant because it wrought changes in 'management' practice *and* in that niche of the publishing industry that has developed to service the needs of management practitioners. In short, we must recognize that *In Search of Excellence* is unusual and rather important because it entered and altered that segment of the publishing industry devoted to business and management, literally, re-writing our understanding of what management books could do and say. And what was it that made the work of Peters and Waterman distinctive in this arena?

My suggestion is that Peters would have been aware of the work of Townsend and, knowingly or otherwise, derived from Townsend the core philosophy that would underpin his expression of the challenge of business excellence and, indeed, his career as a guru. Thus, while Townsend's text is, essentially, a comic work – a book with no sustained or continuing analytical narrative – it, nonetheless, communicates a moral project – a battle against organizational dullness (and dullards) conducted in the name of the consumer. In short, I suggest, that Townsend offered Peters and his insurgents both a voice and outline template for their growing discontents with America's (and, indeed, McKinsey's) corporate elites. Indeed, we would do well to note that the dust-jack of the Book Club Associates edition of *Up the Organisation* (Townsend, [1970] 1971) which I now hold in my hand highlights the importance of trust, vision, values and human agency within an organized context. Furthermore, the text that conveys this understanding, I suggest in a manner that could easily be inserted as the preamble to *In Search of Excellence*:

> The book is NOT about:
>
> a   how to preside with dignity over the mess you've inherited from your predecessors
> b   how to muddle along indifferently.
>
> The book is about:
>
> > how to think unthinkable thoughts and how to do undoable things with a view to:
> >
> > i making an unusual succeed out of a usual situation, or
> > ii making a minor success out of an impossible situation.

It also asks the question. How do you tell when you're on the right track? Answer: Fun, Justice and Success are inextricably intertwined. Fight hard for the first two if you want to deserve the third.

As they developed the excellence project, therefore, I suggest that Peters (and later Waterman) took their cue from Townsend and in channelling this author's ideas (knowingly or otherwise), brought passion, energy and a distinctive voice to a literary genre that, until this point, had been a commercial backwater because it was, frankly, so bloody dull.

In our next section we will offer (perhaps) more concrete arguments for the success of the excellence project, while offering a new and additional speculation on the core of the project's success.

The success of the excellence project

Peters is, publicly at least, humble about his success. In an address delivered to mark what amounts to a new secular festival of business and management, known to some as *Drucker Day*,[8] Peters suggests that the success of *In Search of Excellence* turns on the all-important final 98% that lay-persons call 'luck'.

Peters is, I suggest, quite correct to highlight this often unaccounted feature of our daily lives. Yet in placing this factor as 98% of his guru career he surely over-estimates his dependence on simple serendipity! Peters' modesty aside therefore it will be helpful to observe that, beyond what I call 'dumb luck' there are at least six factors that may be invoked to explain the success of the excellence project beyond the suggestion that it channels the energy and the philosophy of *Up the Organisation*.

Factor one: the McKinsey effect

The excellence project, Peters reminds us, was sponsored by perhaps the world's leading consultancy organization, McKinsey and Co., and carried with it, despite the internal politicking noted above, the public endorsement of 'the firm'. This endorsement, it is clear, did much to recommend the project to businesses, to journalists, to key decision-makers and to the public-at-large.

Factor two: corporate sponsorship

The excellence project, while supported by McKinsey, was, of course, assisted by corporate sponsorship, in cash and in kind. *Dart* and *Siemens*, as we have seen, were instrumental in the early stages of the project. Furthermore, *IBM*, then among the leading US corporations, and by 1985 the most profitable company in the world (DeLamarter [1986] 1988: xiv–xv), featured very strongly in the text of *In Search of Excellence*. Heller [1994] (1995: 63) observes, for example, that '*In Search of Excellence* … had twenty-six references to IBM, all glowing' and adds that Bob Waterman's (1987) *The Renewal Factor*, 'contained thirty-six references' to IBM 'all complimentary' (Heller, [1994] 1995: 71).

In other words, the close involvement of key corporations in the development of the excellence project and the celebration of the potential, latent, within US organizations that was developed throughout *In Search of Excellence* both deserve to be recognized as important influences promoting the endeavour launched by Peters and Waterman.

Factor three: the nationalist trope

In Search of Excellence is framed around a clearly nationalist trope. The context of the excellence project is, of course, framed against a backdrop of social and economic crisis and gives voice to fears about the growing dominance of Japan. And yet the authors begin their account with some 'good news' albeit good news that takes a swipe at the prevailing organizational practices of US management:

> There is good news from America. Good management practice today is not resident only in Japan. But, more important the good news comes from treating people decently and asking them to shine, and from producing things that work.
>
> *Peters and Waterman (1982: xxv)*

Building on these pockets of good news, the excellence project promised to spread the word and in so doing offered the reassurance that the US economy and polity could be changed and renewed.

Peters and Waterman, of course, were not the first to make this promise and sadly they were not the last[9]! Nonetheless, it is worth observing that the commitment to *making America great again* played well across a range of communities, I suggest, because while the excellence project plainly suggested that America's renaissance rested in a celebration of indigenous qualities it simply refused to descend into racist stereotyping. Indeed, I suggest that the precise and careful articulation of this nationalist trope has done much to cultivate a market for the excellence project beyond the shores of the United States.

Factor four: the system is to blame!

Peters and Waterman (1982), as we shall see in our next chapter, suggest that it is what made America strong in the immediate post-war period that made it weak in the 1970s. Thus, the authors argue that from the 1940s, American corporations had used scale and the pursuit of efficiency to win a war and to conquer markets both at home and abroad. Yet, we are told, that too many of these large corporations had later failed to understand that the market had changed even as they seemed to prosper. Despite the preferences and priorities of the leading corporations, consumers had, Peters and Waterman argued, come to demand low prices *and* innovation *and* good quality and had consequently offered their patronage to those overseas competitors (especially the Japanese) that had re-structured their functions and reporting relationships to deliver these outcomes. Yet in haranguing 'the system' for these failings, Peters and Waterman added two important qualifications that, I suggest, have proved vital to the success of their project. First, they were careful to point out that there remained, within US organizations, pockets of excellence that might act as beacons for others. Second, Peters and Waterman provided absolution for their readers and converts. US managers, they suggested, could be forgiven for their adherence to Taylorism and for their commitment to the multi-layered, m-form company structures, which had reserved decision-making powers to, remote, elites because these had – not to put too fine a point on it – worked over a fairly lengthy period of time.

Or, perhaps more plainly, the excellence project attracted converts and main-tained the affiliation of those enrolled within it because it made it plain that while American management had problems, American managers remained the answer!

Factor five: word-of-mouth marketing

In Search of Excellence plainly benefited from the support of McKinsey, from cor-porate sponsorship and from a carefully mediated nationalistic trope. In addition we should concede that, prior to its publication, the core message of *In Search of Excellence* was already familiar to leading executives thanks to a series of work-shops that had been developed within McKinsey and Co., to commercialize the project. Yet it is worth pointing out that beyond these workshops Peters and Waterman had in effect 'primed the pump' for the excellence project by distrib-uting 'mimeographed' copies of their manuscript to a large group of corporate decision-makers. This strategy, which might have been expected to depress sales of the text, it seems, actually acted to expand the market since many of those who received mimeographed copies of the excellence manuscript, later purchased personal copies and perhaps more importantly, purchased multiple copies of *In Search of Excellence* for their colleagues and for friends. Sir Peter Parker, in an in-troduction to *The Art of Japanese Management* (Pascale and Athos [1981] 1986: xv), confides that 'over two years' friends, acting separately had given him no fewer than 'seventeen copies' of *In Search of Excellence* and added that 'I am beginning to take it personally'.

Factor six – storytelling

Offering analytical reflections on the manner in which leading consultants and the organizations they represent have shaped our appreciation of the business of management, Kiechel (2010: 156) suggests that we should pay very close atten-tion to the manner in which Peters builds and sustains his narratives of business excellence:

> Asked to explain the success of *In Search of Excellence* Peters cites ... the
> books' abundance of exemplary tales. This was a first among business

books, he maintains, arguing – mostly accurately – that "Peter Drucker doesn't tell stories".

The ability to tell a story, one rooted in the frustrations and occasional epiphanies in corporate life, launched Peters into celebrity on a circuit that steadily grew on the pattern of his success.

Taken together these six (overlapping) factors offer a plausible, if familiar, rationale for the success of *In Search of Excellence*. Yet this narrative formulation does tend to elide key discussions that, as we shall see, had been circulating – at least among America's intellectuals – since the mid-1950s about the limitations of 'Organization Man'.

Organization Man

In 1956 Whyte [1956] (1961) offered an account of 'Organization Man' and the development of those recent, yet widespread forms of social organization – evident in business, the army and in the seminary – that have, whether or not we choose to recognize this, come to shape our actions and interactions in ways that would have been unfathomable to those born just a few generations before. Reflecting on these developments, Whyte argues that notions of America and of American values have been built on a mythology that pits 'individualism' against 'collectivism'. No good American, he suggests, would ever offer their public support for ideas taken to be 'collectivist' in orientation because America is, of course, taken to be the natural home of the frontiersman, the rugged individualist. Yet Whyte argues that the individualist, frontiersman is a myth. Cornuelle [1965] (1967) concurs with this view. Indeed, he suggests that this culturally, cherished, image truncates American history and elides its language. For Cornuelle [1965] (1967: 21), therefore, Americans are 'a frontier people' and far from being the rugged individualists of popular imagination are, in fact, a people raised on and 'accustomed to interdependence'.

Whyte complains however that despite this history of mutual aid and spontaneous social co-operation the US population is, now, one that works within and is obliged to defer to 'the organization'. Noting the manner in which a public rejection of collectives and collectivism is undone by a general desire to serve 'organizational needs', Whyte [1956] (1961: 17), speaking as an American, argues that 'in our attention to making organization work we have come close to deifying it'. Yet he suggests that this is a strange, and very earthly, deification because a broad commitment to scientism, he warns, has encouraged Americans to indulge the belief that 'organization' is, in (the disembodied) human hands (of the organizational scientist), perfectible. Lamenting this peculiarly secularized deification of (business) organizations, Whyte reminds us that Americans have long since abandoned the 'Protestant ethic' in favour of a 'social ethic' which unlike Protestantism has chosen credit, consumption and debt over modesty, forbearance and frugality. Elaborating on the manner in which the

United States has sought to perfect 'organization', Whyte applauds the work of the Human Relations School since, he tells us, this movement at least offered a legitimate space for social beings. Yet he argues that the substantive changes developed in the name of this research programme have tended to provide, only, a 'sugar-coating' (46) to the mechanistic approaches of Taylor and Ford, which had obliged workers to defer to 'enlightened bureaucrats' (46). Echoing Whyte's analysis, Sampson (1995) offers a similar complaint. He observes that the machine bureaucracies, which by the 1950s, had come to define the American experience of organization have continued to expand. Quoting Sir John Banham (Chairman of Whitbread), Sampson (1995: 206) observes that 'companies like General Motors and Shell had been deliberately designed to limit the power of leaders while their scientific management was meant to be impersonal'. Little wonder therefore that for Banham, Britain was, by the 1970s, a place 'in which people were seen as machines', adding that 'leadership' was something 'best left to the discredited military'.

Acknowledging the very limited challenge that the Human Relations School had laid before those who had made it their purpose to depersonalize social organization, Whyte suggests the need for a more political reading of the core issues that have shaped 'organization man'. Thus, Whyte reminds us that while Mayo and his colleagues had certainly highlighted a need for 'belonging', the Human Relations School had nonetheless insisted that, more-or-less spontaneous forms of social organization such as trades unions were illegitimate!

Offering a broader, more contextual and, we should note, a more political reading and critique of the organizing practices that define the United States, Whyte warned his readers that the assumptions that had nurtured 'the Organization Man' would, in time, come to infect all of society. Indeed, he observed that the Organization Man – trained in engineering, dragooned through a dreary business school curriculum and emboldened in a pompous anti-intellectualism – had in the post-war period become increasingly drawn into policy discussions that would inevitably re-shape 'the arts' and 'education' more generally. Warning us of the longer-term consequences of this process, Whyte [1956] (1961: 97) offered a stark warning: 'Look ahead to 1985. Those who will control a good part of the educational plant will be products themselves of the most stringently anti-intellectual training in the country'.

In an attempt to counter this dystopian future, Whyte takes his cue from Drucker who had, earlier, suggested that managers and policy-makers needed an education, not in the particulars of 'business' but in the larger, abiding truths that are formed through a consideration of what Aristotle (1965) would term 'the poetics'. Thus, Whyte [1956] (1961: 95) suggests that for the businessman (*this was 1956!*) 'the most vocational course' would be 'one in the writing of poetry or short stories'.

We cannot be sure, of course, that Peters was, when developing the excellence project, fully aware of Whyte's warnings and discontents; nonetheless, it is plain that *In Search of Excellence* shares common ground with this text and may be read as an attack on the limited purview of 'Organization Man' – on scientism and on the bureaucrats (petty, petite or otherwise) who had in the post-war period become the custodians of a stultifying bureaucracy, dedicated often to little more than its own reproduction. In this respect we might suggest that the excellence project took root in America and prospered precisely because it offered itself to the public and to policy-makers as a change programme designed to wrest social organization from the bureaucrats, from the accountants and from 'the lieuten-ants' (Whyte [1956] 1961: 46) who had been charged with its reproduction so that this might be placed, once more, in the hands of leaders – rehabilitated be-fore the public and fired with a passion for change. Thus, the excellence project might be read as the triumph of charisma over bureaucracy – an expression of the simple demand that decision-making powers be taken from the mid-level bureaucrat and returned to a newly confident and energized elite, which in being freed from the fetters of scientism would (a) lead from the front in a fashion that would through storytelling (b) offer purpose and a sense of belonging to those who had become disinclined to accept that their lot in life was simply to execute plans developed elsewhere.

Yet no matter how we choose to rationalize the success of the excellence project it is surely ironic that those who had been recruited to bring conceptual sophistication and communicability to the musings of the Organization Practice found that their rendering of the contemporary problems of management had been bested by the contemporaries whom they had been recruited to support. In our next section we will offer an analytical account of *The Art of Japanese Manage-ment,* designed to explore this curious outcome. Perhaps heretically I will suggest that in choosing *In Search of Excellence* over *The Art of Japanese Management*, the US public took a wrong turn, missing the opportunity to pursue, what Sir Peter Parker (then chairman of British Rail) has referred to as 'a social policy of enter-prise' (Pascale and Athos [1981] 1986: xx).

The art of Japanese management

Despite Whyte's concerns over a growing anti-intellectual tide in America, *The Art of Japanese Management* is, we should note, a rigorous and intellectually robust work. In his prefacing remarks for the 1986 edition of this work Sir Peter Parker offers a summary of the book's core concerns and philosophy. He observes that the previously amenable world known to the managerial elites of Britain and the United States had recently ceased to exist. In so doing, however, he alludes to a rather scholarly grasp of English history. Highlighting the central problems fac-ing management in the US Parker observes that 'the west' had continued to view the world 'through Tawney-tinted glasses'[10] (Pascale and Athos [1981] 1986: xvi).

The Art of Japanese Management builds squarely on the McKinsey '7-S' frame-work, unfolds over eight chapters and, we should note, carries an introduction from Ronald Daniel, the managing director of McKinsey and Co., whom we encountered a few moments ago. In his introductory remarks, Daniel insists that support for the McKinsey model should not be read as an attack on 'the analytical methodologies that have been developed, taught and applied during the last three decades' (Pascale and Athos [1981] 1986: xxiv), adding that: 'These methods have contributed importantly to the formulation of business strategies, the development of effective organization structures, and the definition of useful systems for managing businesses large and small. About this there is no doubt' (xxiv).

Nevertheless, Daniel insisted (and here he seems to hedge his bets) that it is 'the absence of, or conflicts within' the 7-S framework 'that accounts for weak corporate performance' (xxiv). Signalling his support for a larger programme of change informed by this framework, Daniel told those preparing to read *The Art of Japanese Management* that he hoped that 'much more reseaach [sic]' would be developed to examine 'the nature of and effect on performance of superordinate goals' (xxiv) and to investigate 'the other so-called soft S's: staff, style and skill' (xxv).

The Art of Japanese Management utilizes the 7-S framework to offer an analytical comparison of the systems of management, said to be characteristic of America and Japan. *Panasonic* headed by Matsushita is offered to us as an exemplar of Japanese management practices while the United States is represented by *ITT,* which at this time was managed by Harold Geneen.

Geneen, as we shall see, comes out of this exercise in comparison poorly. It is worth noting, however, that while Pascale and Athos were keen to highlight the qualities of Japanese management practice, they also chose to celebrate the operation and performance of a small number of notable US organizations. *IBM, Boeing, Procter & Gamble, Delta Airlines, 3M* and *Hewlett-Packard* are, for example, celebrated as high performing organizations who have built success on a balanced embrace of the 'hard' and 'soft' factors of business revealed through the 7-S framework.

At the outset, Pascale and Athos seem to offer their support to the position adopted by Daniel and later echoed by Peters and Waterman. Chapter 1 for example begins by celebrating US business excellence and while noting Japan's growing economic might, reminds us that Japanese business had grown and prospered by adapting US management systems. Yet as the text progresses the position of the authors seems to harden on the qualities of the US system and on its prospects for constructive change. Chapters 2 and 3 of *The Art of Japanese Management,* for example, offer contrasting accounts of *Panasonic* and *ITT,* Matsushita and Geneen. Pascale and Athos acknowledge that under Geneen's management *ITT* had grown to become a world-leading organization. Indeed, for the benefit of those under 50 years of age, it is perhaps worth observing that in 1959 when Geneen joined the company, *ITT* had posted sales of $765.6 million and modest profits of $29 million (with less than one half of this flowing from operating income). Yet by 1977 the company had reported 58 consecutive quarters of growth (and only two instances where growth fell below 11% per annum) – sales of $16.7 billion and earnings of $562 million. Indeed, under Geneen's stewardship *ITT* had become a huge conglomerate with 350 business units across 80 countries (Geneen with Moscow, 1986).

Despite this truly impressive track record, Pascale and Athos complain that Geneen's stewardship of *ITT* focused narrowly on a concern for the hard-s factors. Furthermore, they argue that this focus has, in effect, acted to limit and to undermine Geneen's legacy. Justifying this assertion, Pascale and Athos observe that *ITT* has faltered following Geneen's retirement. Indeed, they suggest that Geneen failed as chief executive, despite his bottom-line successes, because he did not develop an organization and a credo that was sustainable in his absence. Contrasting Geneen's 'aggressive, competitive … forceful [and] downright threatening' approach to management (Pascale and Athos [1981] 1986: 151) with that of Matsushita, Pascale and Athos suggest that *Panasonic* had developed a more balanced and hence a more sustainable business model, one that was, we should note, able to withstand the retirement of key personnel.

Acknowledging that the balance exercised by *Panasonic* is subtle, nuanced and, perhaps difficult for those entrenched in US business to discern and to accept, Pascale and Athos ([1981] 1986: 85) quote Takeo Fujisawa, co-founder of the *Honda Motor Company*: "Japanese and American management is 95% the same and differs in all important respects".

This quotation, of course, jars with comments made in earlier chapters as to the separate but equal capabilities of US and Japanese management and demonstrates, I suggest, a hardening of the authors' position as to the potential of US management and the prospects for the US economy. And yet light remains within this tunnel because there is, still, the suggestion (a) that the United States may be reformed and (b) that the reformation of the United States may be executed in a manner that reflects distinctly American virtues. This light is however all but extinguished in the following chapters which consider the true depth of the US problem. In Chapter 4, for example, the authors begin by telling us that American managers *could* change and *could* learn to manage organizations in a fashion that would secure success inter-generationally. Yet as the book proceeds, Pascale and Athos seem to concede that the realistic prospects for success in this change management endeavour are quite low. Indeed, by Chapter 6, the authors come close to suggesting that US management (presumably beyond the few US exemplars noted above) is plagued by a national neurosis that is manifest in a systemic approach that is short-termist, which indulges macho posturing and bullying, which is inclined to grant rapid advance to those relatively inexperienced in people management and which is only too willing to punish any pragmatic exercise of humanity.

Highlighting the manner in which the normal forms of human decency are squeezed out by the American system of management, Pascale and Athos draw our attention to a *Forbes*[11] articles that highlights 'The Ten Toughest Bosses'. Pascale and Athos do seem to concede that this feature is a piece of journalistic, page-filling whimsy. And at some level this is probably correct. Yet it is also worth observing that the writer retained by *Forbes* simply fails to challenge the conduct documented in the piece. Furthermore, we should note that *Fortune* later ran a very similar piece (see Dumaine and Berlin, 1993) that is similarly inclined to giggle in the face of what is, truthfully, the awful behaviour of those at the top of American business and which concludes by washing its hands of the problem, advising those bullied and abused that they can always quit!

Such abject failures in/of management (and of basic human decency), Pascale and Athos make plain, run contrary to the more balanced and long-term approaches that, we are assured, has allowed the Japanese to 'get everyone in the organization to be alert, to look for opportunities to do things better, and to strive by virtue of each small contribution to make the company succeed' (Pascale and Athos, [1981] 1986: 189).

Chapter 7 of *The Art of Japanese Management* advances this theme further yet expresses it in more cultural terms. Thus, Chapter 7 focuses attention on executives and their conduct and suggests that in order to harvest the small contributions from across the organization that have assured Japan's competitive success, American business leaders would need to become makers of meaning for their colleagues and customers. The problem being, of course, that the American system revealed by Pascale and Athos has already shown itself to be, in effect, constitutionally incapable of true business excellence because it is remote, short-termist, driven by numbers rather than by purpose, and cares little for its employees or, indeed, for its customers!

Given this account of US management, it is perhaps unsurprising that a significant portion of the US public – and especially those *named and shamed* in *The Art of Japanese Management* reacted pretty negatively.

Geneen fights back

In a text published some five years after the first publication of *The Art of Japanese Management,* Geneen casts doubt on 'the Japanese economic miracle' and suggests that Pascale and Athos [1981] (1986) had chosen to see the world not through Tawney coloured lenses but through rose-tinted spectacles. Thus, the differences said to exist between US and Japanese management, are, Geneen insists, altogether less pronounced than we have imagined. And this is probably a fair point albeit one that Geneen fails to substantiate. For example Moriguchi and Ono (2006) point out that the 'lifetime employment' commitment vaunted by many Western commentators on Japan was, in truth, only ever available to a minority of the workforce and was not offered to women. Furthermore, Kamata (1983) suggests that employment within Japan's automobile plants was, for temporary workers at least, brutal and compared unfavourably to the conditions that had prevailed in Ford's factory during the early years of the twentieth century (see Beynon, 1978)!

It is notable however that Geneen chooses not to mention the work of Pascale and Athos, while developing what can only be read as a very muscular rebuttal to *The Art of Japanese Management.* Accounting for Japan's success, Geneen, while studiously ignoring the work of Pascale and Athos, begins by rejecting a cultural form of analysis:

They [the Japanese] undersell us for mundane reasons. Japanese labour costs are far below ours; their factories, built there after the devastation of World War II, are newer, more modern, and far more efficient than ours. It costs them $1,500- $1,800 less to build a car than it costs us. They can afford to invest some of the margin in quality controls that Detroit manufacturers apparently felt were not possible for them up to now.

Geneen with Moscow (1986: 18)

Three points arise however from Geneen's assertion as to the foundations of Japan's economic success. First, Geneen's very public, if veiled, attack on Pascale and Athos seems to be unaware of the argument actually advanced by the authors. Of course, I can understand and I can accept that for personal reasons, Geneen might not have been keen to linger on the precise details of the argument developed in *The Art of Japanese Management*. After all, Pascale and Athos had questioned, very publicly, Geneen's managerial acumen and had made unsubstantiated suggestions regarding his early upbringing.[12] Yet I cannot begin to imagine why a man renowned for his laser-like focus on facts and for his attention to detail would, in the preparation of his (veiled) rebuttal, fail to read the analysis of Pascale and Athos. And yet there is more than enough in Geneen's (implicit) rebuttal of *The Art of Japanese Management* to support this suggestion. Thus, we should acknowledge that in the early stages of their work, Pascale and Athos paused, quite deliberately, to challenge those who had suggested that Japan's economic success depended on poverty wages, poor environmental standards or some other distortion of the terms of trade:

Today, Japan's wages are slightly higher than those in the United States, and the cost of doing business in Japan – with imported raw materials, expensive real estate, and crowded highways – is decidedly higher. American executives complain of extra costs that stem from occupational safety regulations and pollution controls. While initially lagging, Japan's standards are now amongst the most stringent in the world.

Pascale and Athos ([1981] 1986: 20–21)

Second, it is worth observing that while he is plainly unable to countenance, explicitly, the logical conclusion of his own assertion, Geneen's attack on Pascale and Athos, effectively cedes the field to his tormentors. Thus, Geneen, in effect, acknowledges that US managers (guided by his approach and his demands) *had* failed to meet the Japanese challenge and had made poor choices over a prolonged period of time.

Third, we would do well to note that, while refusing to accept the truth of the situation outlined by Pascale and Athos, Geneen chooses to indulge in a little deflection. Indeed, Geneen invokes a trope that deserves to be identified as both grubby and xenophobic to attack those who would question his approach and legacy. Building on an account of America and Americans, which Whyte [1956]

(1961) had dismantled some 30 years previously, Geneen asks (rhetorically), 'would we Americans really want to trade our heritage of personal freedoms and individual opportunity for the ingrown paternalism, humility and selflessness of the Japanese?' (Geneen with Moscow, 1986: 17).

And this is, I think, the crux of the problem. Rather than accept that there was something wrong in the United States and rather than accept that lessons might be taken from Japan, Geneen chose, instead, to rewrite US history, ignoring its interdependent spirit.

Responding to Geneen therefore I will ask, Was *The Western Electric Company*, somehow betraying the core values of America by choosing to place itself within its community as a force for good?

By 1939 and for the benefit of the 29,000 workers (drawn from 60 separate nations) employed at its Hawthorne Works in Chicago, *The Western Electric Company* had:

- arranged, encouraged and managed a company stock participation plan for employees,
- developed insurance plans and saving plans for employees, taking deductions at source,
- operated a non-contributory pension plan,
- maintained a programme of recreational, social and athletic activities including an evening school where 3,000 students received instruction in 45 different subjects (Roethlisberger and Dickson with Wright [1939] 1964: 9).

So, was *The Western Electric Company* un-American?

Should it have been black-listed by McCarthy? Investigated by Hoover?

I will not stoop to answer what is, after all, a series of mocking rhetorical questions. But I will add that in highlighting the virtues of the Japanese approach to management Pascale and Athos *were* (quite unlike Geneen) at least aware of Japan's history and had, albeit coyly, warned that care would need to be taken to ensure that corporate activism did note, over time, develop into an unwholesome corporatism. Nonetheless, the core message of *The Art of Japanese Management* is clear and is clearly rendered in the prefacing comments offered by Sir Peter Parker:

> To concede victory to Matsushita [over Geneen] is to celebrate excellent management. The message is not that only Japanese management is supreme; it is that success in enterprise depends on management above all, and what matters is not whether the management is Japanese, American, British or Ruritanian but that it is excellent.
>
> *Pascale and Athos ([1981] 1986: xix)*

The problem being, of course, that while Japanese managers had (at some level) embraced the outline credo of excellence, so much of American management

had not and could not.[13] Taking issue with those inclined to reject the core message of *The Art of Japanese Management,* therefore, Sampson (1995: 212) reminds
us that the success of the *General Motors-Toyota* collaboration in the NUMMI car
plant offers 'clear proof that GM's past faults were not with the workers but with
the managers'.

Summarizing the core message of *The Art of Japanese Management,* Parker tells
us that the appeal of the text rests on the understanding that this text communicates to the few who were prepared to listen, an appreciation of business founded
on something that *The Western Electric Company* had understood and what American managers had, it seems, subsequently chosen to neglect: that business and
organizational endeavours more generally depend on social co-operation and
reciprocity – on 'the broader awareness that managing means leading and that
managing cannot be disassociated from community responsibilities' (Pascale and
Athos [1981] 1986: xx). In this regard what made *Panasonic's* approach to management special and what made it worthy of further consideration and emulation
was not that it was 'Japanese'. It was instead its public articulation of the understanding that business leadership needs to be enacted within contexts that honour explicitly, plurality, responsibility and social reciprocity. This commitment
to the essentials of business leadership, however, was not foremost in the parallel
analysis developed by Peters and Waterman (1982). Indeed, as we shall see in
our next chapter *In Search of Excellence* 'took the fifth' on the broader context
of American management preferring, instead, to offer a romanticized account,
which while publicly sceptical of the virtues of committee decision-making,
largely ignored those institutional processes and historically developed compromises that have shaped the social structure of US business. This acontextual account of management and change as Chapter 2 will discuss, enabled what might
be termed a 'year zero' approach. The problem being, of course, that this has
allowed the headline elements of the excellence project to be harnessed to larger
changes that are, in truth, contrary to the espoused credo, which Peters and Waterman had developed within the covers of *In Search of Excellence.*

Concluding comments

This chapter has offered an examination of the genesis of the McKinsey 7–S
framework which is, we have suggested, foundational to the excellence project.
Typically, the happy atom is placed before students as a useful heuristic which
captures the social-technical totality of business organizations. While acknowledging the elegance of this heuristic, we have, nonetheless, offered reflections
on the social-political processes involved in the constitution of this framework.
Building on the work of Bruno Latour (1987) we have argued that the ready-
made account of the 7–S framework that is served to students in the textbooks
prepared for their education in 'management' obscures and elides the broader
processes that were involved in its development and articulation. Offering an
account of the controversies and compromises associated with the making of the

'7-S' model we have considered the social-political processes and the broader competitive challenges that shaped the development of this, now, familiar framework so that we might be reminded of the political realities of social organization.

Noting that Pascale and Athos were recruited to the 'Organization Practice' to bring conceptual sophistication and memorability to the nascent excellent project, I have reminded readers that the articulation of business excellence developed by these authors was, ironically, bested by the commercial project later developed by Peters and Waterman (1982). While acknowledging that the relative, and contrasting, fortunes of these texts is, often taken to be, simply, an outcome of nationalist sensibilities, I have gone beyond this rationalization to suggest a different reading of events. I have, therefore, suggested that *In Search of Excellence* prospered in the face of the alternative laid down by *The Art of Japanese Management* precisely because it failed to challenge the deeper, core problems of US business culture, and so, encouraged change and renewal in the absence of a larger root-and-branch reform of American business. In short, *In Search of Excellence* prospered because it was, in comparison to the analysis developed by Pascale and Athos, altogether more conservative! Acknowledging this reality I have suggested that in choosing Peters and Waterman over Pascale and Athos, practitioners and policy-makers have denied themselves the opportunity to develop an approach to management (a) founded on an appreciation of community and based (b) on an understanding of social reciprocity that *just might have* resisted the neo-liberalism that would be unleashed on the West in the 1980s. This is an issue we will pursue in our next chapter. But before we turn to this matter it is, perhaps, worth pausing to offer reflections on the term that has through (casual) application become our central motif. In short it is time to offer critical reflection on the nature and character of the excellence project, which we have suggested took the McKinsey '7-S' framework as its foundation. In other words, what makes excellence a project?

★ ★ ★ ★ ★

The excellence project

The commercial success of *In Search of Excellence* was, as we have seen, unlikely and largely, unexpected. It would be a historical folly verging on teleology, therefore, to suggest that, at the outset, the architects of the '7-S framework' understood that they were embarking on a body of work that would literally re-cast our image of management and which would, furthermore, continue to occupy a central position within the management studies curriculum some four decades after its first articulation.

In retrospect it is, of course, plain that the architects of the McKinsey '7-S' framework *have* engineered, very publicly, a revolution in the ways in which we think about management, talk about management *and* conduct ourselves 'managerially'. Yet the potted history of management which we teach our students tends to elide key processes and in so doing tends to beguile us with its tautologies. In an attempt to challenge the ready-made history of business excellence therefore I have attempted to demonstrate that the excellence project, while offering itself boldly as a plan to revitalize American management in the face of a growing Japanese challenge was, at root, the product of a developing competitive crisis within McKinsey and Co., which despite internal wrangling successfully recruited advocates and clients who provided the resources necessary to allow Pascale and Athos to take this developing programme of work to a wider, non-specialist audience through the publication of *The Art of Japanese Management*. And yet it is apparent that the excellence project, constituted as such in hindsight, was a fraught and uncertain endeavour with fairly modest and local aspirations that might have been stopped in its tracks by initial public and corporate reaction to the work of Pascale and Athos. In the wings, however, Peters and Waterman were waiting – with crucial revisions.

As we shall see in our next chapter, Peters and Waterman had prepared an alternative and, in any sense, a domesticated reading of the challenges of business excellence, more palatable to the American public and its policy-makers. Turning a blind eye[14] to the systemic problems that Pascale and Athos had identified within American culture and within American management, Peters and Waterman offered instead the reassurance that the excellent companies would act as the vanguard of/for transformational change. This selective blindness, as we will learn, plainly appealed to those elites who prefer a romantic and more conservative form of radicalism. Yet it conjured, for the rest of us, new monsters.

Notes

1 I offer no apologies for this 'protracted moment': The Book of Genesis after all spreads its canvas across six days of labour and a day of rest!

2 Company insiders, as Kiechel (2010: 97–98) reminds us routinely speak of the McKinsey and Co. partnership as 'the firm'.

3 Peters and Waterman (1982: 3) render this just a little differently. They suggest that in 1977 McKinsey launched 'two internal task forces' to investigate 'strategy' and 'effectiveness'.

4 Of course, Peters and Waterman (1982) suggest that Royal Dutch Shell offered the team the encouragement necessary to continue with the project.

5 In an earlier work published in 2005 but first drafted to mark his 60th birthday in 2002 entitled *Sixty* (Peters, 2005e) seems more inclined to forgiveness. Here he presents Gerstner's belated cultural conversion to all things cultural as a simple vindication of his commitment to the 'soft stuff' whereas in *The Excellence Dividend*, Peters (2018) is inclined to treat Gerstner's conversion as an opportunity to launch a grander valedictory statement.

6 In an interview with Anthony Gell (June 9, 2014), Peters advances the suggestion less cautiously and simply asserts that he and Bob Waterman were simply the first to use 'excellence' in a business context.

7 Wikipedia an intermittently reliable source has suggested that T J Watson Jr [1963] (2003) of IBM was the first to make business excellence a core element of management. This assertion, however, is mistaken and is based on a very loose interpretation of the three-part philosophy outlined by Watson and owes much I suspect to

Gerstner's (2002: 184) suggestion that IBM is built on three pillars, first of which is, 'Excellence in everything we do'. In fact the philosophy built by the younger Watson suggests that business should (1) respect the individual, should (2) give the best service of any company in the world and should (3) pursue all tasks on the understanding that they may be executed in a superior fashion. There are, it is plain, key affinities between Watson's credo and that later expounded by Peters and Waterman – and this should come as no real surprise since IBM features very prominently within *In Search of Excellence* – yet it is a stretch to suggest that Watson offers, in any developed sense an account of 'excellence'. Indeed, we would do well to note that Watson uses the term only once and in a very conventional manner: 'To maintain our reputation for excellent service, we long ago established high standards for the selection of salesmen and customer engineers' (Watson [1963] 2003: 30).

8 This day has been convened, of course, to mark the enduring contribution made by the late Peter Drucker to the theory and practice of management. The address was delivered on November 6th 2010.

9 This is, of course, a very thinly veiled reference to Trump's, hateful 'Make America Great Again' (MAGA) trope.

10 This rather lovely turn of phrase is, essentially an 'in joke' open only to those who share with Sir Peter Parker, knowledge of the works of the English historian, RH Tawney.

11 This piece appeared in *Forbes* (21/04/1980: 62–65).

12 Pascale and Athos [1981] (1986: 151) develop a deeply unflattering picture of Geneen, suggesting that his focus on the 'hard s' factors and his tendency to dominate and to bully colleagues is a deep-seated reaction to childhood powerlessness. We should note that no evidence is offered to support what amounts to unfounded speculation on this subject.

13 Peters (2018: xiii) suggests a core difference between the Japanese approach to management and that adopted by US counterparts. He tells us that Honda founder Soichiro Honda has observed, 'When Congress passes new emissions standards, we hire 50 more engineers and GM hires 50 more lawyers. Peters provides no source for this observation; nonetheless, Freiberg and Freiberg (1997) offer us good reason to accept that there may be truth in this statement and that legal obstruction may well be a default position for corporate America. Thus, the Freibergs observe that the early years of Southwest Airlines (an organization much admired by Peters) were marked by protracted legal battles launched by industry incumbents who, rather than compete with the new entrant, sought to legislate it out of existence. The Freibergs also note that when this tactic failed, the larger incumbents simply stooped to unlawful price fixing!

14 Given Tom Peters' admiration for Lord Horatio Nelson this is surely more than a little poetic!

2

THE WORKS OF TOM PETERS, 1982–1985

Introduction

In the chapter that introduced this work we observed that Tom Peters has had a profound impact on the world of business and on our daily lives more generally. Indeed, we argued that in the 1980s Tom Peters *entered* the market for management knowledge and in so doing *altered* the way we speak of managerial matters. In addition we suggested that in forging changes to the language of business Tom Peters has made space for new forms of conduct and for new modes of organizing.

In Chapter 1, we extended this analysis by offering an account of the development of the 'excellence project'. Focusing on the McKinsey 7-S framework, which Kiechel (2010: 163–164) suggests is 'the closest thing to an organizing paradigm to be found' in the excellence project, I offered a comparison of *In Search of Excellence* and *The Art of Japanese Management*. In this chapter, I will extend this discussion of the excellence project and will offer an analysis of the eight attributes of excellence that bring order and structure to *In Search of Excellence*. Yet before we turn to this we should acknowledge that, soon, the 'happy atom' will simply drop out of our narrative.

The McKinsey framework features prominently within student textbooks, is used to organize the analysis of *The Art of Japanese Management* and is discussed within the opening sections of *In Search of Excellence* yet it 'virtually disappears' (Kiechel, 2010: 164) from the later works of Peters. Kiechel, for example, observes that the 7-S framework is wholly absent from *A Passion for Excellence* (Peters and Austin, 1985) and from *Thriving on Chaos* (Peters, 1987) and merits just three pages in *Liberation Management* (Peters, 1992), which is, we should note, a mammoth work.

How might this be explained? Two lines of analysis spring immediately to mind. The first of these arguments is, perhaps, 'innocent' insofar as it relates to matters philosophical whereas the second is a little more political.

DOI: 10.4324/9781003188940-3

Our philosophical rationalization of the fate of the 7-S framework in the work of Peters is based on the suggestion that this heuristic may be considered to be, like Wittgenstein's ladder, a tool that may be set aside when its work is done. In this respect it is possible to suggest that the 7-S framework is written out of Peters' narratives of business simply because, having revealed the necessary interaction of the soft and hard elements of business and the important role which the soft-s factors perform in matters of strategic implementation, its work was done. Our second rationalization of the fate of the 'happy atom' is, however, rather more political and makes room for the suggestion that, in the light of his treatment by 'the firm', Peters may simply have been disinclined to continue to share credit for the excellence project with McKinsey, and so, chose to downplay the significance of the heuristic that had shaped his appreciation of excellence. Both arguments have their own merits, of course, and for what it's worth my guess is that we may never *really* know why the 7-S framework was, in effect, dropped by Tom Peters – history being some complex mixture of cock-up and conspiracy! For the moment, therefore, we must continue to consider that which within the covers of *In Search of Excellence* may be established.

★ ★ ★ ★ ★

In my introductory remarks I suggested that it would be a mistake to assume that, everyone recognises the part which Peters has played in shaping the language and practice of business. Some readers, I have observed, may know nothing of the life and works of Tom Peters while others may have an intimate knowledge of his musings on management, even while harbouring doubts about his contribution to this arena. My suspicion, however, is that most readers will fall somewhere between these two poles. In other words, my experience suggests that most people connected with business have *heard of* Tom Peters but, in truth, are not qualified to venture an opinion as to the nature (and quality) of his excellence project because they have no detailed knowledge of the ideas and orientations that underpin his account of the business of management. Recognizing that most readers will have, only, a very limited appreciation of the life and works of this, key, management commentator this chapter, and the one which follows, will offer a review of Tom Peters' main published works on management.

The current chapter will focus on the main texts published by Tom Peters in 1982 and in 1985 whereas our next chapter will focus on the eight, key, texts produced by Peters since 1987. At first glance this division of Peters' work into two chapters – the first dealing with only two texts while the second wrestles with a further eight – might appear unbalanced. Yet first impressions can deceive. In fact, Chapters 2 and 3 have been structured to bring balance to this text when it is considered as a whole. This chapter and the next, therefore, have been crafted to produce an account of the works of Tom Peters which divides:

- jointly *versus* single authored texts,
- early *versus* later 'guru works' (Crainer, 1997),

- those texts that have excited academic commentary and analysis *versus* those that have, in contrast, generated little in the way of academic commentary or review.

Taken together, however, Chapters 2 and 3 should be read as an attempt (a) to explore the key ideas and arguments underpinning this author's works and (b) to facilitate the narrative re-view of Tom Peters' work that will be undertaken in later chapters.

We will begin our exploration of the ideas and arguments of Tom Peters, however, not by considering *his* writing but with the words of two of his (unofficial) biographers – Stuart Crainer and Robert Heller.

Peters' biographers

Prefacing his endorsement of the wit and wisdom of Tom Peters, the cover of Robert Heller's (2000) biography describes this commentator as a 'business *mastermind*' (original emphasis) who has 'transformed the world of business'. Indeed, Heller suggests that Tom Peters stands at the top of an industry which he, in effect, created. Thus, Heller notes,

> Tom Peters built his reputation as the archetype of the evangelical guru on one book, *In Search of Excellence*. Published in 1982, this title has outsold all other management books by millions of copies.
>
> *Heller (2000: 5)*

Stuart Crainer (1997: 7) offers a similar, if more critical account of this man's project and legacy. He observes that

> Tom Peters has spawned an industry – the management guru business – populated by an array of top academics, consultants, a sprinkling of former executives and a fair share of charlatans. Competition [in this industry] is fierce and the pace fast. The world's managers demand a constant stream of books, seminars, conferences, and videos. And they want more. Ideas are packaged and repackaged. Names become brands and every grain of innovative thinking is exploited for all it is worth. The bitchiness of academia is combined with the ruthlessness of the world of management consultancy.

Highlighting the manner in which Peters' reputation and renown depends on his seminars (and on the manner in which these are reported and repackaged for home-viewing), *The Economist* (September 24, 1994) locates Peters as a performer within a branch of the performing arts which it labels as 'management theatre'.

Tom Peters' contribution to the business of publishing is clear and enduring. He has enjoyed mass-market sales for 40 years. Indeed, he, in effect, spawned and raised a market niche that, now, successfully straddles the industry seg-ments of publishing devoted to 'Business' and to 'Self-help' (Micklethwait and Wooldridge, 1997). Peters' contribution to 'management theatre' is similarly clear and uncontested. In Heller's (2000: 5) terms Tom Peters *is* 'the archetype of the evangelical [business] guru'. Yet when it comes time to weigh up Peters' contribution to management thought and practice the tone of the discourse changes. Many, who readily concede that Peters is an evangelist and a per-former of world renown, stubbornly, insist that Peters' self-belief and stage-craft serve, only, to mask the fact that his thinking is cloudy and his analyses limited.

Many of the criticisms made of Tom Peters' works are, we should note, accu-rate and well-framed. However, it would be a mistake to assume that all of Peters' critics are similarly well informed. Some critics, as we shall see, plainly misun-derstand this author's work while others might, more accurately, be charged, simply, with failing to read the work of Peters.

* * * * *

Writing for *The Times* (December 5,1992) Carole Leonard offers a review of *Lib-eration Management* (Peters, 1992), which suggests that she is simply unqualified to publish an opinion on Tom Peters. Leonard tells us that *Liberation Management* is the follow-up to Peters' second text *Thriving on Chaos*, which was produced in 1989. The problem for Leonard's review, however, is that *Thriving on Chaos* was Peters' third text and was, first, published in 1987!

In the inaugural edition of the journal *Critical Perspectives on International Busi-ness,* Joanne Roberts (2005) makes similar errors. Casting a critical eye over the works of Tom Peters, Roberts attacks the publishing interests which, as she sees it, shape and distort the market for management knowledge. She argues that publishers of business books have a taste for particular forms and formats of work (which she disparages). Furthermore, she argues that these publishers, like their commissioning counterparts in the cinematic industry, seem to value the familiar over works of genuine originality, and so, prefer to produce sequels to previously successful 'blockbusters'. Thus, she observes that

> management gurus, assisted by their publishers, adopt certain well-formulated methods to ensure the successful sale of their book. Such meth-ods include the production of sequels to successful books. For instance, Peters and Waterman's (1983) *In Search of Excellence* was followed by *The Passion for Excellence* (Peters and Austin, 1994) and most recently by *Re-im-aging! Business Excellence in a Disruptive Age* (Peters, 2003).
>
> *Roberts (2005: 57–58)*

Roberts may have a point: The publishing industry is pretty conservative and does, indeed, demonstrate a preference for fashionable topics and marketable 'faces'. Yet there are a few problems with the specifics of Roberts' critique – problems which suggest that she is, simply, not qualified to offer an opinion on the work of Tom Peters. Thus, we would do well to note that the 1994 text to which Roberts refers is actually entitled *A Passion for Excellence* and was first published in 1985. Furthermore, the 2003 text, which Roberts lists is actually entitled *Re-imagine* and not *Re-imaging!* Finally, it is I suggest difficult to view *Re-imagine* as a simple sequel to *A Passion for Excellence.*

A sequel is commonly defined as a continuation of an earlier story. Now while it might be accurate to portray *A Passion for Excellence* as a sequel to *In Search of Excellence* and while there are certain thematic continuities that link Peters' first work to his later texts it is difficult to view *Re-imagine* as a simple sequel to *A Passion for Excellence* since this work (as we shall see in Chapter 3) is quite unlike the other texts listed by Roberts in terms of lay-out, tone *and* narrative.

Sampson (1995), normally a reliable chronicler of the nature of managerial practice and its attendant frailties and inconsistencies (see Sampson, 1973, [1975] 1991), makes similar errors as he discusses the work of Peters. These errors suggest that he, too, regards Peters as a writer who must be critiqued but need not be read. For example, Sampson suggests that *Liberation Management* (1992) is a sequel to *In Search of Excellence* (Peters and Waterman, 1982). Yet this claim, of course, overlooks the fact that Peters published two more texts on the business of management during this decade, namely *A Passion for Excellence* (Peters and Austin, 1985) and *Thriving on Chaos* (Peters, 1987). In addition we should note that Sampson draws our attention to a later work of Peters but misrepresents its title! Thus, Sampson (1995: 259) draws our attention to a work entitled 'Crazy times call for crazy organizations' but seems not to understand that this is, in fact, the sub-title of *The Pursuit of Wow* (Peters, 1994).

Recognizing the limitations of many of those commentaries that have sought a critical engagement with Peters, and with the excellence project, this chapter offers:

a   a critical review of the first two key works produced by this author *and*
b   an analysis of key commentaries produced by his critics and detractors.

In this endeavour, and for ease of exposition, I will offer a chronological analysis of Tom Peters' main published texts on management.

Figure 2.1 offers a list of Tom Peters' main texts on management while Figure 2.2 lists those texts, which, for want of a better term, I have labelled as 'minor works'. These minor works are excluded from our present analysis on the understanding that they offer condensed (and/or repackaged) versions of ideas and arguments that have been developed in those texts, here taken to be the major works of Peters. Our analysis commences therefore with an account of *In Search of Excellence* – the text that, in effect, launched the excellence project.

(1982) *In Search of Excellence* (joint with Robert Waterman)
(1985) *A Passion for Excellence* (joint with Nancy Austin)
(1987) *Thriving on Chaos*
(1992) *Liberation Management*
(1993) *The Tom Peters Seminar: Crazy Times call for Crazy Organizations*
(1994) *The Pursuit of Wow!*
(1997) *The Circle of Innovation: You can't shrink your way to greatness*
(2003) *Re-imagine! Business Excellence in a Disruptive age*
(2010) *The Little BIG things: 163 ways to pursue excellence*
(2018) *The Excellence Dividend: Meeting the Tech Tide with Work that Wows and Jobs that Last*

FIGURE 2.1   A catalogue of Tom Peters' major books on the business of management.

(1999a) *The BrandYou 50*
(1999b) *The Project50*
(1999c) *The Professional Service Firm50*
(2005a) *Tom Peters Essentials: Design* (joint with Marti Barletta)
(2005b) *Tom Peters Essentials: Talent* (joint with Marti Barletta)
(2005c) *Tom Peters Essentials: Leadership* (joint with Marti Barletta)
(2005d) *Tom Peters Essentials: Trends* (joint with Marti Barletta)
(2005e) *Sixty*
(2021) *Excellence Now: Extreme Humanism*

FIGURE 2.2   A catalogue of Tom Peters' minor books on the business of management.

In Search of Excellence

In Search of Excellence was first published in 1982 as the collaborative product of Tom Peters and his, McKinsey consulting colleague, Bob Waterman. In our introductory chapter and in Chapter 1, we offered an account of excellence-in-the-making as we considered the economic pressures and the internal machinations that shaped McKinsey and Co., in the 1970s and 1980s. In this chapter we will shift focus slightly. Thus, we commence our critical review of *In Search of Excellence* with reflections on the peculiarities of the socio-economic context that characterized America – and much of Western Europe – during the 1970s and early 1980s.

The recession of the early 1980s

From 1981 to 1983 America endured a deep business recession. Hyatt (1999) paraphrasing Tom Peters has observed that, at this time, America had an unemployment rate in excess of 10% an inflation rate approaching 15% and a banking interest rate in excess of 20%. This set of economic circumstances, the worst America had suffered in five decades led to street scenes which many thought, (or hoped), had been consigned to an earlier period of history. *The Observer* (quoted in Baskerville and Willett, 1985) for example, reported that in Washington DC 17,000 people had queued for up to five hours, to receive food handouts. Similarly the American Bureau of Census Statistics published figures which show, only too painfully, the social impact of this economic dislocation. Thus, the Bureau of Census Statistics observed that in 1983, 34.4 million Americans (12% of the population) were living below the poverty line.

By the early 1980s, therefore, there was for many Americans, the feeling that things were going badly wrong. This feeling was reinforced by the impression that America, and Americans, were suffering while others, (in popular imagination 'the Japanese') prospered.

The Japanese miracle

Fears regarding Japanese economic success and the growing dominance of the Asian economies more generally had, of course, been troubling a number of key commentators and many, ordinary, Americans before the recession of 1981–1983. As early as 1970 Kahn (1970), for example, had published *The Emerging Japanese Superstate,* which argued that Japanese, per capita, income would exceed that of the United States by the year 2000 as Japan rose, inexorably, to become an economic superpower. However, by 1978, Kahn, this time working with a co-author (Kahn and Pepper, 1978) had revised his forecast and was now suggesting that the Japanese economic mission – to catch up with the West – would be accomplished by 1980. This futurology, mocked we should note by two decades of economic stagnation, was in the 1970s both alarming and persuasive. Indeed, it led a great number of industrialists, politicians and policy-makers to ponder the reasons for the success of the Japanese economy and the apparent slippage of America's.

Perhaps the most famous statement on the power and potential of the Japanese economy was written by Pascale and Athos (certainly I cite it rather a lot!) who, as we have seen, applied the '7-S framework' to offer a comparative analysis of US and Japanese management practices. Commenting on the rise and rise of the Japanese economy, Pascale and Athos observed,

> In 1980 Japan's GNP was third highest in the world and if we extrapolate current trends, it would be number one by the year 2000. A country the size of Montana, Japan has virtually no physical resources, yet

it supports over 115 million people (half the population of the United States), exports $75 billion worth more goods than it imports, and has an investment rate as well as a GNP growth rate which is twice that of the United States. Japan has come to dominate in one selected industry after another – eclipsing the British in motorcycles, surpassing the Germans and Americans in automobile production, wresting leadership from the Germans and Americans and overcoming the United States' historical dominance in businesses as diverse as steel, shipbuilding, pianos, zippers and electronics…Japan is doing more than a little right. And our hypothesis is that a big part of that "something" has only a little to do with such techniques as its quality circles and lifetime employment. In this book *we will argue that a major reason for the superiority of the Japanese economy is their managerial skill.*

Pascale and Athos ([1981] 1986: 20–21; emphasis added)

For Pascale and Athos, therefore, Japanese success was taken to be a direct product of Japanese management. Indeed, it was suggested that Japanese business success was cultural at root: 'the Japanese' it was argued had become adept at manipulating organizational cultures (see Fukuda, 1988) and it was this approach to management which had given Japan its economic advantage.

In the early 1980s, therefore, there seemed two routes available to Americans; either they could work *like* the Japanese or they could work *for* the Japanese.

Rejecting such forms of argument and analysis as distorted and unhelpful (in part, no doubt, because it would prove difficult to sell to American managers), Peters and Waterman produced *In Search of Excellence*, they tell us, to educate American managers in the distinctive capabilities of *American* management. In this regard *In Search of Excellence* might be thought of as an attempt to stimulate American managers to renew and to reinvigorate an indigenous, as opposed to a foreign-based, or alien, approach to managing.

To secure this regeneration of the US economy Peters and Waterman documented the practises of a number of key, successful, US companies. In this respect, *In Search of Excellence* is based on a simple, yet plausible idea: that successful organizations share common practices. Indeed, Peters and Waterman suggest that it is what these organizations have in common that (a) explains their business success – their excellence and (b) sets them aside from less successful, less-than-excellent corporations.

Utilizing the McKinsey's 'happy atom' Peters and Waterman argued that America's economic decline was to be regarded as a product of imbalances in the American approach to management. These imbalances, they argued, had developed in the approach to management, which had emerged in American during the 1950s and 1960s. Elaborating on this point, Peters and Waterman argued that in the post-world war II era, many American managers (thanks in part to the peculiarities of the MBA curriculum and the tools provided by the consulting industry) had become fixated on the 'hard-s' factors of business *strategy, structure* and *systems* and had lost sight of the importance of *staff, style, skill* and *superordinate goals* – the 'soft-s' factors required to breathe life into strategies, structures and systems.

To correct these failings and to reinvigorate American business, Peters and Waterman advocated a balanced approach to management. This, more balanced, approach to business, as we have seen, was said to depend on the skills, energy and imagination of managerial leaders who would take primary responsibility for ensuring the productive alignment of the 'hard' and 'soft-s' factors of business.

To demonstrate the manner in which those organizations which balanced the 'soft S-factors' of business out-performed those who focused, only, on a narrower range of 'hard' concerns, Peters and Waterman chose to compose a panel of excellent companies. They formed an initial sample of firms, we are told, by:

- analysing publicly available date on performance
- reviewing the literature on organizational performance published during the previous 25 years and
- engaging in structured interviews.

It is, however, worth noting that what Peters and Waterman pass off as 'a structured interview process' is perhaps less structured and is altogether less systematic than the authors have suggested. Indeed, it is worth noting that close to one half of the excellence panel is built on what the authors acknowledge to be a more limited body of interviews. Furthermore, it is worth observing that seven of the excellence sample could provide no extensive public data on performance because these companies were, at that time, either privately owned or subsidiaries of larger corporations. Nonetheless and despite this absence of data, Peters and Waterman assure us that all of the organizations they chose to highlight as special and distinctive had, in fact, cleared all the hurdles necessary to be labelled, legitimately, as 'excellent'.

Discussing the development and refinement of their sample population, Peters and Waterman tell us that they initially identified an initial group of 75 companies whose rating on six measure of financial performance made them leaders in their respective fields. This first frame, we should note, chose to exclude banks and financial institutions because it was suggested that the regulatory environment shaping conduct within this context was sufficiently distinctive to skew results. Commenting on this exclusion, Peters and Waterman, however, hinted that they would defer the consideration of excellence within banking and finance to a later study.

The financial performance indicators selected by Peters and Waterman to construct the initial sample of 75 companies are as follows:

- compound asset growth;
- compound equity growth;
- average ratio of market to book value;

- average return on total capital;
- average return on equity;
- average return on sales.

From the initial grouping of 75 firms, Peters and Waterman tell us that they subsequently rejected 13 companies as failing to reflect the pattern of American business although it is worth noting that *Schlumberger,* a European high technology company somehow slipped through this screen and was retained within the excellent panel of companies!

Peters and Waterman tell us that they then analysed the remaining 62 cases in the light of the six financial performance indicators noted above. To qualify as 'excellent' the authors decided that each company would have to post financial results in at least four of the six selected measures, which placed it in the top half of its industry. On the basis of this analysis of performance, Peters and Waterman decided that 18 of the remaining 62 companies were (probably) excellent but did not quite meet all of their criteria. A further 30 companies were agreed to be excellent according to the criteria outlined above, while a final grouping of 14 companies were said to represent exemplars of excellence. This graded sample (of exemplars of excellence *versus* simply excellent *versus* probably excellent) we should note was developed by 'boosting' the scores awarded for innovation. Innovation is of course a rather loose term that might encompass all manner

High Technology Firms	Consumer Goods Companies	General, Industrial Companies	Service Companies	Project Management Companies	Resource-based Companies
Allen-Bradley	Blue Bell	Caterpillar Tractor	American Airlines	Bechtel	Arco
Amdahl	Eastman Kodak	Dana Corporation	Delta Airlines	Boeing	Dow Chemicals
Data General	Frito-Lay	General Motors	Disney Productions	Fluor	Du Pont
Digital Equipment	General Foods	Ingersoll-Rand	K-Mart		Exxon
Emerson Electric	Johnson & Johnson	McDermott	Marriott		Standard Oil/ Amoco
General Electric	Procter & Gamble	Minnesota Mining & Manufacturing	McDonald's		
Gould	Atari		Wal-Mart		
Hewlett-Packard	Avon				
Hughes Aircraft	Bristol-Myers				
IBM	Cheeseborough-Pond's				
Intel	Levi Strauss				
Lockheed	Mars				
National Semiconductor	Maytag				
NCR	Merck				
Raychem	Polaroid				
Rockwell	Revlon				
Schlumberger	Tupperware				
Texas Instruments					
TRW					
United Technologies					
Wang Laboratories					
Western Electric					
Westinghouse					
Xerox					

FIGURE 2.3   The Long-List of (62) Excellent Companies organized by sector and listed alphabetically.

Source: Peters and Waterman (1982).

of actions and endeavours. That said, Peters and Waterman (1982: 12 original emphasis) do offer some indication of the manner in which they constitute 'innovation' within the excellence project: '*innovative companies are especially adroit at continually responding to change of any sort in their environments*'. Yet quite how this account of innovation-as-responsiveness might be made the subject of an agreed and reliable process of 'boosting' is left solely to the imagination of the reader. Indeed, while we ponder on the many different ways in which 'innovation' and/ or responsiveness might be scored and boosted we might also speculate a little on the extent to which the nature of innovation within organizations might change if we substitute 'continuously' for 'continually' in the outline definition that is offered to us by Peters and Waterman!

We will return to concerns which arise in connection with this measurement and sampling process in a few moments; for the moment, however, we must continue (a) to outline the identity of the excellent companies and (b) the common characteristics that are said to unify what is, of course, a pretty disparate grouping.

Figure 2.3 identifies the long-list of 62 excellent companies selected for praise by Peters and Waterman. Figure 2.4 lists the 43 companies that were selected for analysis within *In Search of Excellence* while Figure 2.5 acknowledges those 14 organizations taken to be exemplars of excellence.

Peters and Waterman argued that the excellent companies listed in Figures 2.4 and 2.5, despite their quite different industrial and commercial settings, share common attributes. According to the authors each of the excellent companies identified exhibits a culture displaying eight attributes of excellence. The authors, we should note, chose not to elaborate on the contests and controversies that surround the conceptualization of 'culture' (see Collins, 2021c), but chose instead to offer an extended account of the eight attributes which such cultures

High Technology Firms	Consumer Goods Companies	General, Industrial Companies	Service Companies	Project Management Companies	Resource-based Companies
Allen-Bradley	Avon	Caterpillar Tractor	Delta Airlines	Bechtel	Dow Chemical
Amdahl	Brsitol-Myers	Dana Corporation	Disney Productions	Boeing	Du Pont
Data General	Cheesebrough-Ponds		K-Mart	Fluor	Standard Oil/Amoco
Digital Equipment	Frito-Lay (Pepsico)		Marriott		
Emerson Electric	Johnson & Johnson		McDonald's		
Hewlett-Packard	Levi-Strauss		Wal-Mart		
Hughes Aircraft	Mars				
Intel	Maytag				
IBM	Merck				
National Semiconductor	Procter and Gamble				
Raychem	Revlon				
Schlumberger	Tupperware				
Texas Instruments					
Wang Laboratories					

FIGURE 2.4 The Final List of (43) Excellent Companies organized by sector and listed alphabetically.

Source: Peters and Waterman (1982).

The Exemplars of Excellence
Bechtel
Boeing
Caterpillar Tractor
Dana
Delta Airlines
Digital Equipment
Emerson Electric
Fluor
Hewlett-Packard
IBM
Johnson & Johnson
McDonald's
Procter and Gamble
3M

FIGURE 2.5 The 14 exemplars of excellence.
Source: Peters and Waterman (1982).

of excellence are said to exhibit. These so-called eight attributes of excellence are, of course, now central to the excellence project. But they did not always occupy this central position. Indeed, it has been suggested that they were, in fact, a late addition to the project; a pragmatic adjustment occasioned in response to anticipated client reaction to a presentation prepared for the Munich office of McKinsey and Co. in 1979.

* * * * *

By 1979 Peters had prepared a large slide-show presentation designed to illuminate the nascent excellence project and had offered a two-day presentation of the excellence project, *illuminated by a deck of 700 slides* to clients in Germany. The members of *Siemens* who were present for this presentation had warmed to the arguments offered by Peters. Yet he was warned that *PepsiCo,* which had requested a similar audience, would demand greater thematic coherence. In an attempt to provide this coherence, Peters duly developed an outline of excellence around what would soon become, simply the eight attributes of business excellence.[1]

The eight attributes of excellence

(1) **A bias for action**

Excellent companies, Peters and Waterman (1982) argued, engage in traditional planning activities, but these do not bind them, nor do they blind them to the importance of other managerial approaches. Recognizing this, Peters and Waterman argued that an excessive reliance on traditional forms of planning, and a reliance on, 'hard' data analysis delays effective decision-making and discourages risk-taking. Thus, the authors observed that excellent companies avoid *paralysis by analysis* by scrupulously avoiding the use of committees, and by refusing to accept that all decisions have to be backed by 'hard' data analysis.

Instead of making excessive use of committees, Peters and Waterman argued that excellent companies maintain a bias for action, a willingness to try out new ideas and a willingness to take risks. This commitment to action, they argued, is maintained by excellent companies because these organizations form ad hoc groupings of people who *love* to innovate and experiment. Furthermore, the authors suggested that this tendency to action might be contrasted with the approach adopted by other companies who seem to form committees with a brief to *talk* about experimentation.

(2) **Close to the customer**

Excellent companies, Peters and Waterman argued, gear their innovation and their strategies, structures and systems to meeting, and exceeding, the expectations of the customer. Where a product or a system had failed to satisfy customer needs, the excellent organization, Peters and Waterman insisted, would have a simple means of identifying this, and would have a channel to ensure that this information was fed back to the appropriate personnel within the organization, so that the problem would be remedied.

(3) **Autonomy and entrepreneurship**

Excellent companies value entrepreneurship. To encourage enterprise, to encourage people to develop and to try out new ideas, Peters and Waterman argued that excellent companies ensure that departments and units remain small enough to allow for *ad hoc* exchanges and informal networking. From such forms of exchange, we are assured, new ideas and new products are developed which keep the company close to the customer.

(4) **Productivity through people**

While it is easy to mouth the words that people are the organization's key asset, Peters and Waterman argued that excellent companies pay more than lip service to this idea. Thus, excellent companies, we are assured, work to ensure that people are recognized and rewarded for their contribution so that they, in fact, feel valued.

(5) **Hands-on, value driven**

Leaders of excellent companies are just that. They are leaders, not managers. In an attempt to refine the concept of leadership, Peters and Waterman argued that leaders are visible. They manage by walking about. They lead by example.

Maintaining close contact with staff and with customers, leaders work to foster key values ('customers first', 'zero defects') which, we are told, help to bind people together in the pursuit of common goals.

(6) **Stick to the knitting**

Excellent companies, Peters and Waterman argued, remain focused on the key skills of the organization. Contrary to the trend towards the construction of huge, conglomerate, organizations, Peters and Waterman suggested that the excellent organizations were thriving because they understood where their strengths lie, and built on these core strengths to delight their customers.

(7) **Simple form, lean staff**

Excellent companies are staffed by skilful, innovative and committed men and women. In an attempt to maximise the potential of their staff Peters and Waterman argued that excellent companies adopt simple, team-based structures, designed to maximise interaction, and so, innovation. Since the organization is values driven, and staffed by competent and committed employees, the organization does not need to invest (*divest?*) money in the development, and maintenance of a complex bureaucracy designed to oversee the efforts of others. Instead excellent organizations are able to adopt simple (team-based) forms and are able to operate, successfully, with a lean staff geared to meeting the needs of customers.

(8) **Loose-tight properties**

Excellent companies confront and conquer a key paradox. Excellent companies value innovation and risk-taking, and so, they reward free-thinking people who have the courage, we might say, to reinvent the wheel. Yet to reap the rewards of innovation, to ensure that innovation remains customer-focused, a system of control is required. In seeking to channel and to control innovation, however, managers run the risk that they will actually stifle innovation. To overcome this paradox, excellent companies, we are told, work carefully to ensure that staff members understand the organization's values and are oriented to achieving these. In order to encourage innovation, therefore, the managers of excellent organizations make use of a 'loose' system of management. Yet because the organization is values-driven, managers may employ this system of management, safe in the knowledge that the trust this place in their co-workers and subordinates, will not be abused. In short the core values of the organization serve to integrate and to focus, the diverse and autonomous contributions made by the various teams throughout the organizations. Excellent companies therefore reward loyalty and foster commitment by granting freedom and autonomy!

★ ★ ★ ★ ★

On its own terms *In Search of Excellence* is a plausible, perhaps, even a seductive piece of work. After all who could disagree with the idea that successful companies should direct their efforts towards meeting customer needs? And who could disagree with the idea that companies, which demand innovation from their staff must be prepared to reward those forms of conduct and interaction that beget invention? And who, nowadays, would publicly disparage the idea that companies need to strike a balance between the social and the technical, between the 'soft-s' and the 'hard-s' factors, if they are to secure useful outcomes?

Yet in spite of all this seduction, and in spite of the fact that *In Search of Excellence* has, in effect, spawned a multi-million pound industry that includes:

- journals (such as *Measuring Business Excellence* and *Total Quality Management and Business Excellence*)

- copy-cat texts such as Heller's (2002) *In Search of European Excellence* and
- general frameworks designed to promote and applaud key management practices such as the 'European Foundation for Quality Management Excellence Model' there are key problems with the analysis offered by Peters and Waterman.

Dangerously wrong?

Perhaps the most commonly voiced criticism raised against the excellence project appeared in *Business Week* in November 1984 (05/11/1984) as a cover-story entitled 'Who's excellent now?' Reviewing the track record of the companies, which Peters and Waterman (1982) had identified as 'excellent', this headline article observed that, just two years after the publication of *In Search of Excellence*, one third of the 'excellent' firms were suffering some degree of financial distress!

Of course we should not overlook the importance of this analysis and critique. It *is* important (although probably not for the reasons you think) and it has hung around Peters' neck ever since. Yet despite the presumption that this line of critique offers a memorable '*gotcha* moment' it is actually rather limiting as the basis for a critical review of *In Search of Excellence*. Thus, we should note that the *Business Week* attack seems to accept the core elements of the excellence project – that there is a separate and distinctive category of excellent firms who stand proud of their peers – but chooses to mock Peters for making a poor selection!

Building on his years within the US automobile industry, Lutz (2011) offers an account of the excellence project which is similarly strident and, we should note, similarly ill-informed. Indeed, Lutz devotes a whole chapter of his account of the managerial problems that have shaped the US car industry to what he terms 'the failed culture of excellence'.

Lutz never pauses to share with us his understanding of the essence of the excellence project, preferring to dismiss this with a metaphorical wave of the hand as an initiative that is driven by too much money and by a tendency to over-intellectualize the problems and processes of management. He does, however, take great pleasure in listing the bizarre and, often, hubristic decision-making, enabled as he sees it by 'the failed culture of excellence', that has undermined the car business in the United States.

Yet Lutz simply fails to justify his complaints. And these are many! Indeed, Lutz fails to demonstrate that the decision-making processes, which he disparages are actually an outcome of the excellence project. At key points, in fact, Lutz demonstrates that the so-called failed culture of excellence had nothing at all to do with the problems he identifies. For example he suggests that the tipping point for the US car industry occurred sometime in the late 1960s. The problem being, of course, that this point on the calendar pre-dates the birth of the excellence project by at least a decade! In addition, we should note that the attack on 'brand management' within the automobile industry and the remote committee-led decision-making that, he suggests, enabled this flawed management policy is very far from being an attack on the culture of excellence. Indeed, it is very clear that the excellence project was developed to circumvent this form of remote, committee-led decision-making in order to ensure that the customer and his/her needs would remain at the very centre of all business processes.

As Lutz's full catalogue of complaints is revealed therefore it becomes evident that his reflection on the 'failed culture of excellence' is, truthfully (if somewhat ironically), a self-serving *vehicle* manufactured to allow the author to list all those elements of the corporate world that he dislikes. And this is a long list! The problem being, of course, that this list of complaints has been formed in ignorance of the core arguments developed in and through *In Search of Excellence*.

Whitfield, writing for *The Los Angeles Times* (14/04/1985) takes similar cheap shots at Peters and the excellence project. She notes, quite correctly, that Peter Drucker has been foundational to management theory and practice. Yet she uses this fact to speculate aloud on the education that Peters received at Stanford and on his standing as a guru. Reflecting on Peters' analysis of the business of management, Whitfield asserts that Drucker is entirely absent from *In Search of Excellence* and uses this observation to tear down the edifice of the excellence project.

Given Drucker's absence from *In Search of Excellence,* Whitfield asks (rhetorically): What can Peters know of 'management'?

If Peters is ignorant of Drucker what can he know of business? Can Peters really make a claim to guru status if he is unaware of the impact and legacy of Peter Drucker?

Whitfield's concerns would be legitimate and her questions would be fair – if they were at all accurate! Unfortunately, Whitfield's critique demonstrates a basic ignorance of the key facts at hand *and* ignorance of the philosophy that underpins Peters' cumulating predispositions as regards the stature of Drucker's work.

In fairness to Whitfield we should concede that Drucker does not feature prominently within the covers of *In Search of Excellence*. Yet Drucker is *not* absent from the text as she suggests. In fact, Drucker's name appears in the index of this work on a number of occasions.

Responding to the substantive elements of Whitfield's complaints Peters, (some years later) has offered an explanation for Drucker's shadowy presence in his first major work.[2] Thus, Peters tells us that *In Search of Excellence* did not proceed in ignorance of Drucker and his work. The truth, Peters observes, is that *In Search of Excellence* was constructed as a rejection of Drucker and his organizational legacy. Despite Whitfield's attacks on Peters' education and his competence as a guru therefore, the plain truth is that Peters was *not* unaware of Drucker. Indeed, the truth is that Peters had chosen, largely, to ignore the contribution of this individual.

Explaining the calculus underpinning this *choice* Peters explains that, in the early 1980s, he viewed Drucker as part of the problem which the excellence project had been developed to address. Years later, Peters tells us that he returned to the work of Drucker and was, he confides, surprised by the vision and perspicacity of his elder. Since that date Peters has, he tells us, honoured publicly the vision and legacy of Drucker. The point being of course that, despite Whitfield's attack, at no point was Peters simply unaware of Drucker!

Fortunately, other commentators have looked longer and harder at the work of Peters and Waterman and, from an informed position have generated critical reviews on the excellence project, which usefully question its outputs *and* the ideas, orientations and suppositions, which constitute its inputs. One of the earliest of these, more critical, reviews was produced by Carroll (1983) just as the excellence phenomenon began to secure traction in the United States.

A Disappointing Search

Carroll (1983) observes that the excellence project builds on the fearful suggestion, voiced by Hayes and Abernathy (1980) among others, that the US economy was inadvertently managing its way to economic decline. Responding to this warning, Peters and Waterman (1982), as we have seen, offered a critique of the 'conventional' account of management proffered by consultancies throughout the 1960s and 1970s to argue that the accepted, or conventional, approach to management was appealing but flawed, 'right enough to be dangerously wrong, and it has arguably led us seriously astray' (Peters and Waterman, 1982: 29). Noting this critique Carroll (1983) reverses the logic. He responds that the excellence project is alluring but limiting, stimulating but, nonetheless, deeply flawed. Thus, Carroll suggests that Peters' and Waterman's dismissal of American management as practised by earlier managerial 'pin-ups' – the likes of Robert McNamara (of *Ford*) and Harold Geneen (of *ITT*) – is cavalier and is, furthermore, based on sloppy scholarship.

David Guest (1992) has also drawn attention to the quotation highlighted by Carroll and chooses to turn these words back on the authors themselves. Thus, Guest argues that it is *In Search of Excellence* that is 'right enough to be dangerously wrong'. It is *In Search of Excellence* that will lead us seriously astray.

In an attempt to substantiate their charges Guest and Carroll, in common with others (see also Aupperle, Acar and Booth, 1986; Van der Merwe and Pitt, 2003) offer analyses of the many methodological and conceptual failings of the excellence project – failings we should note that the *Business Week* article of November 1984 had either downplayed or simply overlooked.

The methodological critique

In Search of Excellence is based on a sample of highly successful US firms. Peters and Waterman argue that these, successful, firms have attributes in common, which define them and which separate them from their less successful counterparts. Yet there are problems with the sampling technique adopted by Peters and Waterman. For example both Carroll and Guest observe that, in preparing their sample of firms, Peters and Waterman employed unorthodox and largely unscientific methods. Perhaps unsurprisingly, both Carroll and Guest are dismissive of this approach to the calculation and codification of business excellence. They note, for example, that the sample of 'excellent' companies begins with an ad hoc grouping that reflects the orientations and predispositions of journalists and colleagues rather than, say, business fundamentals. Furthermore, they suggest that this initial and ad hoc sample becomes progressively corrupted and skewed as the authors allow their own biases and orientations to adjust the population in a self-serving and thoroughly unscientific manner. Commenting on the outcomes of this questionable process Aupperle, Acar and Booth (1986) offer a very definite judgement on the validity of this so-called sampling mechanism. Thus, they argue that Peters and Waterman have cobbled together a self-serving panel of firms that, simply, lacks the capacity to constitute a model of excellence.

In addition to the design problems noted above, Guest and Carroll observe that the methodology of the excellence project is poorly executed. Leaving aside the fact that financial measures of performance may not offer a true representation of business fundamentals and may be managed to reflect more local decisions relating to taxation and dividend payments, for example, both Guest and Carroll, observe that a great deal of weight is placed on anecdote and idiosyncratic recollection. Indeed, they observe that the data collected on the organizational practices of their 'excellent' organizations is undeserving of this grandiose and pseudo-scientific label for it is, too often, the outcome of a simple chat with a senior executive who would have obvious incentives to portray the organization, and his (very few women appear in this book!) role within the organization, in a positive light.

Finally on the issue of methodology, Carroll (1983) observes that Peters and Waterman fail to study a less-than-excellent population, in tandem with their, supposed, exemplars of excellence. This failure to constitute what amounts to a control group means that we cannot be sure that the attributes of excellence *are peculiar to, and characteristic of, excellent firms*. In this sense the excellence hypothesis is 'non-falsifiable' insofar as the methodology is constitutionally incapable of uncovering information that would refute the idea that excellent firms (a) have attributes in common and that it is (b) these eight attributes which denote and deliver business excellence (see also Rosenzweig, 2007).

Together with such methodological failings there are a range of, related, conceptual shortcomings.

The conceptual critique

In Search of Excellence makes what economists would term an 'heroic' assumption because it suggests that organizational success is, solely, a product of management's energy and commitment. Countering this assumption, Carroll wonders why Peters and Waterman have been so dismissive of factors associated with the success of other notable companies and economies. Thus, Carroll (1983: 79) suggests that Peters' and Waterman's account of excellence is flawed because it fails to recognise the ways in which factors such as 'proprietary technology, market dominance, control of critical raw materials, and national policy and culture' might have a bearing on the fortunes of an organization. Indeed, he continues,

> Unfortunately, the most perfect adherence to the eight lessons [of excellence] will probably not permit 20 years of success against an IBM unless there is some sort of protective technology. Similarly oil companies without access to lower-cost oil supplies will suffer regardless of how well they implement the lessons [of *In Search of Excellence*] (79).

Heller [1994] (1995:63) offers similar reflections on the excellence project, which suggests the presence of dissenting voices ignored by Peters and Waterman: 'Outside opinions of organisations are notoriously unreliable, but a few clear-eyed insiders knew that IBM was seriously deficient on perhaps half of the eight counts [deemed necessary for excellence]'.

DeLamarter [1986] (1988: 3) offers a yet more strident attack on the excellence project and on the supposed virtues of *IBM*. He warns, 'The gullible leading the more gullible, search for corporate "excellence" and say they find the epitome in IBM'. Indeed, DeLamarter [1986] (1988: xvi) disputes the company's carefully managed image as a beacon of values-driven, business excellence. He observes that 'IBM is at times poorly managed, its products inferior, its customers unhappy and its actions ruthless if not illegal'. He concedes that Peters and Waterman suggest that 'IBM's stellar financial performance' (xviii) is explained by the fact that the company 'is action oriented and close to its customers; encourages entrepreneurship, values its people, and sticks to its main business ... and has benefited from a strong central philosophy that was originally laid down by its charismatic leaders, the Watsons' (xviii). Yet he counters that this view is, in fact, 'dead wrong' (xviii). IBM's success is, DeLamarter warns us, not due to 'the healthy interplay of competitive forces' (xviii) but is, in fact, a product of monopoly power and sharp practice. For DeLamarter [1986] (1988: xvi), therefore, IBM, the poster-boy for business excellence, is, in truth, a company that has exploited its monopoly position to compensate for the fact that it is a poorly managed corporation with inferior products and unhappy customers!

Carroll, we should note, chooses not to attack *IBM* in these terms (although concerns over this company's reach and practice are at least implicit in his analysis). Instead, he settles on a more neutral observation. Thus, he argues that *In Search of Excellence* amounts to a bogus prospectus because it fails to acknowledge the range of contextual and environmental influences, which intervene in the conduct of business, and which impact on the opportunities for success. Indeed, Carroll argues that in assigning organizations to a category marked 'excellent', it is unclear whether, what Peters and Waterman have trumpeted as success in business due to the attributes of excellence, might more usefully be considered as business success built on technology, a patented process or, simply, geographic advantage.

Writing in 1992 Guest raises a criticism, whose potential Carroll had fore-seen in 1983. Noting that a number of Peters' and Waterman's companies soon fell from grace (the hollow, if often-repeated criticism voiced by *Business Week*), Guest observes that the authors fail to discuss whether, in fact, all of the eight at-tributes of Peters' and Waterman's excellent organizations are, actually, necessary for business excellence.[3] Given that a number of the attributes do seem to overlap (e.g. attributes one, three and seven do seem similar) might it be sufficient to hit just four of the eight attributes of excellence, as Heller [1994] (1995) suggests, and yet return excellent results?

Van der Merwe and Pitt (2003) also question the extent to which firms would have to exhibit all eight of the attributes discussed by Peters and Waterman. However, the logic of the case put forward by Van der Merwe and Pitt is different to that advanced by Guest. Reviewing the excellence project Van der Merwe and Pitt raise three important objections to the work of Peters and Waterman. First, they observe that, for Peters and Waterman, excellence is discussed in simple binary terms. Like pregnancy, it seems, that you are either excellent or *not* excel-lent, there being no 'in-between' set of circumstances. Disputing the character of excellence (rather than the character of pregnancy), therefore, Van der Merwe and Pitt suggest that business excellence might, more usefully, be construed as a continuum of possibilities.

Reflecting further on the nature of such possibilities, Van der Merwe and Pitt raise a second point of criticism. Noting that Peters and Waterman have produced a cultural appreciation of the business of management, which hinges around leadership, they question the efficacy of the authors' preferred cultural management strategies. Thus, Van der Merwe and Pitt argue that Peters and Waterman portray excellent organizations as culturally unified collectives. How-ever, they counter that this simple-minded celebration of common purpose pre-vents us from acknowledging conflict within the collective, and so, effectively precludes the meaningful analysis of organizational politics. Accordingly Van der Merwe and Pitt suggest that, (despite the discussions which underpinned the development of the 7-S framework and the agreed need to accommodate 'people and power' within the framework), the model of excellence developed by Peters and Waterman, simply cries out for a better appreciation of politics.

On the strength of this more political reading of management and organi-zation Van der Merwe and Pitt raise a third point of criticism, which invites us to consider the wider costs and benefits of the excellence project. Thus, they suggest that a desire to 'stick to the knitting' and to 'get close to the customer' might well visit costs – technically known as 'externalities' – on other groups and constituencies who have been excluded from the analytical frame by Peters' and Waterman's celebration of organizational unity and common purpose.

Maidique (1983) offers a similar line of critique as she, too, focuses on the design problems which limit the validity of the excellence project. In common with Guest, Maidique concedes that *In Search of Excellence* is a hugely popular text. Indeed, she argues that this text is successful because it has (a) a positive message that is (b) written in a conversational style with the aid of (c) colourful, evangelical prose (see also Mitchell, 1985; Hyatt, 1999). Yet, despite this rhetorical power, Maidique complains that *In Search of Excellence* does not stand up to sustained, critical, analysis. Indeed, she argues that the agreeable, if superficial, characteristics of this text act to obscure the fact that Peters' and Waterman's argument is sloppy. Thus, Maidique warns us that *In Search of Excellence* contains many sweeping generalizations and is, furthermore, marred by basic factual errors. Karl Weick is one of the authors on the receiving end of at least one of these sweeping generalizations. Perhaps this explains the tone of Weick's review of Tom Peters' legacy.

Talk and action

Reviewing the managerial lessons of *In Search of Excellence,* Karl Weick (2004), like Guest, argues that Peters and Waterman operate with a poor conceptualization of management. Noting that managing the efforts of others is a social and a political process, rooted in the arts of persuasion, and so, hinged on verbal communication, Weick argues that *In Search of Excellence* is mistaken when it advocates a 'bias for action'. Instead Weick argues that successful managers have 'a bias for talk'.

As a comment on the nature of managerial work this is, of course, a perfectly sensible statement (see Grant, Keenoy and Oswick, 1998; Grant et al., 2004; Collins, 2018). However, as a commentary on the work of Peters and Waterman this criticism could not be more wrong since it is clear that in advocating what has become known as 'a bias for action', Peters and Waterman were, very clearly, telling managers that they would have to make real, personal and sustained efforts to *talk to* customers, colleagues and suppliers. Indeed, despite Weick's attack, the truth is that Peters and Waterman demonstrate, very clearly, their appreciation of the importance of talk and persuasion. Thus, it is clear that that in suggesting the need to talk to customers, colleagues and suppliers, Peters and Waterman advised that managers to create and to propagate stories, which demonstrate the key attributes of excellence and their personal commitment to the quest for excellence. Viewed in these terms, it is clear that, for Peters and Waterman, the essence of management action means talking! Indeed, it is important that we acknowledge that, for Peters and Waterman, such talk would necessarily imply storytelling and myth-making. Despite Weick's attack on the supposedly limiting nature of the action orientation extolled by the excellence project, therefore, it is clear that, for Peters and Waterman, management action *means* managerial talk because the authors recognise that managing is, at root, a social and political process that depends on myth-making and storytelling for the prosecution of its ends.

Set against, what amounts to Weick's blatant misreading of *In Search of Excellence,* Watson's (2001) account of the legacy of the excellence project is more accurate, more balanced and ultimately far more perceptive in its reading of Peters and Waterman. While conceding that this (in)famous text has attracted, deserved criticism for its conceptual and methodological failings, Watson, nevertheless, protests that *In Search of Excellence* is a significant work with hidden depths. Thus, Watson insists that *In Search of Excellence* matters and has an enduring message because it reminds us that management has a moral as well as a technical dimension and in making this point successfully portrays employees as sentient humans, seekers and creators of meaning. In short, Watson suggests that *In Search of Excellence* is an important work for it has popularized a basic and inescapable truth of management: that the meaning of management is, at root, the management of meaning. Furthermore, Watson reminds us that the excellence project is significant because it offers a new identity for management and, consequently, new ways for managers to be at work.

Mitchell (1985), however, sounds a note of dissent. Reviewing *In Search of Excellence* he concedes that this text is significant for it does, indeed, serve to remind managers that managing is a human endeavour. However, he protests that Peters' and Waterman's concern with cultural matters such as stories and symbolism is a triumph of form over substance. Thus, he argues that *In Search of Excellence* has a concern with meaning and identity that is strictly manipulative.

Guilty pleasures?

Thanks to the likes of Guest and Carroll most managers of a certain age can recount the flaws of the excellence project but when quizzed these individuals often confess that they value the text despite its academic failings. Practitioners of management, it seems to me, actually like this text because, as Maidique (1983) observes, it is engaging and easy to read. But, perhaps more importantly, managers like *In Search of Excellence* because it (a) speaks to them directly about the trials they face in a manner which (b) suggests that managers and the corporations they represent are a force for good. Of course this endorsement of the excellence project does tend to imply that managers employ *In Search of Excellence* in the same manner that a drunkard uses a lamp post – more for support than for illumination – but we should not overlook the fact that this insistence that business is part of a moral economy is essentially truthful and was, in the early 1980s a distinctive message.

Yet we should not assume that the core message of *In Search of Excellence* was, in fact, fully adopted in corporate America. Kiechel (2010: 149), for example, suggests that the very forces that removed Peters and Waterman from McKinsey led corporate America to view the excellence project as a form of sentimental populism with little real sales-potential. Indeed, we would do well to note that within corporate America the 1980s were notable, not for a wholesale and wholehearted conversion to the excellence credo but for a merger boom underpinned by 'junk bonds'.

★ ★ ★ ★ ★

Highlighting the extent of the changes made possible by Michael Milken's inno-vative and incredibly profitable (junk bond) financial engineering, Bailey (1991: 74) is careful to remind us that Milken was, at root, an idealist who had imagined that his 'junk bonds' (non-collateralized debt) could be used to build homes and to foster a people's capitalism. And yet despite this aspiration, the instruments of Milken's new democracy were used, not to build homes but to fuel a boom in corporate restructuring that, at its peak in 1986, reached 'fifteen takeovers a day'.

And what did the owners and controllers of these newly aligned companies have in common?

Not much beyond two concerns: First, a willingness to use other people's money to get very rich, very quickly. And second, the obvious and rather desper-ate need for some tool, no matter how weakly conceptualized and executed, that might bring narrative coherence and cultural unification to an organizational formation wrought by and designed to reflect only financial interests.

And what would offer this coherence? Why the excellence project of course!

★ ★ ★ ★ ★

The fact that Peters and Milken found themselves, in the 1980s serving (and of course being enriched by) an agenda that both had publicly disparaged is, perhaps, just another one of those ironies that life tends to throw in the face of idealists. That much of course is metaphysical speculation. What is clear is that by the mid-1980s, Milken, while living the monastic life of a scholar, was richer than Croesus and Tom Peters, prophet of all things cultural and storytelling was in demand and feted worldwide as a guru of management albeit one in the pay of those larger corporate interests that he had, through his work, publicly disparaged.

To feed the demand for his services Peters had embarked on a punishing schedule of domestic and international travel and was offering upwards of 100 seminars a year. To refresh his product and to reflect the demand for further insights on the practice of business of excellence, Peters teamed up with Nancy Austin (Peters and Austin, 1985) to provide, as we shall see, further guidance on the challenges of business excellence.

A passion for excellence

Peters, in common with other commentators who have been styled as manage-ment gurus, has often been attacked as a prescriptive writer. He is, it is claimed, altogether too ready to offer glib solutions to problems that are simply too big and too complex to be addressed in any simplistic or reductionist fashion. At one level, of course, this critique is perfectly accurate. Despite Peters' faith in the unifying benefits of cultural management most organizations *are* character-ized by conflicts over organizational goals and the means to secure such goals. Yet it would be a mistake to suggest that *In Search of Excellence* provides a simple prescription for excellence. It is true, of course, that Peters and Waterman do tell organizations what *sorts* of things they will have to do to become excellent. And it is, equally, true that Peters and Waterman do insist that organizations will have to adopt the core attributes of excellence if they are to retain their customer base. Yet this generalized concern with structure and practice is surely a long way from a detailed and prescriptive account of 'how to be excellent'. Somewhat ironically, however, a prescription for excellence seems to be exactly what, at least, some of Peters' followers were asking for, following the publication of *In Search of Excellence*.

In a follow-up text Peters, working with Nancy Austin (Peters and Austin, 1985), set out to address this demand for additional guidance on what might be termed the implementation of the practice of business excellence. But rather than produce a glib and unhelpful prescription for excellence, Peters and Austin chose instead to reproduce a number of tales of excellence or 'implementation vignettes', which it was hoped would develop a heightened awareness of the organizational processes underpinning the very best organizational practices, which they had claimed to observe.

Gates (1985) summarizes this position rather well. Reviewing *A Passion for Excellence* for *The Financial Post* (a Canadian newspaper) Gates comments,

> If you want a step-by-step solution for your company, forget it. On the other hand, if you want interesting anecdotes and funny asides, combined with what the authors have found to be common ingredients in excellent companies, then, *A Passion for Excellence* may be your kind of book.

Yet *A Passion for Excellence* sought to do more than, simply, add tales of triumph and endeavour to the excellence project. It also modified the excellence project while reaffirming its core message. In this respect we might, while invoking a biblical metaphor, suggest that *A Passion for Excellence* should be considered to be the 'new testament' revision to the 'old testament' of *In Search of Excellence*. In common with the Christian 'new testament', therefore, *A Passion for Excellence* extends, revises and simplifies the excellence credo. Thus, in *A Passion for Excellence*, success in business is said to stem not from eight, but from just two key attributes:

1 Taking exceptional care of customers
2 Innovating constantly

Peters and Austin assure us that if organizations commit to taking exceptional care of their customers, and commit to innovation as the only constant, everything else should fall into place. Just as Christians committed to the single new testament commandment – to love others as thy self – do not need to be told not to steal and not to murder, so too organizations committed to their customers and to innovation do not need to be told that productivity comes through people, or that they must be close to the customer, since these sentiments and ideas are subsumed within the two commandments of *A Passion for Excellence*.

A Passion for Excellence clearly offers itself as an attempt to extend, and to promote, the excellence project, yet it adopts a rather different mode of presentation and persuasion. Where *In Search of Excellence* was based on empirical research (however poorly conceived and executed), *A Passion for Excellence* adopts a different tack, which all but rejects the idea that managers will require empirical proof to persuade them of the vitality, and validity, of the excellence project. In common with a range of business and management books written during the 1980s, therefore, *A Passion for Excellence* eschews theoretical reflection and methodological rigour, in favour of the logic of common sense (Collins 1998).

Management as common sense

In 1985 Peters was, apparently, oblivious to the sociological problems of placing one's faith in simple facts. He simply assumed that his simple facts would be the same as *my* simple facts and *your* simple facts. In a later text Peters (1989: xx) seems to alter his position on the transparency of 'simple facts'. Indeed, in this later text, he concedes the existence of many forms of 'common sense' and notes the ways in which concrete and practical experiences acts to shape what is sensible. Discussing his growing frustration with the managers of America's 'blue chip' corporations, therefore, he looks back on his career as a guru and he confesses that:

> Seminars with *Fortune 500* managers [came to fill] me with despair. They came. They applauded. They bought my books and tapes. But they were a desolate lot. Though I talked common sense … it was not the kind of common sense their companies practised, and they knew what they were going back to.

In 1985, however, Peters and Austin took their cue from Thomas Paine, and so, constructed an idealized and monotheistic account of common sense. Applauding Paine's simplistic commitment to common sense, and to plain talk, therefore, Peters and Austin insist that their book will offer the same – simple facts, plain arguments and common sense ungarnished by abstraction and theorization. They admonish us, too, that this should be enough to persuade anyone, with the courage to drop their defences and their prejudices, of the eloquence of their business mission and the commandments therein. With a sociological sleight of hand, therefore, Peters and Austin, simultaneously, excuse the fact that their book lacks the methodological and theoretical basis required to substantiate their claims, while disempowering those who might wish to dispute their ideas and claims. Yet before we turn to analyse the contents of this work it will be helpful to consider its context.

★ ★ ★ ★ ★

In Search of Excellence was, as we have seen, conceived and published during a time of social change and economic crisis. Indeed, the text was shaped, in important ways, by the experience of recession. Published in 1985, *A Passion for Excellence* looked out on an altogether more buoyant and more optimistic economy than was visible from *In Search of Excellence* in 1982. Yet memories of the recession of 1981–83 still loom large in the text. Introducing *A Passion for Excellence*, Peters and Austin (1985: xviii) note, 'The battering American business took in the seventies and during the 1981–1983 recession (is there anyone who thinks recovery means we're permanently out of the wood?) has humbled virtually every American manager'.

In this, apparently, innocuous statement Peters and Austin, I think, do two rather important things. First, they encourage a particular reading of America's improving economic context. While conceding that America's recession ended in 1983 they are keen to remind us that the current experience of economic success will be fleeting in the absence of a continually, renewing commitment to excellence. In effect, this, apparently, gentle warning as to the future, amounts to an attempt to change the context of the US economy once and forever insofar as it makes the next recession (a) a heartbeat away and (b) an inevitability in the absence of 'a passion for excellence'.

Second, Peters and Austin pointedly observe that American management – or at least that variant of 'rational' American management, which was roundly criticized in *In Search of Excellence* – has been 'humbled'. 'Rational' management, they inform us, has been brought down by the passage of history and by the course of world events. In pointing this out for the reader, Peters and Waterman signal their track-record and their superior knowledge and understanding of the world of business. In the vernacular they have 'put up'; supporters of 'rational' management must now 'shut up' and must submit themselves humbly to a process of management re-education.

★ ★ ★ ★ ★

A Passion for Excellence, as we have seen, begins by acknowledging that the American economy was in a far healthier state by the middle years of the 1980s than it had been at the start of that decade. Yet Peters and Austin are keen to fend off complacency. The economy, they tell us rather pointedly, is not out of the woods. In an attempt to extricate American managers from the metaphorical woods, which *A Passion for Excellence* identifies the authors advocate 'leadership'.

Leadership was, perhaps, under-played within *In Search of Excellence*. Indeed, Peters and Waterman (1982: 11) tell us that they were inclined to place their faith in 'culture' above 'leaders' because the 7-S framework had demonstrated that 'real change in large institutions is a function of at least seven hunks of complexity'. In *A Passion for Excellence*, however, Peters and Austin (1985) suggest that culture and leadership are, in a sense, indivisible. They insist, therefore, that leaders and leadership will provide our deliverance from current *and* future economic threats.

In keeping with their simplified credo of excellence Peters and Austin argue that leadership is to be regarded as the central, and key, component in achieving excellence. Indeed, and according to their sub-title it is leadership, which makes *the* difference.

In an attempt to bring substance to this claim, Peters and Austin (1985) produce page-after-page of stories designed to demonstrate that managerial leadership is a precondition of excellence *and* the means by which a passion for excellence will be sustained. So what does leadership do? What do leaders do?

The practice of leadership

For Peters and Austin the practise of leadership is based on Management by Wandering Around (MBWA). This concept, of course, had been introduced to readers in Peters' first text, *In Search of Excellence,* where it had formed a component of the 'bias for action' attribute. However, in *A Passion for Excellence*, the concept of MBWA moves central stage to become the key factor underpinning managerial leadership, and so, the foundation on which stand the two commandments of excellence.

The concept of MBWA states that mangers cannot lead from the boardroom. While managers can, and must, lead from the front, they cannot lead at a distance. Thus, Peters and Austin argue that managers will only come to be viewed as leaders (and so, will only develop the followers required in values/vision-driven organizations) when they are able to connect with their staff. However, the authors warn us that for some members of the boardroom elite, this approach to leadership may prove to be a difficult and trying process. In an echo of our earlier biblical allusion therefore there is, within this account of the trials of managerial leadership, the suggestion that, for some, a passion for excellence may actually turn out to be a Christ-like passion.

Pattison (1994) takes this analysis of religious imagery somewhat further. Peters and Austin, he argues, do not simply allude to things that have religious connotations. Instead he tells us that these authors literally retell a famous biblical tale – albeit one from the Old Testament

Religious metaphor and allusion

Discussing religious allusion and metaphor in the works of management's gurus, Pattison (1994) argues that *A Passion for Excellence* amounts to a modern, secular, retelling of the biblical story concerning Noah and the flood. Indeed, Pattison suggests that it is the familiarity of this religious tale, which helps to make *A Passion for Excellence* substantial and persuasive in the absence of a programme of theoretically informed research.

The tale of Noah, as you will no doubt recall, begins by observing and recounting the ways in which the inhabitants of God's earth had fallen from grace to become degenerate. Recognizing this degeneracy, the Old Testament tells us that God chose to recommence the business of creation. But to do this – to recreate Heaven on earth, we are told, God, first, had to cleanse His creation of sin.

Knowing that Noah and his family had remained true to His calling in the midst of the Godless depravity that had swept across the fabric of creation, God, the bible tells us, decides to spare Noah and his kin from the flood that he plans as the means of cleansing the earth. He instructs Noah to build an ark. In addition he tells Noah that he must herd animals on to the ark so that these, too, will be spared from the flood. To this end he issues precise instructions as to the size of the ark and the number and type of animals that should be gathered therein.

Noah, as a good and God-fearing man, does God's bidding and is spared from drowning. Those who failed to heed God's warnings and who, consequently, failed to atone for their failings and oversights, we are told, are denied entry to the ark and are, simply, left to perish in the deluge visited on the fabric of God's creation.

Commenting on the rhetorical power of *A Passion for Excellence,* Pattison argues that this text follows and reproduces the essence of the biblical story of Noah albeit in a secularized form. Reducing *A Passion for Excellence* to its elements, therefore, Pattison notes that, in this text, Peters and Austin warn their readers that:

- Changes in markets, technologies, regulation and consumer preferences are ushering in a new era of on-going change and turbulence.
- In the wake of this turbulent change there will be two types of organization: the drowned and the saved.
- Those who fail to heed the warnings – those who fail to prepare themselves for the future –will be lost.
- Those who wish to be saved must 'get on board' with Tom Peters and his excellence project.

Echoing the tale of Noah, therefore, Peters and Austin warn us that there is no way to avoid the challenge, and no way to avoid the pain, which a passion for excellence may bring, because there is no means, aside from leadership, to solve the problems and paradoxes of modern management. And in this we have a further departure from the message of *In Search of Excellence.*

Soft and hard factors

In Search of Excellence, you will recall, emerged against a backdrop of political opposition within McKinsey and Co. It was, furthermore, organized to overcome the opposition of those who had been taught that the executive function revolved around structures, systems, strategies. *A Passion for Excellence*, however, takes this opposition to the orthodoxies of managerial work a step further. Freed from McKinsey's in-fighting and emboldened by the commercial success of *In Search of Excellence* Peters and Austin choose to counter the suggestion that, somehow, the 'soft-S' factors remain subordinate to the 'hard' elements of business. Instead they argue that the 'soft-S' factors must take precedence. 'Soft' analysis is they tell us 'hard'! And on page after page, Peters and Austin celebrate 'soft' analysis as the primary role of the executive. Accordingly, managers are exhorted to follow their instincts – to do the obvious. Likewise they are encouraged to throw off the chains of statistical analysis, so that through 'naïve listening', they might see problems anew and from the perspective of the customer.

This, of course, does not mean that *A Passion for Excellence* is anti-analysis. In fact, the book is highly analytical but in a manner not typically acknowledged by critics. Thus, Peters and Austin undermine the privileged position of 'hard', 'number-crunching', as *real* analysis in order to show that 'soft' forms of analysis are equally (if not more) reliable than those 'hard' analytical techniques taught to Harvard's alumni.

So what do we do with all this information? Well it would be tempting to dismiss *A Passion for Excellence* as a technique-fixated (see Hilmer and Donaldson, 1996) approach to management. But, in truth, such a claim will not stick easily to this text. In fact, there is much within the text of *A Passion for Excellence*, which, at one level, promotes careful, thoughtful and reflective management practise. Every few pages, in fact, Peters and Austin interrupt their stories and reminiscences (dubbed 'implementation vignettes') to issue their readers with questions and topics for *analysis*.

The question we must ask, however, is this: short of exhortation, anecdote and vignettes of excellence in practice, what do Peters and Austin offer on the nature and practice of leadership?

The leadership difference

Peters and Austin argue that managerial leadership is *the* key to excellence. The problem being that aside from making the claim that leadership is, in fact, the difference between conspicuous success and horrendous failure (see Pattison, 1994; Van der Merwe and Pitt, 2003) the authors actually offer little discussion of the debates, which persist on the nature, meaning and effect(s) of leadership. In fact, Peters and Austin seem studiously to ignore the controversies and complexities, which have shaped serious scholarship on the nature and conduct of leadership for perhaps 75 years.

Of course, we should acknowledge that Peters and Austin are in the business of 'popular management'. They did not set out to prepare a textbook for undergraduates on the nature, contours and process of leadership, and so, we have no right truthfully to expect 'the tour' – an analysis of 'leadership studies' that takes us from the field's pre-history (Thompson and McHugh, 1990) through 'traits', 'styles', 'contingencies' and (of course) right back to 'traits' albeit variously couched as 'emotional intelligence' (Goleman, 1995) or 'level 5 leadership' (Maxwell, 2011). And yet in choosing to expound on leadership practice in the context of excellence and in offering this (whatever *this* is) as *the* answer to the contemporary problems of business and management, Peters and Austin do need to offer some acknowledgement that leadership is complex, contested and potentially controversial.

Unfortunately the authors duck this issue and like so many of those who service 'popular management', simply demand that we accept that their preferred view of leadership is correct, universally applicable and adequate to the core problems identified. None of this, however, can withstand close scrutiny and, with apologies to WB Yeats, *Things fall apart; the centre cannot hold.*[4]

Commenting on this centre that now falls apart in the hands of Peters and Austin, Grint (1997b) takes issue with those who place their faith in the virtues of common sense – those who protest common sense reasoning is (a) superior to and (b) exists prior to academic theorizing. Indeed, Grint reminds us that those who protest that 'theory' is irrelevant to their mission and project, have, unwittingly, adopted a theoretical position for to reject the need for theory is to argue that 'facts' stand for themselves – that 'reality' is objective and self-evident to all (see Burrell and Morgan, 1979) – and this is, of course, a view of the world shaped and ordered by theoretical precepts and assumptions.

It is clear therefore that when Peters and Austin assert that leadership is the difference between excellence and mediocrity (where mediocrity equates to failure) they have an obligation to come clean about their preferred model of leadership. Is it, for example, a traits model such as that which would have been familiar to managers in the early post-war period (see Stogdill, 1948)?

Are excellent leaders born?

Are they truly adaptive, decisive, flexible motivators with courage and resolution?

Or is leadership more usefully captured not as a collection of traits (which are too often synonyms for things that men do in the workplace) but in terms of 'styles' that may be learned and refined such that leaders may be, variously, participative, transactional or transformational to name but three of the commonly acknowledged styles?

And given this variety of 'styles' we might reasonably ask, Which 'style' is it that underpins the passion for excellence?

Or is leadership more usefully conceptualized in contingent terms as a process that involves matching the leader to the situation at hand? And does this imply as Fiedler (1967) suggests that a leader should be selected with skills that match the situation?

Or is there a need for a more 'situational' appreciation of leadership contingencies such as that advanced by Hersey and Blanchard (1982), which suggests that the leader may adapt his/her style to accommodate the 'maturity' of employees, switching between 'telling', 'selling', 'delegating' and 'participating' styles?

In response to these questions *A Passion for Excellence* offers only a large collection of proverbial responses (Peters and Austin, 1985: 354–361):

- Leaders listen; non-leaders talk.
- Leaders are humble; non-leaders are arrogant.
- Leaders are available; non-leaders are hard to reach from below.
- Leaders are decisive; non-leaders are arrogant.

- Leaders carry water; non-leaders preside over the mess.
- Leaders are tolerant of open disagreement; non-leaders are intolerant.
- Leaders know when to fire people; non-leaders duck difficult tasks.
- Leaders have plain offices; non-leaders prize the lavish.
- Leaders are straightforward; non-leaders are tricky.

Yet these aphorisms actually do little to answer our question(s). *And we do need answers* because if the practice of leadership is truly central to the excellence project we require some reasoned appreciation of the changes that Peters and Austin would have us adopt and in so doing, model for others.

So, who/what are the excellent leaders?

Brace yourself!

Leaders, it seems are born to *it* and yet can learn to perform *it*.

Leaders are, it seems, assertive, fair, reasonable, decent *and* impatient. Furthermore, leaders match their conduct to reflect the contingencies thrown up by the need to pursue excellence.

In other words, Peters and Austin advance a model of leadership that is based on traits, styles and all forms of contingency but adds to this, a narrative sheen and an emotional gloss.

Leadership is everything and therefore nothing – a recipe for change that lacks all the important (cookery) instructions.

Or with a different metaphor in mind: If leadership is the core of the excellence project and the difference between success and failure it is, despite my earlier promise of civility, difficult to shake the feeling that *A Passion for Excellence* has steered us to the middle of 'shit creek' and pinched the paddle.

Summary

This chapter has reviewed Peters' first two books on the business of management that were co-written with Bob Waterman (Peters and Waterman, 1982) and Nancy Austin (Peters and Austin, 1985). The first of these texts – *In Search of Excellence* – was based on a sample of (supposedly) highly performing firms and claims to have diagnosed (a) the pre-conditions for business excellence and (b) the practices that would sustain cultures of excellence. This book, of course, effectively launched Peters' guru career *and* defined a new market for business publishing.

Perhaps unsurprisingly, giving its academic pretensions, *In Search of Excellence* precipitated a large number of academic reviews. Many of these reviews sought to question the validity of the excellence project, and so, offered reflections on the analytical and methodological shortcomings of this text. However, it is worth pointing out that this text also precipitated a body of more supportive academic and practitioner literature, which sought to apply the lessons of excellence to specific industries (see Miller, 1993; Barter, 1994; Bunz and Moore, 1998) or to different national contexts (see for example Heller, 2002).

Recognizing the trenchant nature of the academic and journalistic critiques visited on the excellence project I have sought to provide an analytical account of *In Search of Excellence,* which nonetheless acknowledges its appeal. To this end I have attempted to explore the book's content within the context of its creation. Furthermore, I have attempted to provide a critical assessment of this work and its legacy while highlighting those moments when Peters' detractors have offered commentaries on the excellence project that are simply ill-informed. The criticisms made of *In Search of Excellence* are reasonable and well-intentioned. *In Search of Excellence* is, in academic terms, a piece of work that is sloppy and hence unconvincing – or would be so if the population concerned itself with such niceties. Noting that the excellence project has proven to be, largely, immune to conventional academic criticism I have argued that *In Search of Excellence* needs to be understood as a moral project which seeks a correspondence not with verifiable facts but with the larger truths constructed in and through those narrative projections that I label 'stories'.

Analysing Peters' follow-up text – *A Passion for Excellence* – I have highlighted the similarities that unite (a continuing focus on leaders, cultures, customers and stories) and the differences (a disavowal of the normal conventions of academic modelling and theorizing) that divide these texts. Noting that Peters and Austin (1985) have rejected academic theorizing in favour of 'plain talk and common sense' I have attempted to uncover the theoretical orientations that underpin (or should that be undermine?) this refinement of the excellence project.

Exploring Peters' and Austin's conviction that leadership is *the* difference between business failure and success I have argued that this text depends on an under-theorized model of leadership. I have therefore attempted to demonstrate the existence of a range of implicit assumptions that give shape and substance to Peters' revised account of business excellence. Indeed, I have suggested that this text remains persuasive and substantial only for so long as this model of leadership remains unnamed and hence beyond sustained academic scrutiny.

And yet, despite my suggestion that the excellence project is invulnerable before conventional forms of academic criticism, debates as to the wit and wisdom of the excellence project do persist and from time to time do intrude on the public understanding of this endeavour. In my closing remarks I will consider two key points of contention that arise in connection with the very foundations of the excellence project. The first of these I will label, the *Business Week* controversy, the second, which I suggest does, in fact, go to the very heart of the excellence project I will call 'the lessons learned issue'.

The business week controversy

In 1984 *Business Week* ran its, now famous, cover-story, which argued that a significant proportion of Peters' excellent companies were suffering financial distress just two years after they had been trumpeted as the very exemplars of modern business practice. This is the critique that most people recall and it is, in truth, often repeated by those who really should know better. For example Charles Handy, perhaps Britain's only management guru (despite being Irish!) has produced *The Handy Guide to the Gurus of Management* for the BBC (first broadcast in 2011), which considers such luminaries as Peter Drucker, Warren Bennis and, of course, Tom Peters. Discussing Peters, Handy offers a sketch of *In Search of Excellence* and gleefully produces the gist of the *Business Week* article. Yet in so doing Handy simply fails to acknowledge that, by this time, Dan Ackman (2002), writing for *Forbes*, had offered an account of this controversy that rebuts it – on its own terms. Thus, Ackman observes,

> *In Search of Excellence* didn't name the biggest companies and ride with winners: In 1982 when the book was published, just three of the 43 companies ranked among the top 25 by sales on The Forbes 500s. And just 22 of the 32 public companies were among the 500 largest. Those 22 ranked, on average, 125th on The Forbes 500s by sales. Over the years the companies grew. By 2002, 24 of the firms were among the largest 500 public companies with an average Forbes 500s sales rank of 99.

Overall Ackman concludes that 'the companies Peters and Waterman called excellent [in 1982] have easily outperformed the market averages any way you slice it'. In response to the question posed by *Business Week* in 1984, therefore, Ackman suggests that, with the exception of Atari and the Wang Corporation (which ceased trading) the companies that are excellent 'now' are the companies identified by Peters and Waterman way back 'then' in 1982. Whether Peters can take any personal credit for this success and whether this success can be explained as a consequence of adhering to the eight attributes of excellence that were outlined by Peters and Waterman in 1982 must remain, as our reflections on 'the lessons learned issue' will make abundantly clear, the subject of on-going debate and conjecture.

The lessons learned issue

The central conceit of *In Search of Excellence* is, as we have seen, pretty straightforward and boils down to two assertions:

1 There are pockets of managerial excellence within a number of prominent US organizations.
2 These special US organizations exhibit forms of conduct, which may be adopted by others.

Reporting an interview conducted with Peters and Waterman in the very early days of the excellence project, however, Kiechel (2010) questions this account of the excellence project. Indeed, he uncovers something truly intriguing which unlike the *Business Week* article has the capacity to cause lasting damage to the edifice of excellence!

Noting the broad-based appeal of the excellence project and the market success of *In Search of Excellence,* Kiechel reminds us that for most US organizations the pursuit of excellence would require far-reaching changes – in effect, a transformation in the very essence of the company. Noting that shifting strategy is 'inevitably easier than changing your culture' Kiechel (2010: 168) tells us that at the very earliest stages of the development of the excellence project (before the book was published and, we should note, when the 'sample' was still of 62 companies) he invited Peters and Waterman to venture an opinion as to 'how the exemplars had become excellent' (168). Kiechel (2010: 168) notes that the authors seemed not to have considered this fundamental point, and later failed to address it within *In Search of Excellence.* Indeed, he adds that at that time Peters and Waterman 'didn't much want to answer' (168) the question. After some probing, Kiechel (2010: 168) observes that

> [f]inally, they allowed that in all but a half dozen cases, the enterprise had been set up that way in the first place. Subsequent generations of management merely had the good sense not to mess with what, say, Messers. Procter and Gamble had wrought.

In other words, and despite the suggestion that others might learn from and in so doing, emulate the best-run American companies, Peters and Waterman seem to have understood, from the outset that the central claim of the excellence project stood on a rather shaky foundation. Thus, Kiechel suggests that in all but a half dozen cases, what Peters and Waterman had found were *not* exemplars of business excellence that others could emulate, but a herd of unicorns, a collection of businesses – successful and significant, of course – but businesses whose cultures, conduct and achievements were truthfully part of their corporate DNA and on that basis could not be replicated!

And with the excellence project now listing 30° to port we must now turn to consider 'the guru works' (Crainer, 1997) of Tom Peters. Chapter 3 will commence therefore with an account of Peters' first single-authored, guru, text entitled *Thriving on Chaos* (Peters, 1987). But you can stow that life jacket because the excellence project, as we shall see, is not in any imminent danger of foundering.

Notes

1 See   www.businessballs.com/strategy-innovation/in-search-of-excellence---tompeters/
2 See https://tompeters.com/2005/11/peter-f-drucker-right-man-for-hisour-times/
3 It is perhaps worth noting that Peters and Waterman (1982: 16–17) do themselves seem to suggest that it may not be necessary to secure all eight attributes.
4 This is of course a reference to the poem, 'The Second Coming' by WB Yeats. The poem is especially suitable for a (re)consideration of the gurus of management insofar as it uses Christian imagery of the Apocalypse and the Second Coming to offer a description of post-war Europe.

3

THE WORKS OF TOM PETERS, 1987–2018

Introduction

Chapter 2 offered a critical, analytical, review of Tom Peters' early writings on the business of management. It considered *In Search of Excellence* (Peters and Waterman, 1982) and *A Passion for Excellence* (Peters and Austin, 1985). It also explored the contexts shaping the development of these texts and it reflected on a range of criticisms that might be raised against the methods, orientations and aspirations of these works. This chapter picks up where the preceding one concluded. Thus, Chapter 3 offers a critical review of the eight, key, texts on business and management (see Chapter 1 for a complete listing of Peters' texts) that Peters has produced since 1987.

For ease of exposition this chapter retains the chronological format employed in Chapter 2. Accordingly, this chapter begins with an account of *Thriving on Chaos* (Peters, 1987) which was first published in 1987 and concludes with a critical review of *The Excellence Dividend* (Peters, 2018).

Thriving on chaos

Thriving on Chaos, as you might properly expect, presents a picture of the world as 'chaotic'. In keeping with Peters' earlier analyses this text offers a starkly dualistic vision of organizations and management that divides the world into two camps: those who will thrive in an age of chaos and those who will fail. Building on this stark and dualistic vision, *Thriving on Chaos* warns us that many contemporary organizations will fail because they are simply unaware of the revolution in management which the 'chaotic' nature of our times call forth. To save these organizations from failure, and in so doing, allow managers to 'thrive on chaos', Peters, now working as a sole author, offers a text with a different format to those considered in Chapter 2.

DOI: 10.4324/9781003188940-4

In Search of Excellence and *A Passion for Excellence* offer, for their time, pretty radical statements on the business of management but they are in format and design utterly conventional books. Both of these texts are presented to readers on the understanding that they should be read from beginning to end in a sequential fashion (with the possible exception of the final 100 pages of *A Passion for Excellence,* which offers specialist advice to educators and which may, consequently, be skipped by the general reader without damaging the integrity of the text as a whole). Compared to these earlier texts *Thriving on Chaos* is unconventional. It does not oblige the reader to follow the linear sequence of an argument that grows as the text moves from its introduction towards its conclusion. Instead *Thriving on Chaos* might be regarded as a manual or as a handbook.

Outlining the rationale that underpins this departure from the conventional narrative form that characterized his earlier work and which, in truth, typifies most texts published in the arena of management and organization studies (this one included!), Peters tells us that his choice of format stems from a recognition of (a) the size of the task that he will outline and (b) the different problems and contingencies that each organization will face. Consequently he informs us that he has prepared a manual for managers – a 'handbook for a management revolution' that, like those prepared for the users of, say, complex technological equipment, will allow managers to select those portions of the text that apply most immediately to the current issues and problems they face.

Introducing the key arguments *Thriving on Chaos,* Peters returns to a familiar theme. Echoing the concerns outlined in *A Passion for Excellence,* which called for what amounts to a 'permanent revolution' in management, *Thriving on Chaos* warns us that we should not think that we can escape the chaos that threatens to envelope each one of us.

Carroll's (1983) critical review of *In Search of Excellence,* you will recall, suggested that a company that was excellent according to the eight attributes of excellence identified by Peters and Waterman would always struggle against an organization with more general factor and/or technology advantages. Responding to this criticism, *Thriving on Chaos* insists that current advantages of size, location, technology or marketing, provide no long-term security in an environment that is, increasingly, complex, competitive and inter-connected. In order to persuade his readers of the veracity of this alarming account of our prospects in this (newly) chaotic world, Peters once again employs the rhetorical device, which he used to good effect in *A Passion for Excellence.* Thus, he threatens us; he wounds our self-image (Jackson, 1996) and then applies the balm of his common sense approach to management to soothe the fears he has introduced. *Thriving on Chaos* begins, therefore, with a quotation from Barbara Tuchman, designed (a) to unsettle those who are complacent as regards the future and (b) to disarm those inclined to disagree with Peters' account of our, impending, futures: 'Three outstanding attitudes – obliviousness to the growing disaffection of constituents, primacy of self-aggrandizement, [and the] illusion of invulnerable status – are persistent aspects of folly' (Peters, 1987: vii, parentheses in original)

In the context of Peters' earlier discussions of excellence (see Chapter 2) the message that we are supposed to take from this inscription seems clear enough: It is folly to deny the scale of the changes facing business. Those inclined to disagree with Peters' analysis of our chaotic future are delusional. In other words: Peters is a guru. Peters knows best. Peters sees further; Peters sees clearly the ways in which the forces at work in our complex and fast-paced economies will impact on every business, every career and on every home and community. And to be fair Ackman's (2002) reappraisal of the enduring legacy of the excellence project does suggest that, from a particular standpoint, this is not, entirely, an idle boast.

Discussing the factors which underpin guru success, Huczynski (1993) observes that while those vaunted as gurus may have no more wisdom than their less celebrated colleagues these honoured commentators do tend to have a knack for communication. Indeed, Huczynski argues that mere authors become celebrated gurus when and where they successfully produce representations of managers and managerial work that resonate with the fears and concerns of their audiences. Thus, Huczynski advises that commentators become recognized as gurus when they succeed in the production of accounts of managerial work that are:

- memorable (hence the focus on alliteration),
- individually focused,
- composed of a number of steps, and
- supportive of the managerial role.

Kieser (1997) endorses this summation, however, he adds a small, but important, rider. He argues that gurus need to 'be lucky' if they are to succeed. In particular he suggests that successful gurus enjoy good fortune when it comes to timing. In 1987 Peters got lucky with his timing. Very lucky indeed!

Black Monday

Thriving on Chaos was first published in America in October 1987. Commenting on the tone and structure of this work Crainer (1997) argues that this was Peters' 'first guru book – and the first he wrote without the tempering presence of a co-author' (205). And it shows!

Like *A Passion for Excellence*, *Thriving on Chaos* was conceived as a book, which would offer advice on the thorny problems associated with the implementation of Peters' preferred approach to management. Observing that Peters had been stung by the criticism applied to his earlier works, Crainer (1997: 206) argues that the 'the roots of *Thriving on Chaos* stretch back very clearly to *In Search of Excellence* – it is basically a lengthy riposte aimed at all those critics who suggested that Peters' theories could not be turned into reality.'

In other times reviewers might have dwelled on the chaotic nature of the text since as Crainer notes '*Thriving on Chaos* is true to its title. It is badly organized with an ornate numbering system for the chapters which defies explanation'

(206). But in 1987, in the middle of the month of October, something happened that would make Peters' analysis of the nature of chaos, and its implications for the practice of management, a hot topic for debate.

Lewis' (1992) discussion of the literary depiction of the modern workplace suggests that, for many of us, Monday is always 'black day', a day over-shadowed with gloom and foreboding, because it signals the start of another tiring and tedious week devoted to the necessary evils of working and commuting. However, Monday, October 19, 1987 was no ordinary start to the working week. 'Black Monday' as this day was soon labelled, was, for many, an especially gloomy start to the working week because, on this autumn morning, the value of stocks listed on New York's Wall Street exchange fell by 20%. Other stock markets, world-wide, we should note suffered similar collapses in the immediate aftermath of New York's (ahem) 'correction'. Perhaps unsurprisingly newspapers spoke of 'meltdowns' as editorials drew attention to the interconnected nature of modern economies. All of a sudden the headline message of *Thriving on Chaos* seemed very real and highly persuasive. Who could, now, reasonably deny that the world of business is complex and chaotic?

Thriving on Chaos, as we have seen, begins by rehearsing Tuchman's warnings as regards the dangers of self-deception and self-aggrandizement. Given this, it may come as a surprise to find that within the first few pages of *Thriving on Chaos,* Peters seems to bestow on himself the elusive qualities of leadership and vision, which in *A Passion for Excellence* he was happy to celebrate in others. In *Thriving on Chaos,* therefore, Peters speaks of *his* knowledge, *his* practice and *his* vision for the future. Indeed, he seems seem to elevate himself above the, in-house, managerial leader that he celebrated in *A Passion for Excellence* to become both 'hero' and 'narrator' for our chaotic times. In *Thriving on Chaos,* therefore, Peters is revealed not as *the guide on the side* but as the *sage on the stage* and from this exalted position, as the paramount business leader, he conveys his stark message: that there are no longer any 'excellent' companies.

Qualifying this headline grabbing assertion, Peters points out that those (like his critics) who have assumed that excellence is a fixed and stable 'state' of being have embraced the three persistent aspects of folly, and so, will surely fail in their endeavours. Other organizations more attuned to the complexity of the business environment, he warns, will prosper because they understand that 'excellence' is a journey not a destination – an on-going process not a state.

In an attempt to help organizations in this never-ending journey, Peters breaks from previous practice. In earlier texts Peters chose to illustrate the problematic nature of organizational change with stories and vignettes and had attempted to use these narratives as a means of fostering wider debate and reflection. Yet in *Thriving on Chaos,* Peters apparently, now, more confident in the role of guru is impatient with this gentler and more facilitative approach. The problems *and* the answers now seem clear to Peters. Consequently he disposes with the questions that were a feature of *A Passion for Excellence* and instead adopts a more prescriptive tone. Thus, where *A Passion for Excellence* offered pauses and questions for reflection, *Thriving on Chaos* offers, instead, a basket of 45 prescriptions designed, we are told, to ensure that managers commit to change as the only constant. Yet there is something rather hollow about a prescription for chaos.

The nature of chaos

In the late 1980s a body of rather complex mathematical thinking known variously as 'complexity science' or 'chaos theory' became a 'hot topic' in many forms of academic and popular discourse. Chaos theory, if you will, became fashionable. In lecture theatres and in bars people discussed chaos theory. Chaos Theory even found its way on to the 'silver screen'.

In the film, *Jurassic Park,* the actor Jeff Goldblum appears as a handsome, if philandering, mathematician schooled in the science of chaos and complexity. All disaster movies, it is said, begin with someone ignoring a scientist and this film is no exception. Thus, Goldblum's character warns the audience, at the outset, that the science of complexity demonstrates that any attempt to regulate the chaotic forces of nature will tend to conclude in catastrophic failure. The problem for the owners of *Jurassic Park*, and for the cast more generally, is that while the fact of this failure is broadly predictable, the nature, flow and consequences of the predicted breakdown are much more difficult to foresee.

Examining the implications of chaos thinking for management practice Letiche (2000) offers a critical appreciation of the science of complexity. He argues that theorizing on complexity and chaos is shaped by a concern with process, emergence and with self-organization. Yet in so doing he reminds us that any casual discussion of 'complexity theory' will tend to obscure the contests that mark this terrain. Thus, Letiche (2000: 545 original emphasis) notes that 'complexity theory can be conceptualised as a collection of new anti-mechanistic metaphors stressing process and *emergence*; it can also be conceptualised as the modelling via (mathematical) computational experiments of how events self-organize.'

Reflecting on the managerial implications of these, now potentially competitive and contestable, metaphors, Grint (1997b) offers a lucid introduction to some of the complexities, which characterize this challenging field. He argues that chaos theory and its, broadly, anti-mechanistic account of the manner in which our world adapts and changes implies six conditions that are critical to organizational analysis. Thus, he tells us that the science of complexity insists (1) that while organization is both predictable and unpredictable it (2) mocks those models that would seek to forge a predictive relationship between a 'cause' and its 'effect'. This, essential unpredictability has, Grint suggests, clear implications for the practice of management. Indeed, he argues that the science of chaos obliges managers to behave with caution because their actions have (3) irreversible consequences that tend to amplify in effect. Furthermore, Grint argues that chaos thinking implies that managers should allow a degree of (4) self-organization and (5) individual discretion because allowing the space for such local and adaptive responses should provide (6) the diversity of responses that are necessary to prevent the organization from suffering a complete and catastrophic collapse.

While broadly supportive of this analysis of chaos and complexity, Burnes (2005) extends Grint's critique. Reviewing the body of literature concerned with 'complexity' and 'chaos', in the context of organization theory, he suggests that organizational commentators have, too often, applied this body of work in a fashion that, either, misunderstands or misrepresents the subtlety and diversity of this arena of scientific endeavour. For example he observes that organizational commentators often render this body of literature in the singular – as complexity theory – whereas the truth of the matter is that this arena of scientific theorizing remains a contested terrain. Thus, Burnes warns us that scientists have produced *theories* of complexity rather than a single theory of complexity that might unite all those interested in this field. Letiche (2000: 545 original emphasis) makes a similar point when he suggests that the field concerned with theorizing complexity is divided by a common language. Indeed, he argues that complexity theory 'can be interpreted to lead to both radical process thinking and to scientific realism. Complexity theorists can discuss *emergence* and self-organization – and actually be referring to very different universes of discourse'. Yet this fact tends to evade organizational commentators operating within 'popular management' who, as we shall see, tend to distort the essential mathematics of chaos.

Pursuing the implications of this distortion Burnes and Letiche warn us that organizational commentators apply their chosen theories of complexity *as if* this science offered only one model of our chaotic world when, in fact, it offers many 'different universes of discourse' (Letiche, 2000: 545). In addition, Burnes (2005) suggests that organizational commentaries on chaos and complexity tend to invoke the science of complexity as a simple metaphor for disorder. However, both Burnes and Grint (1997) protest that scientists interested in the non-linear dynamic processes of complex systems actually have a concern with 'orderly disorder'.

Orderly disorder

It would be fair to say that the ambition of normal modes of scientific theorizing is to generate, through careful and detached observation, models of the world, which can forge a predictive relationship between cause and effect. Complexity theorists, however, reject this orderly account of the world because they argue that systems grow and change in ways, which simply cannot be apprehended by linear models of the world. Yet complexity theorists do recognize that chaos has orderly elements. This recognition, they argue, makes our complex, adaptive systems somewhat paradoxical insofar as they are both orderly and yet disorderly, predictable and unpredictable. For scientists of complexity, therefore, the world is chaotic insofar as complex, adaptive systems tend to elude our attempts to predict, apprehend or, otherwise, control them. Yet at the same time complexity theorists argue that the chaos and turbulence we experience is patterned by a set of 'order generating rules', which are replicated as the overall system adapts. Consequently Letiche warns us that while many organizational theorists speak confidently of self-organization they have, too often, failed to reflect on what such notions of self-organization might imply of and for our notion of self. Mindful of the far-reaching consequences of such, subtle, distinctions Burnes warns us that chaos thinking has been translated, and prematurely transformed, into a body of normative prescriptions, which purports to explain exactly what managers must do to remain competitive in an arena that is said to be newly chaotic, the problem being, of course, that these normative prescriptions have a reductionist concern with prediction, which tends to undermine any attempt to appreciate the fundamental complexity of social organization.

Given these comments on both the nature and the limits of complexity theorizing how does Peters' (1987) attempt to apply the science of chaos to the arena of management actually stack up?

An unsettling world

In our previous chapter we observed that critics of Peters have, too often, failed to acknowledge that this guru has produced accounts of business and organization that, despite flaws in methodology and conceptualization, convey essential truths about the complex and contestable world of management. With this observation in mind it is important that we acknowledge that, at some level, all of Peters' key works on management prior to 1987 have had some flavour of chaos thinking as this has been elaborated by Grint (1997b). Peters' co-authored texts of 1982 and 1985, for example, each recognized elements of chaos thinking insofar as they suggested that the successful organizations of this period recognized (a) the limits of managerial control, (b) the inevitability of self-organization, (c) the vainglorious nature of 'hard' approaches to management, and so, (d) celebrated the virtues of local action, rule-breaking and individual discretion. It is clear therefore that at some level all of Peters' texts on managing seem to recognize at some level the managerial paradoxes, which a chaotic view of the world throws up. And yet other aspects of Peters' work remain linear, mechanistic and, above all, stubbornly anti-chaotic in their orientations and suppositions. For example Peters seems to view 'chaos' as a new development, a new epoch which is, itself, a product of social, economic and technological change. However, Letiche is adamant that chaos is an intrinsic feature of all systems adding that this feature is revealed to us when we apply non-mechanical metaphors to our attempts to appreciate the world. In this regard we might voice the suspicion that, for Peters, chaos remains a simple synonym for disorder. Furthermore, it is apparent that Peters continues to assume that this disorderly world – prone as it is to wild and largely unpredictable fluctuations – may be controlled, culturally, through the elusive qualities of some amorphous thing he places at the head of the organization and labels, carelessly, as leadership.

Pulling these elements of our argument together we can see clear differences between Peters' account of 'chaos' and the works of those who are, truly and thoroughly theorists of the science of chaos. Thus, where Letiche (2000) and Burnes (2005) are clear that complexity thinking has useful implications for organizational analysis because its anti-mechanistic approach reveals the essential complexity that is denied by more conventional modes of thinking, Peters represents chaos not as a mode of thinking, but as a new approach to managing that has been ushered in by the processes of technological change and economic deregulation. Where Letiche and Burnes observe that complexity theorizing challenges our most basic and fundamental assumptions as regards the nature and practice of management, Peters holds to a model of management, which assumes that top-down models of culture change will prevail.

In short, Peters' analysis of the management of chaos might be said to be more contradictory than chaotic: He begins by announcing a new world of chaos but concludes with the assurance that such inherent complexity can be channelled, controlled and, ultimately, may be made to serve the ordering impulse of skilful managerial leaders.

Liberation management

Peters' next offering was published in 1992 soon after the Gulf War that was fought by a coalition of forces in order to secure the liberation of Kuwait from the occupying forces of the Iraqi military. In this book Peters, once again, promises a management revolution. To this end, and reflecting the book's production during a time of war, Peters argues that practitioners of *Liberation Management* (Peters, 1992) should become 'corporate scud missiles'.

Discussing the nature of science and the business of academic writing, Latour (1987) reminds us of the literary tools that scientists of all descriptions deploy in their world building endeavours. Indeed, he argues that all writers – even the most reclusive of this breed – have to be skilled networkers and, to some degree, poets. Elaborating on the reasoning that underpins this claim, Latour tells us that authors have to acquire the skills of the poet and must develop the characteristics of the politician because readers are devious and obstinate contrarians who are naturally disinclined to accept the, perfectly reasonable, statements as to the nature of the world, which scientists (of all types) must toil to prepare.

In an attempt to overcome the objections of these contrary readers, Latour observes that academic authors of all disciplines – whether they be scientists or social scientists – must take steps to:

• Forge alliances with other writers who can provide the evidential support that will demolish the fortress of 'the contrarians'.

A few moments ago, for example, I took steps to build a network that would do just this. For example I drew on the support of Latour in my efforts to convince you, my readers, that we should pause to reflect on the essential nature of academic writing. In addition, I allowed myself a few poetic flourishes: I conjured a collective noun – 'contrarians' – to label and thence to disarm my opponents. Furthermore, I dragged these 'contrarians' from their normal places of business and placed them all in a fortress, which I then scheduled for demolition!

• Convey their now, jointly-authored arguments in a fashion that readers will find pleasing, and so, worth repeating.

To this end, Latour notes that academic authors regularly employ metaphorical forms of expression (such as the metaphor of chaos) and other more poetic flourishes in their analyses. A few moments ago, for example, I took steps to bring a degree of pace and memorability to my analysis of the craft of writing. I gathered, together, all of those inclined to disagree with my work, labelled them as 'contrarians', and placed them in a fortress under siege. It is worth noting – since you cannot see my previous draft – that initially I had placed the 'contrarians' in *fortresses* but I quickly changed this metaphor. Why did I do this? The answer is simple.

First, I need you – dear reader – to agree with me and I quickly decided that talk of *fortresses* strained my metaphor. I am you see not fully confident that my own network has the capacity to fight on a number of fronts and so I am wary of the suggestion that I/we might successfully besiege a number of fortresses at once. And second I decided that the suggestion that there exist many structures raised in opposition to my (perfectly reasonable and sensible argument) would hand the metaphorical advantage back to my opponents. Thus, the suggestion that there exist *many* outposts of opposition to my ideas would, almost inevitably, lead to me being re-cast as '*the* contrarian', out of step with the majority who tend, naturally, to become identified with/as reasoned opinion.

In preparing his commentaries on the business of management Peters, like all authors has taken steps to forge networks with like-minded supporters. And as he expresses his preferred line of argument he has taken time to construct metaphors designed (ostensibly) to convince us, his readers, of the soundness of his case for change. And yet Peters often makes poor choices when it comes to the selection of metaphorical devices. He has, as we have seen, offered metaphors for chaos that turn out to be profoundly unchaotic. Furthermore, he has offered metaphorical references to anal retentiveness that are linked to disturbing images of loosening (see Crainer, 1997). Such ill-advised, metaphorical choices have a tendency to undermine arguments and in Peters' case allow me opportunities for amusing, yet purposeful, diversions designed as invitations to join my network of like-minded free-thinkers! Thus, it is worth observing that Peters' account of the manager as 'corporate scud missile', which features in *Liberation Management* troubles me...and should trouble you.

The scud missile, as you may recall, was a weapon deployed by Iraqi forces in the first Gulf War. Originally developed by the Soviet Union in the 1960s the scud missile was a direct descendant of the German 'V' weapons that rained down on London and the south east of England during World War II. In common with the earlier 'V' weapons, the scud missile is inaccurate, often unreliable and has a limited range. As a battlefield weapon it is, by and large, an unsatisfactory means of delivering conventional weapons technology (have you noticed that the military and the suppliers of military ordnance have a preference for euphemistic language forms that turn the business of killing into a form of applied logistics?). Indeed, Jones (1978) suggests that more people died in the development of the V2 weapon than were killed by its deployment! That said the scud missile does have a use as a weapon of terror and was used by Iraqi forces in 1991 to target (in the loosest possible sense of the term) civilian populations in Israel and Saudi Arabia.

At one level, of course, Peters' support for, what might be termed, a scud missile approach to management is, clearly, a continuation of his support for ways of doing business, which celebrate energy, action and enthusiasm. But surely there must be a better metaphor for this than that of the corporate scud missile?

Does Peters really want us to think of the weapons of the oppressor as his preferred route to liberation?

Does he really think that the future of management lies in the hand of those who – like the scud missile – lack direction, behave erratically and have limited capabilities?

Let us see.

Liberation Management was first published in America in 1992, a decade after the publication of *In Search of Excellence*. In common with this, the first of Peters' key texts on management, *Liberation Management* surveyed an American economy in recession.

Fears concerning instability, dislocation and unemployment obviously play a major role in guru theorizing and we should not under-estimate the extent to which gurus (and politicians more generally) seek to capitalize on our basic fears and insecurities. Nevertheless, Crainer (1997) suggests that *Liberation Management* should be thought of as a product of Tom Peters' own, very personal, insecurities.

Commenting on the genesis of this text, Crainer argues that the origins of *Liberation Management* can be traced back to a televised debate between the author and Robert Reich (who would later become the US secretary of state for labour) that was screened on *CNN* in 1985. Crainer tells us that in this debate, Reich gave Peters a very public and deeply embarrassing lesson on the history of trade and industrial policy. Being, like so many other top management consultants, both intellectually bright and psychologically insecure, Crainer (1997) tells us that Peters decided to remedy the gap in his education, which Robert Reich had, so publicly, exposed. Consequently Peters spent the summer of 1985 attempting to get to grips with economic history and, boldly as ever, began drafting a book on trade policy. This book on trade policy was, it seems, later abandoned but much of the preparatory reading later resurfaced in *Liberation Management*, which as we shall see, makes a return to the basic methods of *In Search of Excellence* despite abandoning much of the headline message of this earlier text.

In Search of Excellence, you will recall, derived its authority from a programme of field research, which sought to construct a model of business excellence by analysing the conduct of managers in a sample of high performance organizations. However, *A Passion for Excellence* and *Thriving on Chaos* both reject such an approach in favour of a line of argumentation that derives its authority from common sense and its content and energy from recounted conversations that had, often, taken place during Peters' seminars. In *Liberation Management*, however, Peters returned to the method of *In Search of Excellence* insofar as he made some attempt to generate data on management and organization in the period, which he described with a metaphorical flourish (of course) as the 'nano-second nineties'.

To assert that this process of data generation conforms to the normal conventions of academic research, however, would be to give it false airs. Too often, what Peters passes off as an authoritative commentary on the actual management practices of a particular organization is, in truth, more properly represented as the outcome of a relatively brief interview with the founder or chief executive – that was, in any case, shaped by Peters' a priori concerns and personal convictions. Indeed, it is important to note that many of the 'interviews' that were conducted within these organized settings had been contracted out to a team of freelance business journalists, unschooled in the rigours of social scientific research who would have, in any case, a vested interest in delivering field reports that reflected Peters' own concerns and preoccupations. As Crainer, one of those involved in the process, acknowledges,

> What is interesting about this approach is that Peters and his researchers often went into the companies with largely preconceived ideas of what they were looking for and wanted to find. The research was to some extent a self-fulfilling prophecy.
>
> *Crainer (1997: 229)*

What was it that Peters wanted and needed to find?

Peters and his team searched for and found (of course) companies with energy and vitality. They looked for and found (to their satisfaction at least) companies that were impatient with bureaucracy – companies that delivered in the absence of traditional organizational structures (and strictures). In short, *they looked for and found (all over again) the very attributes previously lauded as excellent.*

And yet Peters begins *Liberation Management* (Peters, 1992) by noting that his earlier books on management and organizing had all been flawed. Accepting, implicitly, the critiques outlined in our analysis of *In Search of Excellence*, Peters acknowledges that his earlier works had a tendency to 'put the cart before the horse' insofar as they urged managers to get close to the customer and yet failed to acknowledge the ways in which 'structure' acts to obstruct the achievement of total customer satisfaction. To remedy this oversight Peters advocates a more structural form of analysis. Yet it might be countered that this renewed concern with structure amounts to a false dawn because Peters soon announces that it is a commitment to demolishing organizational structures, and a commitment to "necessary disorganization" which holds the key to the revolution required.

That Peters moves so quickly *from* recognizing the importance of 'structure' *to* announcing the need for the outright demolition of such organizational structures is disappointing because in highlighting the limits of his previous 'action orientation' he actually stumbles over (and around) a key criticism that might be attached to most of management's gurus.

★ ★ ★ ★ ★

Discussing the nature of guru theorizing Huczynski (1993) observes that successful gurus devise and market accounts of managerial work, which suggest, somewhat optimistically, that individual managers – when armed with the appropriate tools and technologies – can bring about positive and lasting change within their employing organizations. In a seminal contribution to the field of 'change management' Pettigrew (1985) however argues that this sort of advice is flawed and misleading because it refuses to take account of the ways in which existing organizational structures might act to forestall, or to condition, managerial choices and managerial action. Thus, Pettigrew argues that much of the advice on (how to) manage change is unhelpful because it fails to understand that embedded structures and pre-existing institutional arrangements tend to set very definite limits as regards the viability of certain patterns of action (see Collins, 1998). Pettigrew does seem to concede that management's gurus may well have good reason to be impatient with the limitations of existing structures and policies; nevertheless, he argues that it would be folly to assume that pre-existing arrangements can be changed quickly and/or simply to accord with managerial aspirations.

Discussing the UK car maker, *Austin-Rover*, Williams and his co-authors (Williams, Williams, and Haslam, 1987) offer a concrete example of Pettigrew's core concerns. Indeed, the work of Williams et al., demonstrates the manner in which previous managerial decisions, became embedded within this company's policies and broader institutional arrangements, and in so doing circumscribed subsequent managerial action within *Austin-Rover*. Thus, the authors demonstrate the ways in which particular assumptions concerning market expectations (it had been assumed that the Mini Metro, later renamed the Rover 100 would achieve volume sales) led Austin-Rover's management to make choices as regards production technology (they chose a dedicated production line with tooling that could produce *only* the Metro on the understanding that the car would enjoy mass market sales). Furthermore, the authors observe that these mis-guided assumptions and choices as regards (a) the market potential of the car and (b) the most cost-effective means of producing this vehicle set a context for future decisions which, despite disappointing sales, simply obliged the company to continue to produce the Metro and in so doing prevented managers from exploring new options and new strategic directions.

Surveying this sort of outcome Peters would probably protest that his account of organizational structures has been designed to reveal the extent to which the maxim of traditional economic theorizing: that structure must follow strategy is reversed by the experience of organization. Indeed, Peters argues that there is an urgent need for a remedy for this problematic state of affairs. Yet it is this focus on change (in the absence of a feeling for continuity) and the suggestion that existing organizational structures require outright demolition, which I suggest has prevented Peters from reaching a new and more developed appreciation of the realities of organizational practice. In short, Peters' (1992) account of 'necessary disorganization' fails to develop a proper appreciation of structures in context because:

1   While it would be fair to say that Peters does, indeed, acknowledge that strategy tends to follow structure he tends to treat this outcome as an oversight and error – as a function of managerial ineptitude. Yet in the work of Pettigrew (1985) the links between context and action, and between strategy and structure are explored in ways which suggest that these interesting dynamics constitute a fundamental element of organizational life that will not be wished away by the entrance of a new heroic leader. Thus, where Pettigrew's concern with structures, in context, produces an exploration of the limits and possibilities of action, Peters' concern to develop new structures for an altered context produces only exhortation. And this exhortation, we should note, simply fails to recognize the obdurate nature of existing organizational arrangements.

2   By focusing attention on those organizations whom scant research suggests enjoy the 'necessary disorganization' for future business success, Peters produces an aprocessual form of analysis insofar as he offers few insights on the transition process that organizations, currently chained by their histories and bureaucracies, would be obliged to undertake en route to their supposed liberation.

3   Despite his claim to have rediscovered the importance of structures and the need to reconfigure structural arrangements for future success, Peters offers no meaningful account of the embedded processes and institutional mechanisms (such as trade union collective bargaining and the presence or absence of labour statutes) that variously shape, sustain, and/or challenge *the existing structures of business organizations in context*.

It is ironic therefore that a book, which begins by rejecting both the method and the message of *In Search of Excellence* should culminate in a form of analysis that repeats and compounds the problems identified in Peters' earlier texts. But before we turn to the next book developed by Peters it will be useful to pause to consider the stresses which the production of *Liberation Management* placed on its author.

★ ★ ★ ★ ★

Liberation Management is by the standards of modern business publishing a very big book. Peters claims to be proud of this work and claims to have enjoyed producing it. Yet the joy of writing is seldom unalloyed. In common with all long-term projects the process of writing a book has its highs and its lows. In truth it takes some fortitude to awake each morning knowing that the tyranny of the blank page awaits.

Authors tend to find different ways of expressing the difficulties they encounter as they attempt to record their thoughts and ideas. As you can see, I tend to speak of paper tyrants. George Orwell, famously, spoke of writing as an affliction. In the essay 'Why I write' (see Orwell, 1988) he observes: 'Writing a book is a horrible, exhausting struggle, like a long bout of some painful illness. One would never undertake such a thing if one were not driven by some demon whom one can neither resist nor understand' (187–188)

Friends who are, unlike me, *proper* writers have been heard to speak of 'thin' and 'fat work' as they discuss the trials of authorship. 'Thin work', as you might, expect progresses at a tremendous rate – so fast, in fact, that the author seems compelled to write at the expense of all other necessities. Consequently a 'thin work' may cause the author to suffer an alarming degree of weight loss. 'Fat work', in contrast, tends to proceed slowly and tends to enlarge its struggling progenitor as it refuses to grow. That is to say that a writer confronted by the slow pace of his/her progress may take comfort in/from food as s/he struggles to commit their thoughts to print. Viewed in these terms *Liberation Management* is properly viewed as a 'fat work' but not because it fills in excess of 850 pages (quite a contrast to the 850 word columns that had been Peters' main publication outlet between 1987 and 1992). No, *Liberation Management* is a 'fat work' in the sense that Peters gained 20 lb. as he struggled to complete this text. When we combine the fact of Peters' enlargement with the knowledge that the manuscript was delivered late to the publishers and when we add to this Crainer's (1997) assertion that Peters developed problems with alcohol and chose to enter therapeutic counselling at this time, it seems reasonable to suggest that Peters' joy in penning *Liberation Management* was not unbounded. Indeed, given Peters' experience of writing it seems sensible to suggest that the production of this work may have exhausted Peters, draining him of the energy and inclination necessary to tackle another project in the form of his 1992 text. In this respect the struggle to produce *Liberation Management* may help to explain the character of the texts which Peters offered to the public in 1993 and 1994, and, indeed, every publication since!

The Tom Peters seminar and the pursuit of wow

In the years 1993 and 1994 Tom Peters released two texts on management and managing: *The Tom Peters Seminar* (Peters, 1993) and *The Pursuit of Wow* (Peters, 1994). The first of these texts, it would be fair to say, was dictated rather than written and emerged as an attempt to capitalize on the demand for copies of the slides, which Peters uses to illustrate his seminars. In this regard *The Tom Peters Seminar* might be thought of as a Peters performance event, *circa* 1992, captured, somewhat imperfectly, in print and frozen in time.

The Pursuit of Wow also builds on a stock of material that Peters had, previously, developed for another purpose. Between 1987 and 1997 Peters produced a regular newspaper column that was widely syndicated. By 1994 he had produced 450 of his syndicated columns and had somehow formed the opinion that these would make a successful book project. Commenting on this project of collation, however, Crainer (1997) suggests that *The Pursuit of Wow* fails as an attempt to meet market demand from inventory because only 20% of the book's content, actually, derives from the Peters syndicated column with the remaining 80% of the text being generated anew for the book. That the text produced in 1994 made so little use of the column archive is hardly surprising. Good newspaper columnists produce insights into, and commentaries on, the sights, sounds and travails of everyday life. These columns if they are to attract and retain an audience must sprinkle wit, and where appropriate, anger and indignation over a canvas, which captures the spirit of a particular place and time. Yet, because of this, individual columns seldom survive the process of reprinting. The witty asides and the knowing allusions that captured the spirit of the moment or the cupidity of some individual in, say, the springtime have often lost all reference come the autumn. The result being that newspaper columns, like physical comedy, seldom survive the process of translation. The standard exclusion, it seems to me, applies to both – 'you really had to be there'.

Given the problems associated with translation and repurposing it is, perhaps, unsurprising that readers and reviewers tend to be disappointed by Peters' offerings of 1993 and 1994. That is not to suggest, of course, that the texts of 1993 and 1994 are, entirely, without merit or have no interesting features. In truth the seminar text *is* intriguing (and deserves its place as a 'major' work) because in this work Peters introduces us personally to his redefined market and congregation.

In April 1989 Peters (1989) published a piece in *Inc*, which offered personal reflections on his career. In this article he observes that the heroes of his early works and his role models of/for excellence had been drawn from the senior managers of *Fortune 500* companies. However, he confides that, over time, he had become pessimistic about the future prospects of these very large organizations. Looking back to his second offering on 'excellence' (Peters and Austin, 1985) he tells us that on re-reading this work he can sense a growing disillusionment with America's giant corporations. By the late 1980s, he tells us, he had come to a new appreciation of the world:

> by the time I sat down to write *Thriving on Chaos* in the early winter of 1987 I had a whole new set of role models. The heroes of *In Search of Excellence* – IBM, Hewlett-Packard, 3M – had given way to the likes of *Chapparral Steel* and *Weaver Popcorn*.

In later chapters, however, we will demonstrate that neither of these new heroes features prominently in the storyworld of *Thriving on Chaos* or, indeed, in any subsequent work!

The Pursuit of Wow is, similarly, interesting (and so deserves its position as 'a major work') for it, too, signals key changes in form and other, more minor movements in content, which as we shall see have come to figure more prominently in Peters' later works.

Looking first at the shifts in content: *The Pursuit of Wow* is interesting because it introduces a key theme that has become, more and more, prominent in Peters' work. This theme is 'design'. In *The Pursuit of Wow,* Peters casts a critical eye over product (and service) design and rails against those organizations that, as he sees it, abuse their power. In this respect Peters' text of 1994 echoes many of the arguments put forward by Michael Hammer in his analysis of Business Process Reengineering (BPR) (Hammer, 1990). Thus, Peters argues that America's largest organizations, too often, fail to place the customer at the heart of their business processes and, as a consequence, produce lack lustre service and shoddy product designs. Highlighting, as always, the (supposedly) competitive nature of the modern business arena, therefore, Peters (1994) argues that those businesses that wish to prosper in the future will have to rethink both their product designs and their organizational charts if they are to delight their customers. In short, Peters argues that 'the pursuit of wow' – the ability to surprise and delight customers through such things as design – is to be allowed to shape future managerial behaviour.

On the question of form there is, perhaps less to say: *The Tom Peters Seminar* has, if you are prepared to persevere, 'a beginning', 'a middle' and 'an end'. Taken as a whole the seminar book is hardly compelling but it is, clearly, designed on the understanding that the reader will navigate the text in a traditional manner. That is not to say, of course, that *The Tom Peters Seminar* is just like Peters' earlier texts. The book is, in fact, distinctive in that the text is, thanks mainly to the input of the editorial firm, 'Word Works', an illuminated volume. Where earlier books offered only densely packed text *The Tom Peters Seminar* is illuminated by a collection of legends and inscriptions. This illumination makes the text more welcoming and, at one level, more appealing. Yet despite its decoration, this text simply lacks the energy of the live seminar.

The format of *The Pursuit of Wow* is more interesting and, I suppose, more shocking than that of the seminar text, principally because this text seems to dispense, entirely, with a traditional narrative structure. Thus, *The Pursuit of Wow* is composed of 210 related, yet distinct, elements that, in different ways, celebrate topics such as 'design', 'values', 'empowerment' and the skills of the managerial leader. Each of these elements is listed and discussed with just one aim in mind – to allow the reader access to the tools and insights necessary to delight customers. Yet unlike *The Tom Peters Seminar* there is no 'beginning', 'middle' and 'end'. Indeed, no attempt is made to join the 210 elements of *The Pursuit of Wow* into a clear and consistent narrative.

★ ★ ★ ★ ★

Most books can be represented in linear terms as a journey, if you will, from ignorance to enlightenment, from passivity into action, from loneliness to love. Yet *The Pursuit of Wow* is different. In common with *Thriving on Chaos*, *The Pursuit of Wow* dispenses with a conventional narrative structure. Yet where *Thriving on Chaos* offers itself as a handbook, as a (socio-)technical manual, *The Pursuit of Wow* is, perhaps, more usefully considered to be a spectacle – a hypertextual experience, designed and constructed, apparently, to precipitate the sort of 'yeasty responses'[1] that will make readers and customers, more generally, shout *wow*.

Hypertext is, perhaps, most commonly associated with computer-mediated sources of information such as the encyclopaedia, *Encarta* which Microsoft published between 1993 and 2009. In common with more traditionally formatted encyclopaedias such as the 'hard copy' version of *Encyclopaedia Britannica*, *Encarta* offers a browsing experience, designed to allow users (a) to search for general information on a specific topic and (b) to pursue linkages within the *Encarta* database that allow the browser to develop a more in-depth appreciation, tailored to their specific information needs. For example, a search on 'tartan' might provide an initial entry on traditional Scottish attire, that would then allow the user to refine their search in relation to, say, the clan system, the Jacobite cause, Sir Walter Scott, King George III and football fans.[2]

To facilitate this search capability each *Encarta* entry is designed to provide a cogent response that is concise and hence complete on its own terms. Thus, each *Encarta* entry is designed on the understanding that it could exhaust the curiosity of the user. And yet each entry is also designed to allow for the possibility of on-going inquiry. To this end, *Encarta* is based on hypertext: Its many entries are designed to appear complete at the level of the paragraph and yet each entry, simultaneously, suggests to the user the possibility and availability of more in-depth knowledge that is just a 'double-click' away. In this regard hypertext has an elliptical character.

In making use of this elliptical allusion to describe (some of) Peter's post-1994 works I am trying to suggest that this author's (hyper)texts have a circulating character which (re)combines areas of business and areas of the text that are, more commonly, separated. In this regard Peters' hypertextual narratives are quite unlike his more orthodox narratives: They do not conclude with a 'full stop', rather they tend to 'tail off' elliptically…as they suggest the prospect of additional information and the possibility of future enlightenment.

The circle of innovation

In common with the texts published in 1993 and 1994 *The Circle of Innovation* (Peters, 1997) is probably best thought of as (yet) another by-product of Peters' work as a management performance artiste. Introducing this text Peters tells us that *The Circle of Innovation* consists of his preferred seminar slides, some additional explanatory text and, we are told, the combined knowledge acquired from the 400 seminars he has offered since the publication of *Liberation Management*. The sub-title of *The Circle of Innovation*, which like *The Pursuit of Wow* eschews a normal narrative structure, in favour of a more hypertextual format, is, 'You Can't Shrink Your Way to Greatness'. This, however, seems to contradict Peters' support in *Liberation Management*, for those organizations that had pursued a strategy of downsizing their corporate staffs. Furthermore, this sub-title also seems to cause tensions with the support for radical decentralization that is evident in *The Circle of Innovation* itself. But we are not allowed to mention this. In a typically grand and dismissive gesture, Peters tells us that all bets are off! His work *is* inconsistent, he tells us, because the world is!

But surely *IBM* and *Johnson and Johnson* have been recommended to us as organizations guided by stable, commonly held cultural credos?

★ ★ ★ ★ ★

In *The Circle of Innovation*, Peters' commitment to 'excellence' is finally and formally abandoned. Innovation, it seems, is the key to future success. However, we should note that while such pronouncements often generate useful headlines – principally because they excite the passions (and scissors) of the world's business journalists (see Collins, 2007) – they are seldom accurate as representations of Peters' texts. Thus, we should note that, despite Peters' disavowal of excellence it would probably be more appropriate to say that, 'excellence' (striving to satisfy customers), becomes subsumed by 'innovation', since those factors, previously, regarded as being central to excellence – skunkworks, leadership, cultural management and change – now form the core of Peters' new and preferred buzzword. In this respect *The Circle of Innovation* despite its headline claims must be read as a continuation of the key ideas and arguments that have shaped Peters' work since the 1980s. However, we should acknowledge that these continuities can be difficult to discern because this time around Peters' business beatitudes (Collins, 2000) are packaged differently: They are now surrounded by photographs, by bold type. by bold phrasing (*yikes!*) and by what, it seems, is to be regarded as bold, profound and innovative thinking – to 'think revolution not evolution', to work on your own ideal and not the ideal of someone else, to make mistakes, to bloody your nose, to innovate, I-N-N-O-V-A-T-E.

To convey the need for radical, business change Peters employs the eponymous 'circle of innovation'. This diagram (see Figure 3.1) presents an unbroken circle of innovation marked with 15 way-points. Through this device Peters seeks (a) to demonstrate the text's impatience with traditional narrative structures and (b) to highlight the core factors that, as he sees it, must underpin the process of innovation. Thus, Peters' circle of innovation celebrates women as a market and as a business resource. In addition, the text highlights the need for boldness as it waxes lyrical about the need for erasers and the power of mistakes. Furthermore, *The Circle of Innovation* raises a rhapsody on the power of love.

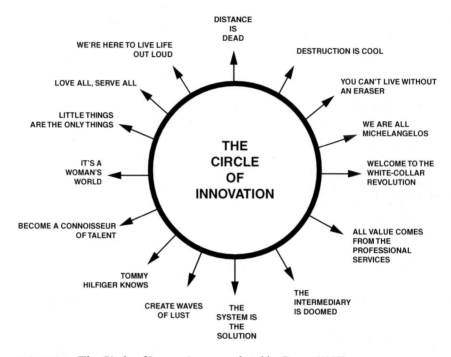

FIGURE 3.1 The Circle of Innovation as rendered by Peters (1997).

But there are problems with this account of innovation which cast doubts on the power of 'love'. If inconsistency is the order of the day every lover is, surely, a potential love-rat! Indeed, we might suggest that an endorsement of inconsistency is nothing more than a self-serving excuse for the failure to develop a sustainable social policy of enterprise that would provide wages sufficient to raise a family!

Re-imagine

Peters' 2003 offering entitled *Re-imagine* continues in much the same vein as the other texts produced since 1994, while amplifying many of the movements and trends that have been evident in this author's work since the publication of *The Pursuit of Wow*.

In common with Peters' seminar text (Peters, 1993), *Re-imagine* was 'dictated' rather than 'written'. Indeed, Peters (2003) tells us that he filled around 37 audio-tapes with his thoughts on the business of management and then passed his words to a team of editors and designers who, duly, produced a first draft for his inspection. Given the primary role accorded to design (and designers) in the preparation of this text it should come as no surprise that *Re-imagine* is a large and colourful text. It is, in fact, much larger than any of Tom Peters' previous texts and in my hands seems to be about the size (and weight) of an elementary, 'international' student textbook. In common with these 'international' textbooks *Re-imagine* offers a full colour presentation. Indeed, it is richly and vividly illuminated with photographs, selected it seems, to illustrate or to emphasize some aspect of Peters' text. Yet despite its appearance this is no textbook. *Re-imagine* does not offer a full, rounded or balanced exegesis on the business of management. It does not provide readers with a coherent introduction to the complex and varied literature on management and managing. Indeed, actually reading this book may be about the last thing you are supposed to do. In short, *Re-imagine* is probably best thought of as a 'coffee table book'.

★ ★ ★ ★ ★

The *Concise Oxford Dictionary* defines a coffee table book as 'a large, lavishly illustrated book'. When used in the context of everyday speech, however, these allusions to size and illustration take on particular connotations, which question the essential nature and function of such books. On my bookshelves I have a large and diverse collection of texts. I have, as you might expect, all of Tom Peters' books and pamphlets on management. I have read each of these texts on a number of occasions. However, I will confess that I do not really enjoy reading these works. Sorry Tom: It's work!

I *do* enjoy the fiction of John Steinbeck and the non-fiction works of George Orwell. And when I get the chance to read a book, solely for my own enjoyment, I often select and re-read one written by these authors.

On top of my bookshelves – because my shelves simply cannot accommodate them in any other way – I also have a number of the large and lavishly illustrated works that the *Concise Oxford* labels as 'coffee table books'. My current favourites among these coffee table books are *The Racing Bicycle*, edited by Moore and Benson (2012), which includes a bike designed and built by a friend, and *Hinault* by van Gucht (2015). I was given these books as Christmas presents some time ago but I still look at them regularly, mainly because I derive pleasure from their lay-out and photography, and in the case of *Hinault*, the iconography! And this, I suppose, is the thing that distinguishes my 'coffee table books' from the other texts on my bookshelves. I *read* Steinbeck's fiction, I *study* Orwell's essays but I *look at* my coffee table books.

The fact that I employ these books in different ways does not, I think, reflect badly on me. I do not use Steinbeck's talents and abuse those of van Gucht because, the truth is that, coffee table books are not, actually, meant to be read! Instead these texts are supposed to be held, admired and appreciated for their beauty as objects with an intrinsic artistic merit.

Beauty, famously, is said to be in the eye of the beholder so I will not seek to impose my aesthetic sensibilities (or lack thereof) on you the reader. Bike porn is, I accept, a specialist and highly expensive perversion (largely beyond my means!).

You must judge for yourself the extent to which Peters' text provides a pleasing addition to the world of internal furnishing. For the moment, however, I will endeavour to maintain the symmetry of our chapter. I will, therefore proceed as if *Re-imagine* text was meant for reading by offering an analysis of its contents.

★ ★ ★ ★ ★

Re-imagine, in common with all of Peters' texts produced since 1993, represents an attempt to capture the drama and energy that those who attend Peters' seminars report as, perhaps, the defining feature of his stage performances (see Collins, 2021a). To this end *Re-imagine* is built around, and derives its energy from the 'stories' and 'rants' – Peters' apparently bad tempered complaints about the foibles and frailties of modern corporations and modern corporate thinking – that are used to introduce the various component parts of this work.

Of course *The Tom Peters Seminar* (Peters, 1993) was, similarly, built around the 'stories' and diatribes that Peters uses to convey his concerns to a live audience. Yet *The Tom Peters Seminar* fails to capture the essence of Peters' seminar performances because, through the processes of transcription it has been channelled into a rather traditional, linear format that is quite unlike the creation that emerges when Peters interacts with his audience. This recognition of the difference between speaking to and writing for an audience, between living in the moment and merely recounting events in print may help to explain an important feature of *Re-imagine*: its annotations and 'side bars'. Thus, *Re-imagine* continually directs the reader's attention to 'marginal notes', designed, it seems, to expand or to explore an element of the main body of the text. These 'marginal' features of the text work to reacquaint areas of the text divided by the normal conventions of typography *and,* as in everyday speech, provide the reader with pleasing digressions and diversions (see Collins, 2021d) which s/he may choose to follow as preferences dictate.

Reflecting the analysis, first introduced within *In Search of Excellence* (Peters and Waterman, 1982) *Re-imagine* devotes a whole chapter to stories and story-telling. In this chapter Peters insists, quite correctly, that the art of management and the arts of the storyteller are indivisible. Those with the best narratives, he tells us, have the most committed employees and the most ardent customers. Yet despite this rhapsody on the art of the storyteller, *Re-imagine*, as we shall soon learn, actually offers few real stories. And those, few stories that Peters actually relays are seldom particularly memorable.

Perhaps the fact that Peters' dictated this text explains the paucity of stories. Perhaps Peter's growing frustration with the corporate world and his increasing willingness to season his prescriptions with bad tempered ranting explains the absence of plotting and characterization in this narrative. Whatever the reason, one thing is clear: Many narratives with the clear potential to become both entertaining and (from a managerial perspective) productive stories are either stripped of necessary motive and characterization or are cut short, and are therefore robbed of the resources necessary to produce a conclusion that is in any sense satisfactory. For example, discussing what might be termed 'the economics of experience', Peters introduces a short section of text, which bills itself as a story. And yet he fails to keep to keep this promise, and delivers instead a summary of events that breaches the covenant formed between storyteller and audience that is brokered whenever a tale is introduced (Collins, 2018, 2021d):

> Joe Pines tells a wonderful story about a next-door neighbour of his in Minneapolis. Robert Stephens owns a small business that installs computer-telecommunications systems. So-called "local area networks," or LANs. The company name was to the point: LAN Installation Company.
>
> Fine. Accurate.
>
> But over the back fence, Joe and his techie neighbour got to talking about the "experience thing." (Quite a push for a "techie") To make a long story short, LAN Installation Company morphed … hold onto your hat … into *The Geek Squad.* That is the talented techies, who had done good work, now emphasized the fun, energy, excellence, reliability … *the experience provided* … behind what they do. To keep on with making this relatively long story very short, their business quickly grew from 2 percent of Minnesota's LAN installations to 30 percent.
>
> *Peters (2003: 121; emphasis and ellipses in original)*

Joe Pine may well have a great story. There is after all enough on the page to suggest an epic-comic tale of self-identifying *geeks* who 'pivot' their business offer to capture nearly a third of the market. But Peters has failed the (promised) tale because in a large format book that extends over more than 350 pages he feels the need to cut to the chase, to get to the takeaway, to cut the story short, with the problem being that in cutting the story short there is no longer a tale to be told, recalled and shared.

Skipping to the takeaway – *IT company stops selling wiring, starts selling experience and cleans up* – could be forgiven, once or twice. But within *Re-imagine* this is not an isolated experience. Time and again promising tales are failed by Peters and become instead blander narratives – reports that simply lack memorability and portability.

Commenting on the book's structure *The Economist* (December 20, 2003) confirms the 'coffee table' status of the *Re-imagine* and warns,

> This is clearly not a book that is meant to be read – not at least by the traditional method of starting at the beginning and proceeding to the end. Its remorselessly shrill tone, alternating between the shocking and the motivational…could easily cause a normal brain to explode after half and hour's continuous exposure. No, this is a book for dipping into for five minutes at a time in search of nuggets of wisdom, a sort of "daily reader" for followers of Mr Peters' brand of management religion. It may well achieve its goal

of taking management ideas to a new younger audience, aged around 30, being famous for their short attention span and need for instant impact and gratification.

And in a parting shot notes, 'if the medium is the message, the message in this case is that business thinkers such as Mr Peters have become a lot less coherent than they were [some] years ago.'

The Little BIG things

In *The Little BIG Things* Peters (2010) turns his back on the coffee table format adopted for *Re-imagine* (Peters, 2003) to offer a more conventionally sized book. Yet despite this reduction in scale *The Little BIG Things* remains unconventional. This is a book which, like *The Pursuit of Wow* (Peters, 1994) grew from, and which attempts to repurpose, a series of 176 'blogs', posted between July 2004 and July 2009. Recognizing the difficulties associated with this translation and repackaging exercise, it is perhaps worth noting that *The Little BIG Things* adapts and trims these blog posts to offer just 163 ways to pursue excellence.

Highlighting the ways in which this text builds from the message of *In Search of Excellence* (Peters and Waterman, 1982) and the lessons learned since the 1980s, Peters suggests that *The Little BIG Things* has been produced to remind readers that while the central problems of management are easily stated and resolve to (something like): *finding and securing ways to connect with colleagues and broader groups of stakeholders in order to offer goods, services and experiences that make customers mouth the word 'wow'*, most people simply don't 'get it' and cannot or will not live up to this obligation.

Elaborating on this point, Peters argues that his readers, his clients and his *Twitter* followers seem to *get the point* at an intellectual level but too often fail to recognize that excellence is a deeper commitment that begins within the next minute, the next meeting. Thus, Peters suggests that too many of his 'followers' cannot commit themselves to be the change they would see in others.

In an attempt to move his readers from intellectual agreement and (in any sense) casual assent to the challenge of 'excellence', to a more fulsome commitment to change, Peters offers 163 ways to pursue excellence. And to this end the book offers advice on 163 little things (including the measurement of your actions) that you might incorporate in your daily engagements and routines. Yet Peters offers the assurance that these small steps and small changes will be recognized and will be valued by others. Just as 'soft' is 'hard' so the little things in life and in business – small courtesies, thank-you notes, a clean washroom, a coiled hose-pipe – become, we are told, little, big, things.

The Little BIG Things is in common with all those texts produced by Peters since 1993, not a book to be read in a traditional way. No attempt, for example, has been made to enforce a conventional narrative structure on the topics selected for consideration. The book is, Peters (2010: xxv) tells us – *and remember you cannot wash your mind's eye* – a book to read 'while sitting on the toilet'. It is, furthermore, offered and designed to 'induce you to take action, to try out one of these "little BIG things" maybe even eventually include it in your own canon' (xxv). That said the book *is* loosely arranged into 41 sections, which address, briefly, a range of now familiar topics related to 'customers', 'action', 'leadership' and 'change' and a number of perhaps more surprising topics related to 'words', 'lunch', 'others', 'yes' and 'no'. Between these sections Peters offers 'special sections' on 'the recession', on 'Charlie Wilson's war', on 'equations' and on (my favourite) 'guru gaffes'. The latter 'special section', we should note, gleefully documents the many different ways in which management's gurus tend to misunderstand and misrepresent the core problems of business.

Despite the absence of a linear narrative structure *The Little BIG Things* continues to explore the core tenets of excellence – as a social practice – first laid down in 1982 and refined in 1985. It is, of course, structurally similar to *The Pursuit of Wow* (Peters, 1994) and to *Re-imagine* (2003). And yet it is (somehow) better than both of these works. It is, as we shall demonstrate in later chapters, altogether less shrill in its tone, in part, because it usefully integrates a large collection of stories that are genuinely engaging and, often, pretty amusing. This tone and approach is carried into Peters' next offering *The Excellence Dividend* (Peters, 2018).

The excellence dividend

The Excellence Dividend overlaps considerably with *The Little BIG Things*. Indeed, both texts represent attempts to develop excellence as a lived philosophy. In addition, both are richly illustrated by a useful collection of tales. Although it is worth observing that *The Excellence Dividend* actually reproduces a number of the tales rendered as examples/exemplars in *The Little BIG Things*.

The Excellence Dividend, like *The Little BIG Things*, also appears to have been produced, as it were, by accident. Yet where *The Little BIG Things* is derived from some five years of blogging, *The Excellence Dividend* appears to have grown from, what became, a week-long lecturing commitment at the University of Auckland Business School and draws, we are told, on 'fifty years of material' (Peters, 2018: 455).

The Excellence Dividend is, perhaps, more tightly structured than *The Little Big Things*. It offers, for example, just six sections on 'execution', 'excellence', 'people', 'innovation', 'adding value' and 'leadership excellence', and is geared, as the sub-title informs us, to meet the tech tide with work that wows and jobs that last. Each of these six sections we should note begins with an illustrative story and then develops (within the confines of the topic under consideration) a linear narrative designed to explore core concerns. In this regard *The Excellence Dividend* is a hybrid. It is if your mind's eye can cope with the image, a 'toilet-reader' that requires follow-through!

And yet I do wonder about the title and the so-called dividend of excellence.

★ ★ ★ ★ ★

Peters trades in fear and hope. This is not a criticism. It is instead a simple statement on the ways and means of guru theorizing. As he introduces *The Excellence Dividend,* therefore, it should come as no surprise to learn that Peters pauses to reflect on the developing tech-tide, which in an echo of *Thriving on Chaos* (Peters, 1997) threatens to drown us.

Peters offers the assurance, however, that there are grounds for optimism; there is, we are told, a dividend derived from the core teachings of excellence that can be applied to offer meaningful work and security in employment during our turbulent times.

I would like to believe this. As someone who has been 'redundant' and who now falls within the age range where the prospects of securing similar employment post-redundancy diminishes rapidly, I would like to believe that I can, indeed, offer myself to employers as a disciple of excellence, as a valuable branded identity. Indeed, I would like to be reassured that a commitment to excellence (as the next call, the next meeting, the next 5 minutes) will build my identity in the eyes of my current (and should the need arise) future employers. But all the evidence suggests otherwise because the painful truth is that in the British economy as in the US economy, work and poverty, over-worked parents and hungry children now go together. Furthermore, Peters' blandishments regarding brands and branded identities, as we will see in later chapters, simply fails to acknowledge the corrosive nature of insecurity that has been wrought in the name of employability.

Thus, I ask, What is the excellence dividend?

And as we prepare to mark the 40th anniversary of the excellence project when might we expect the first cheque?

Am I suggesting that Peters is to blame for the state of the economy? Hardly.

Am I suggesting that he is to blame for our deregulated market economies and for the manner in which the tax and benefit systems have been redesigned to disadvantage the poor and to reward the wealthy? No. Peters has, as far as I know, never held an elected office.

And yet Peters *is* part of the system; he has advised those who have designed 'the system' and he is, despite his most recent work (Peters, 2021) and despite a romantic attachment to small courtesies and to small acts of kindness, a part of the systemic change process that has allowed business to remove itself from any meaningful commitment to community or to social enterprise.

★ ★ ★ ★ ★

In *Sixty* (Peters, 2005) a work first penned in 2002; offered on-line in 2003 and later self-published under a *skunkworks* imprint, Tom Peters offers 60 'TiBs', 'things I believe' or if you prefer, 60 small articles of faith which since they have guided Peters' life and career are offered fraternally as nuggets of wisdom. Many of these 'TiBs' crop up in other works and feature, for example within *The Big Little Things* and in *The Excellence Dividend* (and that is why *Sixty* has been placed in the canon of 'minor works').

One of the 60 articles of faith shared by Peters is concerned with healthcare and with the healthcare system. Peters warns us that many Americans are killed by simple failures of management within the healthcare system. He suggests, not unreasonably, that the biggest boon to public health would be, not another educational programme around, say, the perils of sugar and/or the need to take exercise but a programme of radical management reform designed to make our hospitals safer, cleaner; more reliable as organized systems. I happen to agree with much of this. In fact, I will readily concede that Peters' focus on the normal accidents (see Perrow, 1979) that are, it seems, everyday features of healthcare in America is truly insightful. Indeed, his reflections on the failings of healthcare management offers, I suggest, a very worthy exercise not in problem-solving but in problem identification (see Schön, 1979) which, if implemented, could have very real, immediate and lasting benefits. And yet there is within all of this a huge and gaping hole in the analysis.

Accepting Peters' call for radical reform of the US healthcare system, accepting that we might now cash the excellence dividend, I ask, Is healthcare, in fact, a single system that will bend to Peters' headline message?

And I ask, Who will get behind the outline agenda for change that Peters suggests needs to be implemented?

Given the entrenched and vested financial interests that shape healthcare and which torpedoed 'Obamacare' who will steward the change process that Peters advocates?

Now at this stage Peters would, I guess, roar his discontents: *Do you think people should just continue to be killed?*

And in this imagined response his (out)rage is, of course, quite correct. Who, indeed, believes that a hospital visit should be more risky than is necessary?

Yet, beyond righteous indignation and a commonly held sense of horror, what does Peters actually offer as the first steps to the reform of healthcare?

A commitment to innovation? Perhaps.

A commitment to the customer? Almost certainly.

But what might this mean? Indeed, what might this mean – concretely?

The painful truth is, I am afraid, *not much* because it is plain that in the absence of a more developed analysis of social organization, its contests, its obduracy, Peters' horror(-stories) and exhortation simply lack the power to overcome the entrenched interests that accept hospital deaths as normal accidents and compensation as a cost of business.

What then is needed? Change obviously – but any useful agenda for change must begin, I suggest, with an account of 'structure' in 'context' that would offer the tools and understandings necessary to explain the obdurate nature of 'the healthcare system'.

That Peters still fails to grasp this after 40 years as a guru, and that Peters still fails to grasp this despite his very clear appreciation of the human costs of healthcare mistakes, is, I fear, his legacy and, in a classical sense, his ultimate tragedy.

Summary

This chapter has offered a critical review of the key works on management produced by Tom Peters between 1987 and 2018. Chapter 2, you will recall, spent a fair amount of time detailing the academic criticism that was voiced in opposition to the excellence project as this was detailed in and through *In Search of Excellence*. Discussion of the academic reaction to Peters' 'guru works' (Crainer, 1997), however, is more-or-less absent from this chapter, largely because the academic establishment has tended to ignore the more recent works produced by Peters. That is not to say, of course, that Chapter 3 is devoid of academic commentary. In fact, I have sought to demonstrate the ways in which academic analysis of the controversies associated with such things as 'chaos' and 'structure' offers the insights necessary, both to reveal and to pierce, Peters' rhetoric on the nature of business and the conduct of management.

In the chapter that follows we will move on from the chronological method of analysis employed in Chapters 2 and 3 to develop, further, the concern with narrative, which was (for example) signalled in our discussions of *Re-imagine* and *The Excellence Dividend*.

Notes

1 This is another example of Peters failing the metaphor since yeast is an organism that consumes its own environment and in so doing causes its own demise. In this regard about the last thing that anyone could want of an organization is a yeasty response!
2 Followers of the Scottish national football team are known as 'the Tartan Army' and unlike other groups in this setting are known for being noisy and boisterous but friendly and as Douglas Adams might have put it, mostly harmless!

4

AN INTRODUCTION TO
ORGANIZATIONAL STORYTELLING

Introduction

It may be useful, briefly, to recap – to trace the steps of the analysis we have developed so far.

In my introductory remarks and in Chapters 1–3 I have attempted to establish Tom Peters as a key shaper of management thought who has had a significant influence on the practical endeavours that now constitute what we, too casually, refer to as 'management'. Despite the misgivings and objections of others I have insisted that Tom Peters is, quite correctly, labelled a guru of management. Indeed, I have gone further. I have argued that Tom Peters is *the* guru of management (Collins, 2007) – the prototype who became the archetype of management's gurus (Collins, 2021a).

Peters' position as *the* guru of management, I have argued, grows from his role in the formation of 'the excellence project' and, beyond this, his role in the development and dissemination of 'popular management'. Following Latour's (1987) advice to study 'science in the making', to examine controversies at that point when reputations are in a very real sense made, I have traced the development of the excellence project within the context of the consulting industry and in the light of McKinsey's attempts to reposition itself as a leading agency within this arena. In addition I have considered the formation of the 7-S framework and the excellence project's initial, public, articulation within *In Search of Excellence*. I have also explored the continuing development and refinement of this project during the past 40 years.

While observing that the core ideas associated with excellence have often been dismissed by academia, I have insisted that the excellence project is significant and is worthy of sustained critical analysis. Indeed, I have argued that the excellence project matters because it has had an enduring impact on the

DOI: 10.4324/9781003188940-5

manner in which managers now account, publicly, for their practice. In short, I have attempted to show that the excellence project is central to our understanding of the practice of management: It has effectively redefined the 'functions of the executive' (Barnard [1938], 1968). Tom Peters matters therefore because his attempts to work with and through *the lumps of complexity* that constitute the social organization of the workplace have advanced and cemented the understanding that managers are architects of moral economies, world-builders, meaning-makers, story-tellers!

In this chapter I will provide critical reflections on organizational storytelling and through these critical reflections, a preface for Chapters 5–8 which will examine Tom Peters' storytelling practices. These prefacing remarks are necessary because while most executives and academics now tend to concur that 'management' is, indeed, a social-political process rooted in and dependent on that form of persuasive talk that we reduce, so easily, to 'organizational storytelling' (Collins, 2018, 2021d), such agreement tends to obscure more fundamental differences that persist as to (a) the nature of stories (b) the practice of storytelling and (c) the potency of such narrative forms within (and across) a variety of organized contexts. In an attempt to reveal the presence of these (often obscured) academic debates *and* their importance for 'practical' endeavour this chapter will offer a map of the intellectual landscape of organizational storytelling and in so doing, will provide a route out of the debates that mark this terrain.

To place useful way-markers on this map, I will contrast 'sensemaking' and sensegiving' accounts of storytelling. In addition, I will consider Boje's (1991) 'terse tales' and the 'ante-narrative' perspective (Boje, 2001) developed as a response to the top-down, controlling and monological narratives preferred by 'popular management' and by *the Sloane Rangers* (Collins, 2003). Finally I will offer an account of the methodology which I have used to extract stories from the written work of Peters. But before we can turn to the processes of extraction and curation, which underpin my analysis of Tom Peters we must, first, pause to trace the development of storytelling perspectives within the field(s) of management and organization studies.

Organizational stories as a focus for inquiry

In recent years, scholars of organization and management have demonstrated an increasing interest in, and concern for, organizational narratives and stories (see Boje, 1991, 2001; Boyce, 1995; Gabriel, 2000; Collins and Rainwater, 2005; Monin and Monin, 2005; Collins, Dewing and Russell, 2009, 2015; Driver, 2009; Fear, 2014; Collins, 2018, 2021b, 2021d). This interest does not, of course, imply that narratives represent, somehow, a new development (see Czarniawska, 1997, 1999; Currie and Brown, 2003; Sims, 2003; Collins, 2007). Indeed, Latour (1987) points out that (even) scientific papers demand to be read as a form of Greek mythology insofar as the subject under study (assisted perhaps by catalytic reagents) must overcome any number of trials and ordeals in order to establish its

nature and its worth to humanity. Latour's narrative reading of scientific endeavour reminds us therefore that contemporary interest in all things narrative should
be understood as reflecting a concern with 'narratology' (Brown, 2006) – the belief that a systematic study of narrative theory and narrative practice can precipitate accounts of organizing practices that insofar as they 'embrace pluralism and
subjectivity' (Brown, 2006: 732) offer theoretical enlightenment and prompts to
practical action. Viewed in these terms the contemporary upsurge in narrative
forms of analysis within academia may be read as signifying a growing disillusionment with the 'mainstream' (Grant et al., 2004) or 'orthodox' (Llewellyn,
1999) methodologies and theories that underpin organizational studies.

Contrasting 'mainstream' perspectives with their 'narrative' alternatives,
Tsoukas (2005) complains that 'behaviourist' and 'cognitivist' accounts of change
tend to dominate organization studies. Reflecting on the differences between
these perspectives he observes that 'behaviourist' models of organization suggest
that managers act 'according to habit, instincts, or environmental determination'
(97). Yet he warns us that in adopting this perspective behaviourist models tend
to regard organizations as being static. Consequently behaviourist accounts of
organization treat change as an episodic disturbance – an exception to the stable
norm.

Behaviourist models, as the label implies, assume that humans, merely, react
to stimuli. Cognitivist frameworks, however, protest that humans act intention-
ally. Yet Tsoukas argues that we should not allow this headline difference to mask
the common orientations that these models actually share. Thus, he observes that
cognitivist models of change, like their behaviourist counterparts, remain predicated on stability and so treat change as an episodic disturbance. Indeed, Tsoukas
reminds us that cognitivist accounts of organization assume that change – as the
movement towards a new and stable equilibrium – occurs when managers, as the
controlling minds, intervene to alter the cognitive maps, which individuals use
to process information.

Taking issue with such accounts of change Tsoukas argues that a 'discursive', or narrative, appreciation of the dynamic processes of organizing offers
clear analytical benefits because it problematizes those elements of everyday
life – organizations, change, technology, structures and the environment – that
behaviourist and cognitivist accounts treat 'ostensively' (Hopkinson, 2003), as
stable, uncontested and pre-existing. Within a narrative approach, therefore,
the normal analytical orientations and presumptions that bring structure and
fixity to the worlds preferred by behaviourists and by cognitivists are re-cast:
nouns become verbs; 'things' become 'practices'. Quite unlike the 'behaviourist'
and 'cognitivist' alternatives, therefore, narrative accounts of managing and organizing construe organization in dialogic terms, as an arena where temporary,
and somewhat transient, meaning is 'continuously constructed through the jux-
taposition of competing views' (Hopkinson, 2003: 1944). Thus, in a narrative
reading of management, that which was previously stable, and yet subject to
episodic disturbance – namely, 'change' – is transformed to become 'the process

of constructing and shaping new meanings and interpretations of organizational activities' (Tsoukas, 2005: 98).

And yet the narrative account of organization remains a broad church. Acknowledging the many roots that might nourish a discursive approach to the study of organization Rhodes and Brown (2005) suggest that narrative appears and is variously constituted as:

1   A form of data
2   A theoretical lens
3   A methodological approach
4   Some combination of 1, 2 and 3.

Llewellyn's (1999) analysis, however, invites us to modify this taxonomy. She agrees with Rhodes and Brown that humans are predisposed to think in narrative terms. Furthermore, she agrees that narrative forms of analysis do, indeed, offer academics and practitioners powerful insights into organizing processes. Thus, Llewellyn reminds us that 'orthodox' academic texts seek 'facts', 'truth', 'answers' whereas narrative accounts of organization explore contests, perspectives and the constitution of truths. Contrasting this orthodoxy with a 'counter-narrative' alternative, Llewellyn advocates the development of forms of inquiry designed to reveal the poetic and political choices that shape the collection and arrangement of what are, too often, presented as 'findings'. Unlike Rhodes and Brown (2005), therefore, Llewellyn is suspicious of narrative as 'data'. Latour (1999) shares this concern. He suggests that 'data' must be rendered in order to demonstrate the processes associated with its careful and deliberate fabrication. Thus, Latour prefers the term 'sub lata', which he translates as achievement.

Despite this dispute as to the nature of data, however, it is, nonetheless, true that supporters of 'counternarrative' approaches tend to agree that narratology offers a productive mode of inquiry. Narratology, we are told, reveals our organizations, ourselves and our texts (see Brown, 2006; Haynes, 2006, 2008; Musson and Duberley, 2007) to be multi-discursive effects that are liable to revision and/or contestation. Expanding on this Rhodes and Brown (2005) suggest that narrative approaches highlight:

•   Temporality – reminding us that while we tend to speak of organizations as entities, or stable 'things', a narrative approach insists that social organization is a fluxing product of space and time. Thus, narrative perspectives highlight the local and the peculiar and would tend to eschew any search for a larger and more singular truth.
•   Plurality – demonstrating that the narrative ordering, which portrays organizations in institutional terms is, but, one of the available means of structuring our realities.
•   Reflexivity – challenging us as academics with a licence to speak on matters beyond our own life experiences and biographies, to recall that we must

always take care to recognize that, in spite of our claims to knowledge, truth and validity, the narratives of organization that we construct remain temporal products – products, indeed, which have tended to manufacture coherence by silencing or subordinating competing perspectives (see also Brown, 2000; 2003; Buchanan, 2003; Collins and Rainwater, 2005).
• Subjectivity – warning us that social organization is a narrative co-creation, a product of interwoven perspectives and subjectivities (Shotter, 2002).

Highlighting the different ways in which these perspectives and priorities have been operationalized, Rhodes and Brown (2005) suggest that narrative studies of organization tend to exhibit one or a number of core thematic concerns. Thus, Rhodes and Brown suggest that narrative studies of organization reflect a concern with:

1 sensemaking,
2 communication,
3 learning and change,
4 politics and power and
5 identity and identification.

Beigi, Callahan and Michaelson (2019) revisit the work of Rhodes and Brown (2005) and in so doing offer an empirical analysis of developing trends in academic research on organizational storytelling. Building on an initial keyword search of those publications featured in 'web of science', Beigi and her colleagues offer analytical reflections on some 40 years of organizational storytelling scholarship and an analysis of 165 papers published between 1975 and 2015.[1] Their work, they tell us, confirms the core analysis developed by Rhodes and Brown (2005). Yet Beigi and her co-authors suggest that the themes outlined, above, now need to be revised in order to accommodate the manner in which scholarship on organizational storytelling has developed in the decade between 2005 and 2015. Charting this development chronologically Beigi at al., note that only two papers on organizational storytelling are thrown up by their search terms prior to 1990. They observe, however, that between 1991 and 1995 a further ten papers were added to the canon with a further 14 added between 1996 and 2000. Between 2001 and 2005 19 more papers on narratives of organization were published and between 2006 and 2010 a further 39 papers were produced. This growth has continued, we are told, with the publication of a further 81 papers on organization storytelling between 2011 and 2015.

Reviewing the approaches adopted by the authors of these papers, Beigi et al., suggest that 39 of the 165 papers (24%) demonstrate a critical sensibility. Noting that of these 39 papers, no fewer than 32 were published after the review conducted by Rhodes and Brown (2005), Beigi and her co-authors advise that it is, now, necessary to reconstitute the core themes listed above. To this end Beigi and her co-authors dispense with the 'communication' theme that was noted by Rhodes and Brown (2005) preferring to offer four, more critical themes, namely,

- sensemaking and subverting;
- change, learning and challenge;
- power and dissent;
- identity, identification and alienation.

The authors warn us, however, that we should not construe these themes as simple dualities. Indeed, they suggest that we should expect to find many tales within and between these contrasting thematic poles.

The contribution of Beigi and her colleagues is interesting and very worthwhile. Yet while their four preferred themes may well reflect the developing trajectory of academic scholarship we should be wary of indulging the suggestion that all of those now concerned with the power of stories at work have embraced the narrative agenda outlined in their four thematic dualities. It is clear, for example, that many of the texts prepared for practitioners or for the 'popular management' segment of the publishing industry, continue to embrace a cognitivist world-view and so regard stories as a simpler and (apparently) more innocent form of *communication* that usefully fosters 'change', 'development' and 'strategic alignment'. We will reflect further on the tension that this cognitivist focus on 'communication' highlights between sensemaking and sensegiving perspectives on organizational storytelling in a few moments. But to enable this we need to offer some further reflection on the very nature of stories.

The nature of (organizational) stories

Commenting on the stories that feed and advance the critical concerns of those who have contributed to the development of the academic study of organizational storytelling, Beigi, Callahan and Michaelson (2015: 449) tell us that organizational storytelling is an ongoing process of narrative sensemaking, meaning construction and knowledge management among and between the members of an organization. They add that such stories are of central importance, both practically and intellectually, because they allow individuals to understand the past, to share the present and to shape the future.

This statement has much to recommend it. It is, of course, elegant and poetic. It is also plausible inasmuch as stories are generally taken to be central to sensemaking processes (Weick, 1995), which shape and reshape our understanding of our pasts in order to provide orientation and animation within our presents that may be carried into our futures. And yet this putative definition of stories and storytelling does tend to indulge the elision of key debates on the very nature of 'the story'. The key problem being that the divisions *within* critical scholarship and *between* critical scholars and more managerialist (or orthodox) commentators will remain opaque for so long as we indulge this process of elision. Accordingly, we will now consider the different ways in which stories have been constituted within the broad(er) literature concerned with organization and management.

Enactment and interpretation

Beigi and her colleagues (2019) highlight the central role which sensemaking performs in the narrative accounts of organization that have developed over the past few decades and in so doing draw attention to the manner in which our worlds, and in a very meaningful sense, our-selves are constructed in and through stories. In popular management sensemaking is often misconstrued as a response to 'a problem' or as a simple process of interpretation. Within popular management therefore the processes of sensemaking are often misrepresented as some*thing* that leaders may learn to channel, to change, to redirect. Recognizing that 'sensemaking' is a complex and challenging concept, and one that is often – and wrongly – reduced to a species of 'interpretation', we will take a small (if painful) diversion to consider the short life of Lauren Wright. In our next section therefore I will offer a story about the life and untimely death of a child.

I offer this tale because it will, I trust, offer a memorable account of sense-making processes that, (like all 'good' stories) will lodge in the mind, travelling with you as you consider the work of Tom Peters. As I prepare to tell this tale, however, it may be useful to acknowledge that my approach here is unusual and perhaps just a little controversial.

★ ★ ★ ★ ★

Middlebrook (1980) in his history of the bomber raids on Hamburg that in 1943 led to the development of a new word – *feuersturm* (firestorm) – offers his readers an indication of the problems that arise when we seek to account for the experiences of others. Reflecting on the sheer scale of his task he concedes:

> In dealing with a city of nearly two million persons which had nearly 10,000 tons of bombs dropped upon it during a short period, the scale of events was too vast to allow a full coverage in any one book.
>
> *(Middlebrook, 1980: 144)*

Commenting on the methodological approach he has developed in the face of such a broad canvas Middlebrook acknowledges a range of viable choices and pauses to explain his own:

> Different authors will use different methods to deal with this problem. This book will use a combination of general description and resumé – both based on reliable sources – and personal account of survivors. Journalistic-type descriptions of events will not be employed; I was not there and I prefer eyewitnesses who were there to provide their own first-hand images (144).

Middlebrook, we should note, also offers a very stark reminder as to the limitations of his methodology: 'please remember that it is only the survivors that speak to you. The dead suffered even greater horrors' (144).

Middlebrook is, of course, a serious and accomplished historian. His warnings as to 'method' are sensible, useful and appropriate. Yet I will ignore his counsel: In fact, I will use, quite deliberately, aspects of the journalistic technique rejected by Middlebrook because I do not want, simply, to report the death of Lauren Wright. Instead I will tell you a story of her brief and terrible existence.

And why will I put you through this? The answer is, of course, quite simple: I need you to feel Lauren's pain, her suffering, her loneliness, her powerlessness so that you will grasp in a real and very visceral sense the manner in which stories retain the capacity, sometimes literally, to move us.

★ ★ ★ ★ ★

Lauren Wright (RIP)

Lauren Wright died quietly at home on May 6th 2000.

Lauren had learned to be quiet. She had learned, painfully, that being quiet – keeping a low profile – was the only sensible course of action in a world populated by adults who were variously violent, indifferent or, if genuinely concerned for her welfare, too easily ignored.

Six-year-old Lauren had been it seems, as much as anyone could hope to be, 'a normal child'. But she had become nervy and withdrawn since her step-mother, Tracey Wright, and Tracey's children from a previous relationship had come to live with Lauren and her father, Craig on the Norfolk-Cambridgeshire border.

It is thought that Lauren died as she had lived – suffering quietly at home – having succumbed to catastrophic internal injuries caused by her step-mother who, two days before, was seen by her own children to punch Lauren twice in the abdomen. This assault, this final assault, was sadly but one violent indignity in a terrible catalogue of degradation that the court would learn Tracey had inflicted on Lauren.

A post-mortem examination conducted on Lauren's remains revealed that this once healthily, chubby, child weighed just 28 lb (12.7 kg) at her death. This is, we should note, the normal weight of a four-year-old child. The post-mortem examination also revealed in excess of 60 bruises on Lauren's tiny, hungry frame. In court testimony, a physician suggested that Lauren's injuries were not untypical of those suffered by individuals involved in collisions with moving motor vehicles.

In October 2001 a custodial sentence of 15 years was handed down to Tracey Wright by a court in Norwich. Craig Wright, her father, was not found to have assaulted Lauren but was held to be woefully neglectful, and was therefore found guilty of a lesser charge of manslaughter. He received a custodial sentence of five years. Both Tracey and Craig, we must assume, now walk among us.

During the trial it became known that Lauren had been seen by social workers and by a policeman (called to investigate an unfounded allegation of sexual abuse made against Lauren's birth-mother) on three occasions in the 12 weeks prior to her murder. In addition it was revealed that neighbours and teachers had also tried, and failed, to alert 'the authorities' of their suspicions of neglect. Indeed, two physicians – a General Practitioner and a paediatric specialist – had independently examined Lauren in the months prior to her killing and had, separately, formed the opinion that she was being abused. Lauren, however, was not removed from the family home. Why not?

Following the convictions of Tracey and Craig Wright, Norfolk's senior social workers held a press conference. It was acknowledged that mistakes had been made and it was accepted that lessons would need to be learned. This is, nowadays, a familiar narrative. Indeed, it is, I suggest, now so familiar that it might be considered to be a meaningless and deeply insulting cliché!

While expressing genuine regret those entrusted with Lauren's care protested that they had quite simply failed to make sense of what was going on. This may be true at one level of analysis. Those entrusted with Lauren's care had failed, as it were, to connect the dots that would have allowed them to see – to understand that Lauren was being harmed by her step-mother and neglected by her father. But this manifest failing in the management of Lauren's case does not amount to a simple failure in sensemaking.

Commenting on the narrative processes that we employ – literally – to make sense of our worlds, Weick (1995) reminds us that the world(s) we live in are noisy and potentially bewildering. Our lives are he reminds us, defined by complexity and marked by ambiguity. On a day-to-day basis therefore we must navigate our lives under conditions, which because they are so noisy, complex and ambiguous, simply threaten to overwhelm us. To allow us to get on and to get by, Weick suggests that we tell ourselves stories. These tales, Weick argues, are helpful if artful *constructs*, which filter the complexity and in so doing reduce the ambiguities that would otherwise engulf us. These simplifying narratives, however, do not interpret the world. We do not react to 'the world'. And we cannot respond to 'problems' which are present and stable before us. Situations only become problematic, Weick observes, when we have taken the time to construct an event, to respond to processes in a manner that suggests the need for resolution. Thus, there is, prior to the moment of 'problem identification', a period of creation and invention, enacted by cues, which deems some aspect of our lives to be in need of rectification. Challenging those who believe that we may teach 'problem solving' in some simple, mechanical fashion therefore, Weick argues that we cannot 'take stock'. We cannot 'step off' to catch our bearings. We are, in fact, so wrapped up in our own rigamarole[2] that the thought and hope of a dispassionate and objective 'interpretation' is, if not, pitiable then certainly laughable. Recognizing the dynamism of our daily travails and the vain hope of a clear and dispassionate 'interpretation', therefore, Weick argues that we are obliged *to enact* sensible environments.

Enactment is, for Weick, an inventive process, which filters the complexity of our daily lives. This filtration process, we should note, defines situations as 'problematic' and in so doing suggests courses of action designed to solve the problems created by our attentiveness. Summarizing the processes that render our worlds knowable and hence our lives, as it were, liveable – navigable – Weick (1995: 17) tells us that sensemaking is (1) grounded in identity construction (2) retrospective (3) enactive of social environments (4) social (5) on-going (6) focused on cues and (7) driven by plausibility rather than by accuracy.

Sensemaking is, therefore a process rooted in, dependent on and enabled through storytelling. In our attempts to come to terms with the day-to-day complexities of our lives we are, Weick observes, obliged to construct and to tell ourselves tales about who we are, about what we are doing and about *why all of this matters*. These tales, we should note, respond to cues and as they do so they enact scenarios which provide orientation and animation. In this regard the tales we tell are designed (however loosely and however selfishly) to articulate our private difficulties and, indeed, our larger public concerns.[3] They are not, therefore, driven by 'interpretation' nor are they guided by cold, hard facts. Instead our narratives are driven by ideas, orientations and presumptions that, however fantastical they may seem to others, are plausible within the context of our constructed identities, within our own sense of self.

Turning this appreciation of the narrative construction and constitution of reality to address the death of Lauren Wright we are now in a position to reassess the claim that this poor child died because social workers 'failed to make sense of events'.

It is of course, worth pointing out that Norfolk's social workers did not kill Lauren. No, Lauren died because her step-mother punched her. Indeed, we should be clear that Lauren died because her step-mother punched her twice and *hard*, so hard, in fact, that her intestinal system collapsed and, in effect, fell apart over a terrible, painful period of 48 hours.

Yet, we should note that despite the reported concerns of teachers, neighbours and at least two medical practitioners, Lauren was present in her home and had remained under her step-mother's hateful gaze. Why was this so?

Lauren was at home and died at home *not* because those within Norfolk's social services who were entrusted with her care failed to make sense of what they saw and heard. No. Lauren was at home on May 4th and died at home, alone, on May 6th, 2001 precisely because her social workers had failed to undertake the imaginative leap that would have allowed them to understand that her relationship with her step-mother was intensely problematic.

Lauren was at home and died at home, alone and in pain, therefore because her social workers preferred to enact a world wherein she was not understood to be 'at risk'. In this enacted world the red flags – the signs and symptoms of abuse (so clear in retrospect) – were not so much (mis)interpreted as they were, instead, embedded within a co-constructed narrative that simply imagined a more agreeable world for poor, lonely, pitiful Lauren.

Lauren died; Lauren was killed; Lauren was murdered by her step-mother (*do you see how a few words here or there can make a big difference to the tale?*) because those entrusted with her care *made sense* of her life and in so doing enacted a world that rendered her pain, her hunger, her tears and her fear largely unfathomable – simply unthinkable.

In our next section – and having, I hope, established the power of stories and the nature of sensemaking processes – I will consider the manner in which those who advise on the business of management have sought to lever the realities of sensemaking to make new worlds and new realities for others. Thus, we will explore the divisions that persist between sensemaking and sensegiving accounts of organizational storytelling.

Sensemaking and sensegiving

It would, I think, be fair to suggest that 'popular management' narratives take the gist of Weick's (1995) account of sensemaking yet translate this and in so doing traduce what is actually a complex and highly sophisticated form of analysis. Indeed, we might venture that 'popular management' creates a world where *because* each of us is obliged to navigate and to construct our lives in and through narrative there exists an opportunity to channel, to steer, to direct and to change the narratives that shape our lives for larger, managerial, ends. For those inclined to advance the aims of 'popular management' therefore stories derive from sensemaking processes but may be redirected to become a sensegiving apparatus. In this regard 'popular management' while speaking of narratives and stories actually adopts a cognitivist perspective. It suggests that *since* all of us are obliged to construct and navigate our lives narratively and *since* action in organizations stems from such narrative constructions, managers *should* intervene in organizational processes to adjust the mental processes of colleagues and employees.

This process of mental adjustment calls on words such as 'narratives' and 'stories' and suggests that managers should craft and deploy stories that have been designed to allow the realization of those goals preferred by organizational leaders...even if these run contrary, it seems, to the immediate or longer-term goals of those caught up in the process (see Pettigrew, 1985). Yet the underlying approach is, in the terms preferred by Tsoukas (2005), 'cognitivist' rather than 'narrative'; there is neither dialogue, discussion, nor any real contest or contrasting opinion. There is instead the simple presumption of mental re-programming. The problem being, as we shall see, that such sensegiving accounts (of storytelling) blithely presume that managers can readily change the modes of organizational enactment that are preferred by their colleagues and subordinates. And this presumption is mocked by experience!

Making sense for others

Esler (2012) captures the essence of sensegiving approaches, or if you prefer: cognitivist appropriations of narrative rather well. He suggests that managers can *make things happen* by using stories to change how people think about their work, feel about their products and act towards customers. He is, however, keen to point out that such outcomes will materialize only so long as the tales, crafted and rendered, have been designed to colonize the consciousness of the audience:

> The secret weapon of storytellers throughout the centuries has been to create a story which sticks in the mind, just as a successful musician will write a pop song with a melody so powerful that you cannot get it out of your head. Germans call this an *Ohrwurm,* literally an "earworm", or "earwig", which won't stop wriggling whether you like it or not, until it worms its way into your brain. Successful leaders work hard at creating an "earwig", or they employ others to do it for them. They spend a lot of time wondering how to communicate their leadership story and subvert the counter-stories told against them.
>
> *Esler (2012: 19; original emphasis)*

Denning (2001) offers a concrete illustration of Esler's argument. In *The Springboard,* Denning, observes that in his time with the World Bank he had tried and failed to convince his colleagues of the virtues of a key infrastructure project designed to bring clean water to the villages and homes of those living in the developing world. Denning concedes, however, that nothing – not charts; nor reports; nor statistical analyses – would persuade his colleagues until that is, he happened on a tale, which, in simple human terms, illustrated the efforts that women and small children in parts of Africa have to exert, daily, in order to collect and to carry water.

Reflecting on his performance of this tale, Denning argues that his story acted as a 'springboard', an emotional lever for action, because it demonstrated to those who remained unmoved by logical argument and rational calculation that something *could* and *should* be done. Thus, Denning's 'springboard story' *caused and allowed* change. Importantly, it removed those cognitive obstacles that had prevented colleagues from supporting the infrastructure programme that he knew to be necessary.

Taken together Esler's 'earworms' and Denning's 'springboard stories' suggest that poetic tales have a capacity to adjust mental models because they (a) tap emotions (b) to shape understanding and in so doing (c) precipitate action. Indeed, it is worth observing that Denning's 'springboard stories' *do things* because they plant and propagate mental modes, which humanize events and in so doing, make real, problems which had hitherto appeared to be, merely, abstract or somehow far-removed from other more pressing or more local concerns. Yet we should not assume that all those who would endorse a 'sensegiving' account of storytelling actually agree on what stories can do within the workplace nor should we assume that making sense for others boils down to a straightforward process of 'communication'.

Tom Peters as we argued earlier and as we shall see in the chapters which follow this, places storytelling at the very core of managerial work. Indeed, for Peters, storytelling is essentially synonymous with managing. Stories he suggests occupy this pivotal position because they retain the capacity to bring order, coherence and direction to the seven lumps of complexity that constitute business organizations. Indeed, it would not be an exaggeration to suggest that Peters elevates organizational storytelling to the level of mythology.

Reflecting on the inquiry process that led the Organization Practice to focus on the challenge of implementation and hence the search for excellence Peters and Waterman (1982) offer the following insights on the (often overlooked) structure of the corporate world:

> As we worked on research of our excellent companies, we were struck by the dominant use of story, slogan, and legend as people tried to explain the characteristics of their own great institutions. All the companies we interviewed, from Boeing to McDonald's, were quite simply rich tapestries of anecdote, myth, and fairy tale. And we do mean fairy tale. The vast majority of people who tell stories today about T.J. Watson of IBM have never met the man or had direct experience of the original more mundane reality. Two HP engineers in their mid-twenties recently regaled us with an hour's worth of "Bill and Dave" (Hewlett and Packard) stories. We were subsequently astonished to find that neither had seen, let alone talked to, the founders.
>
> *Peters and Waterman (1982: 75)*

This is an important confidence. It demonstrates, I suggest, Peters' growing appreciation of the moral purpose of managerial work. Indeed, it is worth observing that in an attempt to capitalize on this growing appreciation of the power, which stories have to unsettle mental models, Peters elevates organizational narratives from the prosaic realities of day-to-day exchange, re-presenting these to us as myths and fairy tales. Thus, Peters reminds us that stories are not the subordinate partners of 'hard' data. They are not *just* anecdotes. Stories, for Peters, are not ephemeral little snippets of talk. Instead he demonstrates that organizational stories persist and prevail over other apparently more serious forms of communication. Indeed, he hints that tales become powerful and arise as guiding forms of mythology when they embody and personify good choices and correct decisions within contexts otherwise notable for flux and ambiguity.[4]

Denning accepts elements of this approach. Yet he seems to reject the broader cosmology of Peters. Thus, Denning suggest that stories perform, only, an ancillary organizational function. For Denning therefore, stories exercise their cognitive effects only at key junctures. Thus, where Peters comes close to the suggestion that stories actually constitute the organization in a very real and enduring sense, Denning seems to insist on a separation between managerial 'talk' and managerial 'action'. For Denning, therefore, springboard tales are useful as projects commence or stall because they can help to engender a common sense of purpose. But springboard stories, Denning insists, will not dig wells. At some point, he argues, the talking needs to stop and the digging needs to start. Peters' account of the organization as a mythical structure, however, suggests that we should reject this bifurcation. For Peters therefore 'talk' and 'action' are inseparable because managers need to sustain and, periodically, will need to repair and/ or renew the moral projects that they are obliged to construct in and through stories. In a challenge to Denning's attempt to separate talk and action, therefore, Peters suggests that what gets done is whatever has the narrative resource necessary to sustain action!

And yet doubts remain as to the long-term viability of the moral project(s) that Peters would advance. Indeed, as we shall see, advocates of a sensemaking account of storytelling suggest that stories, far from being simple tools of cognitive adjustment are, in fact, local products and projects, which remain stubbornly resistant to the top-down direction that is required for sensegiving narratives to prevail.

Stories as polyphony

Sensegiving accounts of organizational storytelling generally concede that it can be a challenge to change the mental models that people use to guide their conduct. Indeed, you will recall that Esler (2012) suggests that managers may have to take steps to subvert the narratives developed by, say, competitors, managerial rivals, or trades union officials. Nonetheless, advocates of 'sensegiving' generally assert that managerial leaders – when appropriately trained and supported – may use stories, reliably, to control the cognitive models that we use to shape our working lives.

In contrast sensemaking perspectives on storytelling challenge management's monopoly on sense. Where those inclined to a sensegiving account of storytelling view stories as managerial fabrications, as levers for cognitive change, those inclined to a sensemaking account counter that organizational stories are natural resources – spontaneous elements of social life which well up from the bottom of organizations. In broad terms, therefore, the sensemaking account of organizational storytelling suggests that the stories which we tell ourselves, and others, are important practically and analytically because they offer us crucial insights into the complexities of management and the, essential, plurality of social organization. Where sensegiving perspectives portray stories as managerial tools that may be deployed to control others, therefore, those inclined to a sensemaking perspective counter that stories – whether these appear as simple anecdotes myths or fairy tales – provide employees with a focus for dissent and a basis for resistance (Boje, 1991, 2001; Gabriel, 1995, 1998, 2000).

★ ★ ★ ★ ★

Gabriel (2000) has been especially keen to explore and to reveal the subversive potential of organizational storytelling. His analysis begins by observing that a discontent with modernist scholarship has redeemed the 'story' from its position as a quaint subordinate to the facts of 'history' such that stories are now widely acknowledged to be, not merely reflections of organizational life, but creators of organizational meaning and organizational realities.

Challenging the sensibilities of modernism and positivism, Gabriel insists that the study of storytelling is a serious and worthwhile, academic endeavour. Yet he reminds us that not all narratives qualify as stories. In addition, and in contrast to those who would advocate a sensegiving perspective, Gabriel argues that stories do not always and everywhere generate and sustain meaning. Indeed, he reminds us that while stories are portable they are often modified as they travel. Turkina [2014] (2015) concurs and yet offers an indication of steps that may be taken to create and to preserve organized myth-making.

In a wonderfully rich, if painful, rendering of the life-stories of the dogs selected and trained by the scientists of the Soviet Union for research into the viability of human space flight, Turkina reflects on the manner in which the authorities used the dogs' endeavours to create a mythology that might speak for the whole of the Soviet Union.

> Laika, Belka and Strelka – these are the most famous space dogs. Today they are household names: in whichever language these words are spoken, everyone understands that you are talking about the first travelers to reach orbit. These dogs are the characters in a fairy tale that was created in the USSR: they are the martyrs and saints of communism. Their fate is the embodiment of a utopian consciousness, the ideal of a society that lived in the future, a society whose aim was to turn a fairy tale into reality.
>
> *Turkina ([2014], 2015: 9–10)*

Elaborating on this myth, Turkina reminds us that the Laika, Belka and Strelka were perfect heroes for a recently formed nation with a contested past and yet the official promise of a shared and glorious future. The dogs selected for experimentation possessed, she tells us, all of the qualities necessary for heroic myth-making: They were small, were tough and, in being strays and foundlings, had enjoyed no early advantage in life. Furthermore, they were photogenic. Thanks to Dr Pavlov, Laika, Belka and Strelka were also eminently trainable. Indeed, they were like the Soviet future, perfectible. And they were mute.

This latter point is, I think, crucial for Laika's status as a cultural icon for in being mute, this officially, heroic little dog could not, later, betray or disavow the project. Furthermore, it was only natural that others would speak for her, narrating her heroism for the more general edification of the population.

Boje's (1991) analysis of narratives and 'narratology' takes this concern with plurality and with narrative control as his central motif. Unlike Turkina however,

Boje is centrally concerned with human subjects who have an alarming tendency to interpellate the narrative projections of their masters. Yet Boje's (2001) more recent contribution to this arena places serious conceptual divisions within the heart of the sensemaking account of storytelling.

Ante-narratives and Terse Tales

Following Weick's (1995) account of sensemaking, Boje observes that, on a day-to-day basis, people confront a key problem: how to make sense of a 'complex soup' of ambiguous and half-understood problems, events and experiences. Reflecting on this problem of ambiguity, Boje suggests that people construct and retrace their lives, retrospectively, through stories. For Boje (2001), therefore, stories have a particular significance and a distinctive meaning. Indeed, Boje warns us that we must distinguish 'stories' from 'narratives' if we are to understand the richness of organizational sensemaking.

Narratives, he argues, stand aloof from the flow of experience. Narratives are, he warns, plotted, directed and staged to produce a linear, coherent and monological rendering of events, while 'stories are self-deconstructing, flowing, emerging and networking, not at all static' (Boje, 2001: 1).

This suspicion of 'narrative' is, I believe, usefully located as a reaction to (and rejection of) the narrative understanding of organization, which comes to us from sources such as the *Harvard Business Review,* (see also Collins, 2003; Collins and Rainwater, 2005). Reflecting on the approach adopted by publications such as *Harvard Business Review,* Boje warns us that academic analysis has, too often, confused stories with more linear and monological narrative forms. Indeed, he complains that 'so much of what passes for academic narrative analysis in organization studies seems to rely on sequential, single-voiced stories' (Boje, 2001: 9). In an attempt to provide an alternative to these monologues of business endeavour, Boje introduces the concept of the 'antenarrative', which, he argues, resituates the concerns of the field of organizational storytelling, directing inquiry towards a concern with flux and emergence. This focus on flow and fragmentation has, as we shall see, a profound effect on Boje's antenarrative conceptualization of stories.

For Boje (2001), 'antenarrative' has two elements. The first element proceeds from the assertion that 'stories' precede 'narrative'. Thus, Boje suggests that stories are 'antenarrative' insofar as they come before the processes of staging and directing, which, as he sees it, lead to the development of 'sequential, single-voiced', top-down 'narratives'. The second element of Boje's antenarrative conceptualization calls on the rules of poker. Here an 'antenarrative' represents 'a bet' (or 'an ante') that retrospective sensemaking may emerge in the future from 'the fragmented, non-linear, incoherent, collective and unplotted' (1) stories, which come before corporate monologues.

This account of stories and narratives, of course, overlaps to some degree with the account offered by Gabriel (2000). In common with Boje, Gabriel observes that stories offer local and intimate accounts of situations, events and predicaments. Indeed, Gabriel is clearly aware that storywork – the art of constructing meaningful stories – is a delicately woven product of intimate knowledge. Furthermore, we should note that at one level of analysis Gabriel (1998, 2000) agrees with Boje that a story represents a speculative bet on the shape of the future. He tells us, for example, that when a storyteller announces a tale – and so seeks the temporary suspension of the normal rules of conversational exchange – s/he forms a covenant with the audience which promises to trade amusement/enlightenment/edification for a prolonged, if temporary, and attentive silence (see Collins, 2018, 2021d). It is also worth noting that Gabriel shares Boje's conviction that it is, vitally, important to distinguish 'stories' from other 'narrative' forms. Yet at this point the accounts of storytelling prepared by Boje and Gabriel diverge quite fundamentally.

Commenting on the craft of storytelling, both Boje and Gabriel have complained that it can be difficult to unearth good stories and talented storytellers in organizations. Indeed, each has suggested that it is becoming, increasingly, difficult to witness organizational storytelling in its naturally intimate surroundings. This shared recognition of poetic decline, however, takes Boje and Gabriel in opposing analytical directions.

Lamenting the perceived decline in organizational stories, Gabriel (2000) simply renews his commitment to the understanding that stories are rare and special forms of narrative with definite characteristics. Drawing on Aristotle's (1965) classical formulation he argues that stories – properly so-called – exhibit a number of key characteristics. Stories, he tells us:

- involve characters in a predicament
- unfold according to a chain of events that, in turn, reflects the structure of the plot and the essential traits of the characters involved
- call on symbolism/symbolic factors
- indulge poetic embellishment and narrative embroidery
- have a beginning, middle and an ending
- seek to convey not simple facts but more general and enduring truths.

Elaborating on the significance of this final, discriminating factor, Gabriel tells us that:

> stories purport to relate to facts that happened, but also discover in these facts a plot or meaning, by claiming that facts do not merely happen but that they happen in accordance with the requirements of a plot. In short, stories are not "just fictions" (although they may be fictions), nor are they mere chronologies of events as they happened. Instead, they represent poetic elaborations of narrative material, aiming to communicate *facts as experience,* not facts as information.
>
> *Gabriel (2004: 64; original emphasis)*

Boje, however, adopts a rather different approach which, in effect, seeks to re-define the very nature of organizational stories. In an initial move, Boje (1991) suggests that the four words which announce: 'you know the story' constitute a poetic tale. Later in a more radical move, Boje (2001) suggests, as we have seen, that stories should be regarded as those special forms of narrative that exist *prior* to the crystallizing processes of casting and plotting. Gabriel, however, disputes these moves. For Gabriel, stories – despite literary deskilling – represent a rich and, in any sense, a vital resource for organizational theorists. And on this matter he and Boje are in perfect agreement: stories are interesting because (freed from the over-reaching ambition of cognitivism) they allow us to experience the dynamic flow that is social organization. But for Gabriel plots, staging and direction need to be recognized as constituting the central characteristics of stories. Taking issue with Boje's first move, therefore, Gabriel protests that while the, so-called, 'terse stories' observed by Boje represent, perhaps invitations to recall a pattern of events or a particular rendering of a tale, they are not, properly-speaking, stories. Stories arrange characters and events according to a plot and move through a number of stages until a satisfactory resolution is achieved but Boje's 'terse tales' do none of this. They will, therefore, fail as projections of sense precisely because they lack 'performativity, memorableness, ingenuity and symbolism' (Gabriel, 2000: 20). Similar concerns, as we shall see, apply to Boje's (2001) antenarrative conceptualization of organizational stories.

Boje's suspicion of narrative monologues stems from a concern that academics and business commentators have been, altogether, too keen to endorse sensegiving accounts of storytelling and have, as a consequence colonized the organizational world with tales that are linear, single-voiced, top-down in their orientation and so cavalier with the concerns and orientations held by others. Noting both the practical consequences and the analytical limitations of such sensegiving accounts of storytelling, Boje (2001) suggests that we should be suspicious of corporate plotting and should, instead, embrace antenarratives which as the name suggests come before the crystallizing processes of plot formation. Yet this antenarrative conceptualization, while well-intentioned, remains I believe unhelpful and broadly unconvincing.

★ ★ ★ ★ ★

I am, I must acknowledge, prepared to concede that Boje's (2001) antenarrative concept usefully directs our attention to the contested sensemaking processes that circulate as organizational members attempt to come to terms with novel events. Furthermore, I accept that as organizational members begin to narrate novel events there may be a period when the meaning(s) and/or the significance of such movements and moments remain volatile and subject to sudden plot changes. But I find it difficult to accept the utility of a narrative that rejects the strictures of plot, place, time and characterization and yet continues to require these very elements!

Boje tells us that his antenarrative understanding of storytelling shares common ground with that outlined earlier by Gallie (1968). Indeed, Boje tells us that, in common with Gallie, he defines stories as follows:

> A story describes a sequence of actions and experiences done or undergone by a certain number of people, whether real or imaginary. These people are presented either in situations that change or as reacting to such change. In turn, these changes reveal hidden aspects of the situation and the people involved, and engender a new predicament which calls forth thought, action, or both. This response to the new situation leads the story towards its conclusion.
>
> *Boje (2001: 22)*

Yet this quotation – this affirmation of an antenarrative sensibility – seems to contain all the features that we would normally associate with a more conventional definition of storytelling! Thus we have people who change and develop as they encounter events. In other words, we have characters! Furthermore, we have a changing situation that becomes a predicament calling forth thought, action or both as we work towards a conclusion. In short we have a plot. Indeed, we appear to have a very conventional plot – a plot with a rhythm, a plot with a heartbeat, a plot that Booker (2004) observes is, literally, typical of storytelling the world over!

Despite my very real affection for Professor Boje therefore, I suggest that an antenarrative tale is simply a reduced and compromised version of a more conventional narrative. To my eyes (and ears) therefore, Boje's antenarrative amounts to a failed tale that might more usefully be regarded as being – at best – a 'proto-story'. To elaborate on this point our next section will consider a number of alternative, if related, narrative forms, namely, the 'reports', 'opinions', 'proto-stories' and 'poetic stories' outlined by Gabriel (2000).

Reports, opinions, proto-stories and poetic tales

Reports

Pursuing the analytical boundaries that separate stories from reports Gabriel argues that reports are monological in character. Reports, he insists, invite factual verification. Reports seek and reference *the* truth whereas stories seek larger and more general *truths*. Where reports trade in facts and seek recourse to *the* truth, stories are Sillitoe (1979: 9) tells us, 'a pattern of realities brought to life by suitably applied lies'.

Opinions

Opinions are superficially similar to stories. Both, for example, may contain factual and symbolic materials. However, Gabriel's (2000) analysis suggests that 'opinions' seek to 'tell' rather than to 'show' the audience what has happened. Consequently 'opinions' may lack the qualities of seduction necessary to convince others that the events under scrutiny are fully relevant to their concerns or, somehow, consonant with their experience.

Proto-stories

Classical formulations of the poetic tale, as we noted above, suggest that stories develop an interaction between scene, actor and plot that proceeds to a satisfactory conclusion. Taking this into account, 'proto-stories' may be considered to be proto-typical of poetical tales insofar as they contain some but not all of the elements necessary to the fulfilment of a story. Thus, proto-stories may have some level of characterization but will remain incomplete and broadly unsatisfactory because, for example, they lack a plot device that can deliver a useful ending. In this regard proto-stories represent 'stories-under-construction' inasmuch as future rehearsal, character development and/or embellishment may produce those missing elements that make the proto-typical narrative unsatisfactory in its raw and undeveloped form.

Poetic tales

Poetic tales are similar to 'reports' insofar as both narrative forms will contain or convey 'facts'. Yet where 'reports' exist ostensibly to convey 'facts', poetic tales will embed such certainties within narratives that seek a connection with larger or more general truths.

Facts, of course, matter to storytellers and may need to be addressed directly within the narratives constructed. But such facts cannot be allowed to intrude on the preferred arrangement of narrative resources. If empirical facts dominate, the story will become, simply and blandly, a 'report' and, as Sillitoe (1979: 9) reminds us, the 'laws of fiction' dictate that a tale that gets too close to *the* truth 'loses its air of reality'. Poetic licence and embellishment are, therefore, central to stories and pivotal to the art of the storyteller. Highlighting this fact Gabriel (2004) tells us that poetic tales will call on one or a number of ('6F') factors, as listed below.

Framing – where the narrative may be constituted to ensure that certain characters, events and understandings are central to the drama. For example in classical renderings of *Batman*, (if such things truly exist) Bruce Wayne is generally portrayed as a rich, morally up-right (if dark and brooding), champion of law and order whereas his opponents are cast as criminally insane, amoral and freakish. Yet the recent film *Joker* which traces Arthur Fleck's descent into madness and his adoption of 'the Joker' alter-ego offers an intriguing counterpoint to the standard *Batman* narrative. Thus, *Joker* frames Fleck – disregarded and mistreated by society – more sympathetically. Indeed, it invites us to view Wayne's father as a selfish, arrogant and privileged member of 'the 1%', the elite that has become the target of the *Occupy* movement.

Framing devices are important within the art of storytelling because they shape and alter our understanding of characters, casting individuals as 'central characters' or 'bit-players'. Additionally it is worth pointing out that framing devices, as we have seen with our *Joker* example may portray individuals, variously as 'heroes' or 'villains', *vainqueurs* or victims.

Focusing – Gabriel's 'framing' and 'focusing' devices overlap to a considerable degree. After all to frame an individual or an event in a particular fashion is, of necessity, to focus on certain components of the scene. In this regard it may be useful to observe that in order to feel sympathy for the character of Arthur Fleck; in order to indulge the belief that his actions are, in the context of his own mistreatment, somehow justified and/or vindicated, we must be prepared to overlook the fact that he is – albeit from a place of pain and desperation – a murderer who has killed in cold blood and who has, albeit unwittingly, incited violent public demonstrations that will, doubtless, lead to more deaths.

Filtering – We could, of course, continue to draw on *Joker* in order to consider the filtering processes that may be invoked in the name of poetic licence but this would soon become tiresome (especially if you dislike the film or, indeed, if you are unfamiliar with it). I will therefore direct your attention from the processes of 'framing' and 'focusing' that we have employed to highlight and to reconsider elements of characterization in order to highlight the ways in which *events* may be filtered to a achieve a particular poetic outcome.

In the novel *If Not Now, When?* Primo Levi [1986] (1995) offers an account of a group of Russian and Polish refugees who came together as a *Partisan* force during Second World War in order to oppose the Axis forces. The novel, based on a true story, chronicles, as you would expect, the dangers, privations and, indeed, the moral struggles that must be endured within what is now termed 'asymmetric warfare'. Levi, we should note, does little to spare his readers from the horrors of war. Through the character Dov, who in a particularly striking scene is sent to muster the *Partisans*, Levi shows us, for example, 'the peasants of Rovnoye, men and women, collected in the square with their hands bound' (64). He shows us, too, the 'SS squad, pointing their weapons, forcing them all [the villagers of Rovnoye] to climb into a wagon' (64). Furthermore, he makes us aware of the 'men of the auxiliary militia, Ukrainians or Lithuanians, taking armfuls of shovels from a shed, and loading them into the wagon' (64), which would soon 'go off towards the gulley to the south of the village, followed by the SS, laughing and smoking' (64).

Levi makes it plain that the men and women of Rovnoye understand, fully, their intended fate: There 'wasn't a soul in…all the occupied territory who didn't know the meaning of shovels' (64).

Dov and his fellow *Partisans*, muster, arm themselves and pursue the wagon in an attempt to disrupt the plans of the SS. They fire on the SS and on their grave-digging auxiliaries causing a temporary disruption to their murderous plans. Yet 'the crash of grenades and orders shouted through a loudspeaker' (67) are heard even as the *Partisan* force breaks off its attack. Men and women, Levi tells us, soon (re)appear with their arms raised. They are searched by laughing SS men who question them and line them up against a wall.

At this stage of the tale, however, Levi the narrator who endured horrors similar to those suffered by the lost souls of Rovnoye intervenes. He tells us, in essence, that he will apply a filter to his narrative: 'what happened in the courtyard of the Novoleski monastery will not be told here' (67). Justifying this omission he tells us, quite straightforwardly that his tale has another purpose: 'this story is not being told in order to describe massacres' (67). Yet as the chapter concludes Levi hints at the events which he has, nonetheless, refused to describe: 'The Germans stayed on till nightfall to blow up what was left of the monastery' then 'went off carrying their dead with them and the machine gun' (67).

Fading – It is it seems the fate of women and old men to be invisible. In many films, for example, old men are simply absent and women, if present, are reduced to bit-players, the love interest, a form of set-dressing or, worse still, 'eye-candy'. As we shall see Tom Peters, Casting Director for the storyworld of management has problems with casting and falls, all too readily, into those patterns which make women (and those from the BAME and LGBTQ communities) invisible. Of course, it (almost goes without saying that) our storyworlds need not to be like this. Choices may be made which, in a variety of ways challenge and in so doing over-turn the processes that cause certain faces to fade away or into the background. For example the 1980s film *Ghostbusters* was recently re-made with a cast of female 'ghostbusters' who were, in a reversal of prevalent stereotypes ably assisted by a handsome and hunky, if alarmingly dim, male receptionist.

Of course, the 'trolls' who populate social media hated the idea of this re-casting experiment and its product. But I do not care much for the opinion of those cowardly racists and misogynists who populate *Twitter* with their vile projections. But I will pause to point out (a) that all forms of storytelling depend on 'fading' as a narrative device and (b) that challenging the (unwritten) rules of narrative construction, which demand that 'ghostbusters' are male, or which insist that James Bond cannot be black remains, often and obviously, a fraught but, nonetheless, worthwhile endeavour.

Fusing – Good storytellers understand those details that are central to their narratives. They also recognize those characters and events that are, consequently, marginal to the plot. In many cases the fusing processes which, variously, compress temporal differences or which act to remove characters from the stories rendered are fairly benign. Thus, it is worth observing that when screenplays are developed from novels and/or factual accounts, events and characters are often cut to produce a cinematic experience that will not exhaust or otherwise try the patience of the audience. In other circumstances, as we suggested above, processes which fuse and in so doing cause certain groups to recede from view are altogether more problematic.

In contrast to my more political account of 'fading' (above) I will satisfy myself here with a simpler and more factual account of 'fusing'. John Berendt's ([1994] 2009) *Midnight in the Garden of Good and Evil* is a non-fiction work which deals with a murder. The book has been very successful, spending 216 weeks on the *New York Times* best sellers list. In 1997, perhaps unsurprisingly, a film adaptation of this book, directed by Clint Eastwood was released. This film, it is worth noting, cuts or combines many of the characters who feature in Berendt's book, reducing the original cast-list of 106 players by half!

Fitting – The satirical publication *Private Eye* (1535: 18) offers a very useful illustration of the exercise of poetic licence. Indeed, through an exploration of the manner in which dramatists may choose to embroider historical events *Private Eye's* reviewer of television programmes offers a very clear example of the liberties (actual and metaphorical) necessary for the exercise of a poetic licence.

Discussing the television drama *The Crown,* the reviewer highlights the manner in which the facts of history may be edited to fit the needs of drama. Thus, the reviewer whose services are retained by *Private Eye* observes:

> History records that Mark Thatcher got lost during a car rally in January 1982, a year in which the Falklands conflict ran from April to June. Not, though, in season four of *The Crown* where these events overlap – just as in the final episode of the season, Margaret Thatcher's resignation and Princess Diana's solo trip to New York now takes place across the same weeks, rather than 21 months apart.

Private Eye's anonymous (but delightfully forthright) reviewer is, we should note, unconvinced by these elisions and by the dramatic devices that the screenwriter, Peter Morgan, has developed to make a drama from the history of Britain's royal family. Indeed, *Private Eye* is actively hostile to Morgan's preferred plotting device. He is, we are told, a 'Pound Shop Freud' (18). Nonetheless, and despite the complaints voiced by some in Parliament that *Netflix* should screen a warning to the effect that *The Crown* is a drama and must not to read as an historical documentary or 'report', *Private Eye* acknowledges that Morgan's 'chronological liberties' (18) develop not as a result of historical ignorance or ineptitude, but as a consequence of 'a rigid episode structure' (18) that has been constructed to deliver the drama. This episode structure we are advised requires 'two storylines entwined to interact ironically or metaphorically' (18). Thus, the chronological collapse that combines Mark Thatcher's misadventures with the much larger misadventure that was the Falklands conflict comes about because Morgan 'needs to pretend the PM's [Prime Minister's] son went missing so that, with Prince Andrew about to get his chopper out[5] over the South Atlantic, HMQ [Her Majesty the Queen] and her PM can simultaneously be mothers with sons in jeopardy' (18).

Let's take a moment to pull the threads together of what has been, I acknowledge, a pretty complex set of arguments and some pretty harrowing examples:

- All academic narratives depend on tools and techniques that would be familiar to the storyteller.
- In recent years stories have been redeemed and rehabilitated within academia. While some do still speak pejoratively of 'anecdotal evidence' and

in so doing suggest that stories are subordinate to more orthodox forms of academic discourse, a growing band of serious scholars has demonstrated that stories are central to sensemaking processes and are, in any sense, vital constituents of organizational life.

- The prophets and proselytizers of 'popular management', while appropriating the language of narrative and narratology, tend to proceed from a cognitivist position and so continue to regard stories as a form of communication that may be used to reconfigure the cognitive maps of their colleagues and customers. This is not to suggest, of course, that all who would advance a sensegiving appreciation of organizational storytelling actually share a common frame. Indeed, we have explored tensions evident between Denning's more functional account of sensegiving and Tom Peters' reflections on social organization as a product of myth-making.

- Observing tensions between those who would advance narratology I have noted the contrasting analytical preferences of Gabriel (2000) and Boje (2001). Exploring these choices I have sided with Gabriel and in so doing have chosen a structural account of storytelling, which is rooted in an interaction between scene, actor and plot, that draws on 'symbolic resources' in order to seek a connection, not with cold hard facts, but with the larger truths which emerge from the artful interweaving of facts and fictions. In short I have argued that stories indulge embellishment and invite a consideration of thoughts, feelings, sights, sounds, light and shade that would be, for example, unwelcome in 'reports' (see Collins, 2021d).

- Finally: while our actions and our identities are truly shaped by the stories we tell (and hear) I have argued that our stories (when freed from cognitivist presumptions) remain local, organic and polyphonic in character. In this respect the intentions of any particular storyteller may be subverted and/or rejected by audiences disinclined to accept the plot, characterizations and/or moral advanced.

Armed with this summary we will now turn our attention to the methodology that underpins my account of the practices and preferences that shape and deliver the storyworld of Tom Peters.

Curating the storyworld of Tom Peters

In an attempt to chart, describe and analyse the stories that Peters' constructs for his readers, the ten works, previously, identified as major elements of Tom Peters' canon of management have been subjected to a detailed analysis which might, usefully, be termed a 'forensic reading'. Following Gabriel, this re-view of Peters' texts sought to identify those narratives which because they:

- place characters in predicament
- unfold in a manner that reflects the structure of the plot and the essential traits of the characters involved

- depend on symbolic resources
- proceed to a satisfactory conclusion
- seek a relationship with a deeper and more enduring truth than is achieved through mere factual verification might, properly, be characterized as poetic stories.

To assist with the process of charting these tales, and to facilitate subsequent verification of this process, a cataloguing form similar to that employed by Gabriel (1995) was developed. This form collected information detailing:

- The location and opening words of each tale identified.
- The main characters and dominant theme of the tale under scrutiny.
- The underlying emotional qualities of the tale – whether pride, sadness etc.
- The dominant narrative type – whether tragic, comic etc.
- The position of the author in the tale.
- The presence/absence of women within Peters' storyworld.
- The extent to which Peters' storyworld corresponds with the catalogue of common organizational stories suggested by Martin et al. (1983).

Readers may well protest that my attempt to signal the dominant narrative type of the tale under consideration runs contrary to the celebration of plurality developed through my comparison of sensemaking and sensegiving perspectives insofar as it appears to downplay the ways in which stories might be subject to alternative readings or re-views. Yet in response to this (anticipated) objection I suggest that it is perfectly possible to recognize, simultaneously, the feasibility of alternative readings *and* the intention of the original storyteller. Thus, my attempt to chart the dominant narrative type of each tale encountered should be read as an attempt to name the author's intention and is based on an analysis of the story in its context. That said, the cataloguing exercise did reveal a few instances when Peters failed in his storytelling endeavours. A very few stories, as we shall see in the next chapter, have therefore been catalogued as 'ambiguous' because in these instances Peters seems unable to *give* a clear sense of his intentions and orientations.

Eight of the ten 'major works' – those texts published between 1982 and 2003 – were scrutinized according to the terms described above during the summer months of 2004 for a project developed to mark the 25th anniversary of the excellence project that would later be published as *Narrating the Management Guru* (Collins, 2007). On average it took some five days of labour to catalogue and to chart the stories contained in each of these eight texts. Subsequent reanalysis and verification of this initial cataloguing took a further 15 days. The remaining 'major works', published in 2010 and 2018 respectively, were scrutinized during the summer months of 2020 to bring the catalogue up-to-date and to prepare for the 40th anniversary of the excellence project in 2022. Since these texts were smaller than many of those researched in 2004 (and have looser narrative structures) the process of extraction and curation was executed more quickly.

Thus, it required just five days to extract and to curate the tales identified in the texts published in 2010 and 2018.

In spring 2021 the two catalogues of storytelling were combined. This exercise which took around a week revealed one or two errors in the gross story-count and in the calculation of story-types from the first cataloguing exercise. These very small errors, arising mainly due to mistakes in transcription are marginal in their effects and have no significant analytical consequences for earlier work. Nonetheless, they have been corrected for this volume.

In total it took some 13 weeks of labour to create (and to correct) the catalogue of Peters' storytelling endeavours that will be reported in the four chapters which, after a brief summary, will follow.

Concluding comments

This chapter has been designed to explain the core debates, which while central to the academic analysis of organizational storytelling are often ignored by managerialist scholars. Managerialist scholars share, with 'popular management' a normative appreciation of the nature of management and organization, and so, tend to assume that sensegiving narratives arrayed to highlight the 'needs' of the organization and 'the imperatives of competition in a globalized and digital age' are sufficiently persuasive to alter the mental modes that shape conduct within organized settings. In an attempt to reveal the debates that underpin academic theorizing in this arena and which (should) condition our understanding of (a) the nature of organizational stories and (b) their efficacy, I have examined the battle lines formed between sensemaking and sensegiving perspectives and between the classical, structural account of storytelling and Boje's (2001) preferred antenarrative perspective.

Throwing my weight behind a critical, structural, sensemaking perspective I have attempted to demonstrate the power of organizational storytelling *and* its limits. In addition I have considered the processes (of fitting, fusing, fading etc.) that may be deployed to allow storytellers to forge a connection between their aims and our concerns.

To provide an objective foundation for the four chapters which follow I have, in addition, offered an account of the methodology that I have used to support my indexation, curation and critical reflection on Tom Peters' storyworld. This analysis of Peters' storytelling practices and preferences will unfold in our remaining chapters. Chapter 5 will commence this mapping exercise by offering (a) a count of the stories that shape and underpin Tom Peters' narratives of business and (b) an examination of the story-forms preferred by *the* guru of management.

Notes

1 As humans we are inclined to see patterns in events – processes within individual actions. This is especially the case, I believe, when we are directly affected by events or implicated in processes. I am, of course, inclined to agree with the analysis offered by Beigi and her colleagues yet I will confess that I am surprised to find that three (if

not four) of my own papers seem to have been excluded from their reflections. Three of these papers (Collins and Rainwater, 2005; Collins 2008; Collins, Dewing and Russell, 2009) have 'organizational storytelling' listed in the keywords that are used to aid abstraction and searching services. I might have expected therefore that these papers would have shown up in the initial search conducted by Beigi and her colleagues. The fourth paper (Collins, Dewing and Russell, 2015) does not have 'organizational storytelling' in its suggested keywords. It does, however, contain 'narrative' as a keyword and since the paper offers a re-view of a public inquiry report that has been designed to reveal its dependence on the storyteller's tools – namely, plotting and characterization – I might reasonably have expected that this paper, too, would have been thrown up by the authors' collective search activities. This end-note is, however, a quibble, literally superfluous to the main body of the chapter and does not, I stress, detract at all from the thrust of the analysis which usefully demonstrates that there has, indeed, been an increase in academic scholarship on storytelling *and* a shift in its problematics.

2   I owe this phrase to the Scots band The Trashcan Sinatras and have pinched it from their rather wonderful song entitled 'Circling the Circumference'.

3   This is, of course, a nod to C Wright-Mills (1978) and his famous work, *The Sociological Imagination*.

4   Turkina [2014] (2015) offers a footnote which is both pertinent and delightful: Her text suggests that the Soviet Airforce might now be viewed as an early pioneer of 'excellence' since in 1936 it adopted a song (which later became their official march). This song, as we shall see below, encouraged recruits to accept that they were embarking on an epic project that would make them heroes – mythical figures for future generations of Soviet citizens:

We were born to make fairy tales come true
To overcome distance and space
Our intelligence gave us steely hand-like wings
And a fiery engine instead of a human heart.

5   Prince Andrew piloted helicopters for the Royal Navy during this conflict and was obliged to use his *wasp* helicopter as a decoy target in order to protect naval shipping from missile attack. The gratuitous (but genuinely funny) reference to Andrew getting his chopper out is, of course, not strictly related to naval aviation. It is instead a very deliberate attempt to highlight Prince Andrew's friendship with Jeffrey Epstein and the suggestion (strenuously denied of course) that he shared Epstein's predilection for sex with vulnerable minors.

5
TYPES OF ORGANIZATIONAL STORIES

Introduction

In the remarks designed to introduce this book I argued that stories are, for Tom Peters, central to the work of managing. Stories occupy this central position in Peters' thought and practice because they offer an intimate and purposeful connection with the moral economy of the workplace and in so doing enable a shift *from* simple control and compliance measures *to* policies and projections designed around commitment to customers, to change and to any manner of unspecified 'competitive imperatives'. Many commentators have, of course, made similar claims as to the nature of Peters' works but few, if any have placed their assertions on an empirical foundation. In this chapter we will prepare this empirical foundation as we begin to probe the stories that Peters has used to communicate the excellence project.

In Chapter 4 you may recall that I offered an introduction to the debates which should, but often do not, feature within accounts of organizational storytelling *and* an account of the methodology that underpins our analysis of Tom Peters' storyworld. Accepting that stories do project *and reflect* core assumptions, priorities and preferences this chapter will build on my critical reflections and on the methodology outlined in Chapter 4 to:

a   chart the presence of organizational stories in each of Peters' key works published between 1982 and 2018.
b   highlight a decline in Peters' storytelling between 1985 and 2003 and a more recent, and sustained revival in his storytelling activity.
c   document and analyse the key story-types preferred by Peters.

DOI: 10.4324/9781003188940-6

The storyworld of Tom Peters

Gabriel (2000) argues that stories are special types of narrative. Stories, he insists,

- possess distinctive structural characteristics,
- depend on the indulgence of a receptive audience and
- provide a connection to enduring truths that remain beyond the reach of simple facts.

Thus, Gabriel argues that poetic tales:

- involve characters in a predicament;
- unfold according to a chain of events that, in turn, reflects the structure of the plot and the essential traits of the characters involved;
- call on symbolism/symbolic factors;
- indulge poetic embellishment and embroidery;
- have a beginning, middle and an ending;
- seek to convey not simple facts but more general and enduring truths.

Echoing this structural analysis, Price (2019) and McBeth et al. (2014), nonetheless, suggest an additional consideration. They observe that stories are not so much told as they are, in truth, re-told. In this regard stories may be considered to be, in the terms preferred by McBeth at al. (2014) cognitively hot, or affect laden, insofar as they harness ideas and well-rehearsed tropes, made familiar, for example, through upbringing and experience as they attempt to come to terms with novel situations and on-going events.

Many commentators, as we have seen, have suggested that Tom Peters builds and depends on storytelling to cement and to convey his excellence project. This much is now taken as fact. But is the work of Tom Peters truly rich in storytelling? And if it is, how do the tales rendered actually construct and narrate the business of management?

In this chapter we will offer a response to these questions. We will begin by charting the presence of stories within Peters' major narratives of business.

Losing the plot?

Utilizing the methodology outlined in Chapter 4, Figure 5.1 (below) offers a simple count of the stories that have appeared in Peters' major works on management since 1982. Figure 5.1, as you will see, also offers a little context insofar as it offers some indication of the size (page count) of each of the major texts scrutinized.

In Chapter 4 we argued that Tom Peters' commitment to organizational storytelling is drawn into the orbit of a cognitivist analytical approach and so struggles

Text	Total Number of Stories	Page Count
In Search of Excellence	137	322+36
A Passion for Excellence	165	422+25
Thriving on Chaos	117	523+02
Liberation Management	114	763+34
The Tom Peters Seminar	41	291+03
The Pursuit of Wow	57	326+08
The Circle of Innovation	38	499+21
Re-imagine	44	352
Little Big Things	114	538+29
Excellence Dividend	105	460+34

FIGURE 5.1   A count of stories in the key works of Tom Peters.

to address issues of conflict and plurality. Nonetheless, Figure 5.1 demonstrates that Peters has indeed called on the arts of the storyteller to convey the excellence project. Yet Figure 5.1 also demonstrates variability in Peters' commitment to storytelling. Indeed, we can see that Peters' early (and co-authored texts) are comparatively rich in stories with *In Search of Excellence* (Peters and Waterman, 1982), for example offering 137 tales while *A Passion for Excellence* (Peters and Austin, 1985) offers the reader no fewer than 165 stories of managerial endeavour. There is some evidence here (and in our previous chapter) to substantiate the suggestion therefore that the excellence project has indeed used stories to provide a (moral) foundation for its claims and projections. Yet we must also concede that the figure of 165 tales rendered within *A Passion for Excellence* represents a peak in Peters' storytelling. This peak, we should note, has been followed by a shallow decline in Peters' storytelling until the early 1990s and by a subsequent and steeper decline between the mid-1990s and 2003. In contrast to the trend reported by Collins (2007, 2008), however, the two major texts produced in 2010 and 2018 signal something of a return to form for Peters insofar as each is comparatively rich in stories. That said neither *The Little BIG Things* nor *The Excellence Dividend* reaches the high-water mark that is *A Passion for Excellence* (Peters and Austin, 1985).

Writing on the eve of the 25th anniversary of the excellence project, Collins (2007, 2008) surveyed Peters' work up to 2003 and suggested that *the* guru of management had 'lost the plot'. Rationalizing this decline, Collins suggested six potential explanations for what had been up to this point a sustained and significant decline in Peters' storytelling. The first two of these six explanations, as we shall see, reflect on the changing nature of organizational life whereas the final three invite reflection on Peters' changing concerns and orientations. The third explanation tendered is slightly different and reflects, to some extent, the intersection between the worlds of management and the celebrity world of the management guru inhabited by Tom Peters. Thus, Collins (2007) suggests that the recorded decline in Peters' storytelling post-1985 may be interpreted as:

1   Reflecting a simple decline in storytelling within organizations that is, itself, a product of work intensification (consequent, ironically, on the prosecution of the excellence project) and the associated narrative de-skilling of the population at large.

2   Signalling – despite the headline advice offered by the excellence project – a generalized decline in managerial commitment to storytelling which, if accurate, would simply lead to Peters having fewer tales to report.

3   Highlighting Peters' own disquiet as regards the catalogue of tales available to managerial leaders and his preference for a studied silence over a headlong rush into cliché.

4   Suggesting a shift in Peters' preferred communication strategy and his growing belief that a more directive engagement with his audience is now sufficient to secure that which was previously entrusted to the power of (sensegiving) tales. In this regard the steep decline in Peters' storytelling evident from the mid-1990s until 2003 may be read as a signal of Peters' impatience and an indication of his growing willingness, simply, *to report* the actions necessary to secure the changes which he views as necessary.

5   Highlighting Peters' growing separation – both physical and social – from the everyday dynamics of the workplace and its storyworld.

6   Suggesting a more fundamental disavowal of the belief, central to the excellence project, that organizations may be channelled and changed through the careful manipulation of their storyworlds.

To these speculations we might, now, add reflections on the writing process that Peters has adopted in the context of his life as a globe-trotting celebrity performer.

★ ★ ★ ★ ★

Commenting on the development of *The Tom Peters Seminar* (Peters, 1993) and *The Pursuit of Wow* (Peters, 1994), Tom Peters takes a few moments in his acknowledgements to credit those who have assisted in the development of these texts. This is of course quite normal. Many books contain segments of texts, which offer thanks to editors, agents and spouses among others. But in the texts highlighted here, Peters takes this to a new level and in so doing chooses to acknowledge what amounts to a team of scribes working under his direction. For example in *The Pursuit of Wow,* Peters tells us that Donna Carpenter, Tom Richman and Sebastian Stuart were in fact his writing partners. And in *The Tom Peters Seminar* (Peters, 1993: 292) he acknowledges Donna Carpenter, Tom Richman and Charlie Simmons as 'de facto coauthors'. Indeed, he later confides that 'Paul Cohen, Liz Mitchell and Randy Patnode, of our newsletter team, are coauthors of several of the stories that appear in these pages' (292). This multiple (co)authoring process, I suggest, may help to explain the decline in Peters' storytelling notable at least until 2003. Thus, I suggest that in sub-contracting elements of his narratives to employees, Peters may have partnered with de facto co-authors who lacked his commitment to storytelling and who were, in truth, more inclined to build their narratives around a more conventional style of *reportage*.

The six speculations offered by Collins (2007) and the suggestion that Peters' decline as a storyteller may be a product of (tacit) co-authoring practices must, now, be reviewed and reconsidered, however, in the light of what is (see Figure 5.1) a marked and sustained increase in the stories presented within the most recent works of Peters. Thus, we should note that compared to the narrative impoverishment of *Re-imagine* (Peters, 2003) which has just 44 tales, *The Little BIG Things* (Peters, 2010) and *The Excellence Dividend* (Peters, 2018) are, in fact, rich in storytelling resources, offering as they do 114 and 105 tales, respectively.

How might we account for this change? It may be helpful to consider the origins of Peters' most recent works.

★ ★ ★ ★ ★

The Little BIG Things is, at root, an edited collection of blog posts which Peters began publishing in 2004. *The Excellence Dividend*, however, has different roots. It builds, we are told, on Peters' collection of 300 important quotations (Peters, 2018: 456). These quotations, gathered and curated over the life of the excellence project in order to illustrate and to illuminate Peters' seminar presentations, Peters tells us, were assembled to fulfil the terms of his adjunct appointment to the University of Auckland Business School and have subsequently been published in book form. Given the origins of these texts, it is tempting to suggest that Peters' latest books, exhibit more tales simply because they are rooted in forms of engagement (and indeed literary genres) that lend themselves to storytelling. This is, at one level, an appealing rationalization. Yet there remains a significant problem with this line of analysis: It cannot bear comparative analysis, and so, cannot stand alone as an explanation for the changes observed in Peters' storytelling activity. Thus, we should note that *The Tom Peters Seminar* (Peters, 1993) was designed as an attempt to capture the energy and vitality of Peters' live seminar events and yet features only 41 stories. Similarly *The Circle of Innovation* (Peters, 1997) consists of a collection of the slides (and quotations) that Peters uses to illuminate his seminars plus some additional, explanatory text and this text features just 38 tales! It would appear therefore that we need an explanation for the resurgence of stories within Peters' work that goes beyond a simple account of the origins of these most recent texts.

In Chapter 6 I will suggest that authors of management texts, in particular, have to be cautious of writing themselves into the dramas they present. Nonetheless, it is worth observing that on the eve of the 25th anniversary of the excellence project I looked upon Peters' declining catalogue of storytelling and voiced the opinion that he was, by this stage, 'out of step with his own philosophy; out of touch with the realities of modern working; *and* out of ideas' (Collins, 2007: 145 original emphasis).

In the remarks that introduced this text I offered an apology for this (sort of) commentary. In retrospect my words (especially the final four) were, frankly, pretty unkind. I do regret this summary judgement on Peters' 'gurudom': It was rude and somewhat exaggerated. Furthermore, I regret these words *here and now* because I find that they place me in the story of the excellence project.

I am aware, you see, that Tom Peters read my book[1] and the words I now regret. I understand too that he was not impressed and, frankly, I do not blame him for this. And yet, given the evident resurgence of Tom Peters' storytelling, I find it difficult to avoid the speculation that my (stinging) words may have impacted on Peters' subsequent conduct. In an earlier chapter, we observed that *Liberation Management* (Peters, 1992) was first prepared as an attempt to respond to criticisms which Robert Reich had voiced in connection with Peters' appreciation of policy matters. Given this, there is, I suggest, room for the speculation that my critical reflections on the occasion of the excellence project's silver jubilee may have persuaded Peters that, in the preparation of subsequent texts, he simply needed to renew his commitment to storytelling.

Yet while it is useful to note Peters' return to the arts of the storytelling and while it is interesting to speculate on an explanation for this shift and renewal, it is important to acknowledge that, on its own, the cataloguing exercise documented in Figure 5.1 actually does little to probe Peters' practices and preferences. Stories are not just objects to be counted. Stories have subjects and themes which, as we shall see, bear and reward closer scrutiny. To enable this more in-depth (and more worthwhile) analysis we will consider the core poetic tropes, which, as Gabriel (2000) suggests, bring structure to our storyworlds.

The poetic tropes

Stories are very special forms of narrative. Unlike 'reports', which seek correspondence with 'the truth', stories Gabriel (2000) reassures us, seek a connection with deeper and enduring *truths*. In this regard poetic tales are unique and yet generalizable.

Reflecting on the characteristics of these special narratives, Gabriel (2000) argues that 'proper' stories will call on a number of eight 'poetic tropes' or generic attributions as they attempt to make events meaningful. Outlining these poetic tropes, Gabriel suggests that poetic tropes are the attributes which breathe life into stories and which give them the capacity to communicate experience. Poetic stories therefore tend to attribute:

1   Motive – which might variously define events to be accidental or incidental.
2   Causal connections – which outline the cause and effects of actions.
3   Responsibility – where blame and credit are allocated to actors and actions.
4   Unity – such that a group comes to be defined as such.
5   Fixed qualities – such that heroes are heroic and villains are, well, villainous.
6   Emotion – to describe the emotional characteristics of actions.
7   Agency – whereby volition is variously raised or diminished.
8   Providential significance – which is important in certain tales, where higher forms may seem to intervene to restore justice and order to systems to the characters and events, which constitute the tale.

The careful organization of these tropes, Gabriel notes, enables the construction of many different plots and characters. Indeed, he observes that authors can structure the poetic tropes to produce a number of different 'poetic modes', designed variously to inculcate pride in, or to bring laughter forth from, the enraptured listener.

Documenting the main poetic modes, Gabriel notes that a tale may be (a) epic, (b) tragic, (c) comic or (d) romantic depending on the construction and organization of tropes, characters and events. We will consider these main story-types in our analysis of Tom Peters' storyworld. Recognizing a particular pattern of practice within Peters' storytelling however, we will add a further sub-type, namely, the tragi-comic tale.

To guide our reflections on Tom Peters' storyworld, however, we must pause, briefly, to offer reflections on the characteristics of the key poetic modes and our additional sub-type. To aid understanding I will offer illustrations of each of the five poetic modes selected for analysis. These illustrations are, as we shall see, drawn directly from the work of Tom Peters.

The poetic modes

The epic form

The epic story-type circulates widely in published accounts of organization and management. In this managerial context 'epic' tales typically concern themselves with the lives and endeavours of those who have, variously, led, changed and/ or 'saved' organizations (see Collins and Rainwater, 2005). Epic tales often have simple and rather linear plot-lines. Indeed, epic tales tend to devote little time to the intricacies and complexities of character development. Instead they focus on action, movement and achievement. And as these tales move towards a satisfactory closure they invite the audience to honour the efforts and/or characters of those revealed to us through the drama.

Two examples drawn from *In Search of Excellence* (Peters and Waterman, 1982) will be used to illustrate the epic story-form. The first of these tales invites us to admire the manner in which *Hewlett-Packard* commits itself to outstanding customer service whereas the second offers what has, thanks to Tom Peters, become a familiar (but effective and deeply symbolic) tale of (in this case) a Chief Executive who takes time from his exceptionally busy day to demonstrate, to his customers and to his staff, the importance of exemplary, personal service:

> We dropped by a small calculator and electronics store the other day to buy a programmable calculator. The salesman's product knowledge, enthusiasm, and interest in us were striking and naturally we were inquisitive. As it happened, he was not a store employee at all, but a twenty-eight-year-old Hewlett-Packard (HP) development engineer getting some first-hand

experience in the users' response to the HP product line. We had heard that HP prides itself on its closeness to the customer and that a typical assignment for a new MBA or electrical engineer was to get involved in a job that included the practical aspects of a product introduction. Damn! Here was an HP engineer behaving as enthusiastically as any salesman you'd ever want to see.

Peters and Waterman (1982: xviii)

In teaching workshops for clients or students, we often use a case built around Delta Airlines' unique management style. We who travel a lot are apt to tell a story or two about the material assistance we have gotten from Delta's gate employees while scrambling to make a last-minute connection. The last time we did it, one executive raised his hand and said, "Now, let me tell you how it really is at Delta." As were preparing for what was clearly to be a challenge to our thesis, the individual went on to describe a story of exceptional service from Delta that made ours pale by comparison. His wife had inadvertently missed out on a super saver ticket because the family had moved and, owing to a technicality the ticket price was no longer valid. She called to complain. Delta's president intervened personally and, being there at the time, met her at the gate to give her the new ticket.

Peters and Waterman (1982: xx–xxi)

The comic form

In literary circles, comic tales are generally taken to be those special narratives that conclude with an improvement in the fortunes of the central character. In Gabriel's schema, however, this resolution is adjusted to reflect, I suggest, the realities of the organizational settings that shape his concerns. For Gabriel, therefore, comic tales are defined by the production of the involuntary response that we name 'laughter'. A single example drawn from *The Circle of Innovation* (Peters, 1997: 254 emphasis and ellipses in original) should suffice as an illustration of the comic story-form in the work of Tom Peters.

The tale reproduced below is hardly laugh-out-loud funny but it is 'comical', I suggest, because it tells us something about the essential (ir)rationality of human actions and, by implication, the human condition:

Some recent experiments have begun with self-scanning at grocery stores. For some reason ... FREAKING HUMAN BEINGS ... we love to scan our own groceries. The force is so strong that in several places where the experiment is taking place, people choose to wait in the longest line for the privilege of ... scanning their own groceries ... and then bagging them themselves.

254 (emphasis and ellipses in original)

The tragic form

The 'tragic' tale, in contrast to the comic form, is defined by its tendency to visit a reversal of fortunes on the main character. Thus, where the 'epic' tale is said to invite us to admire and to celebrate the deeds of its central character, and where the comic tale invites joy and laugher, 'tragic' tales induce feelings of loss and pity.

The tragic tales that Peters renders tend to revolve around poor customer service and/or business opportunities lost due to arrogance and hubris. I will illustrate the tragic story-form with a string of tales taken from *A Passion for Excellence* (Peters and Austin, 1985). The tales reproduced below which appear, we should note, pretty much back-to-back across just a few pages of the text, suggest that (less-than-excellent) organizations often belittle, infantilize and, at times, dehumanize their customers. Indeed, the fourth tale reproduced offered below may be read as (a) confirming these tendencies while (b) suggesting that the processes of business education act to reproduce exactly this state of affairs:

> A sophisticated design engineer in a technology-based company plays a variation on the theme: "We designed a major fix to be applied in the field to one of our sophisticated machines. Then we engaged in a debate on whether or not we should send a letter out, along with the changes to the manual, explaining why we had done what we'd done. The vote was close to unanimous – 'Don't confuse them out there; they're not all that bright.'"
>
> *42*

> A few days before Nancy was to leave for a week's vacation in Mexico, she stopped by her favorite photography shop to pick up her newly repaired camera. The sales person disappeared into the back of the store to look for it, but returned empty-handed, explaining that the camera was not there. Could she be mistaken? Was this really the store that repaired it? (A telephone call the previous day had confirmed that the camera was indeed repaired there and was indeed ready.) A second search ensued. No camera. Nancy finally asked for a loaner to take on vacation (a courtesy normally extended to customers). The salesperson hesitated, then remarked: "How am I to know to that you don't already have your camera and are just trying to rip us off? I have to protect the store, you know. And since you don't have the service claim number, how can you expect me to find your camera – if it is here, which I doubt. You should have come in sooner, not just before you have to leave."
>
> Everyone's entitled to a bad day but this was too much. A loaner was eventually granted. Two weeks later the missing camera was found (it had been "misfiled"). P.S. Nancy now has a new favorite photography shop (42 parentheses in original)
>
> Fredonia French Jacques, a patient representative for twenty-five years, writes about hospital care from the patients' (customers) point of view.

Here, a patient speaks for himself: "I'm brought into this hospital real sick and someone asks me a whole string of dumb questions. I tell them I feel like I'm going to faint and fall to the floor. I come to, and someone's saying, 'You can't lie here!' My wife starts to help me up. The voice says, 'You can't lift him!' "They take my clothes away. My wife gets told to take home anything that's worth anything: my watch, my ring, my wallet. They say they can't be responsible. I put on this gown split down the back. It doesn't have buttons, and they make you wear it backwards. My backside's always hanging out or I'm clutching at my gown with my only arm. See, the other one has an IV in it and I have to push that pole along every time I get up to go to the bathroom or brush my teeth." He continued: "They come in and say they're going to take my teeth out. Can't go to surgery with them. Trouble is that they take them out an hour before, so that when I kiss my wife good-bye, there's nothing to buck up against. I'm embarrassed, and they don't give them back until I'm awake, and who knows how many people gawked at me with my mouth hanging open."

43 (parentheses in original)

The setting now shifts to a classroom at the Stanford Business School in 1983. A team is discussing Disney's obsessive commitment to park cleanliness and customer friendliness. "I've honestly never seen a scrap of trash in either park," a normally sceptical MBA candidate says. She polls the fifty-person class. All agree. Then the team playing the role of the "cynical consultants" rebuts the Disney presentation. They attribute the Disney parks' success to better locations and a couple of good real estate deals. The debate heats up. Many join in. A Sloan Program student, a fast-tracker from General Motors, heads the "cynical consultants" team. He turns serious now; this is not classroom exercise anymore. "Anybody can provide a clean park," he maintains. Therefore the explanation for Disney's success must be the real estate, the access to capital, pure and simple. And what about McDonald's? Might cleanliness and uniformly high standards of service have anything to do with their success? Again, "No." Why? "Anyone can do that." Tom, who has been observing this exercise in his professional capacity, is incredulous. He stammers, "Anyone can, but only McDonald's does."

44

The romantic form

The 'romantic' form as you might expect deals, broadly, with love; with affairs of the heart. Gabriel observes that this story-form is rarely uncovered within organizations by researchers. Commenting on this finding, Gabriel suggests that this outcome may reflect a common cultural assumption that matters of the heart are inappropriate within an environment framed, publicly, by serious and rational decision-making. Indeed, Gabriel argues that romantic tales are seldom unearthed through processes of workplace research because those engaged in this research, too often, fail to develop the rapport that is necessary to allow respondents to render such tales with confidence in settings that, daily, suggest that 'feelings' lack legitimacy in this context.

I have no concrete illustrations of the romantic story-form to offer you because there are literally no examples in the storyworld of Tom Peters. We will return to this issue in a later chapter when we ask what this sort of finding might tell us about the authenticity of Tom Peters' storyworld. For the moment, however, we must complete our tour of the poetic modes.

Tragi-comic tales

The tales we have identified as being of a tragic-comic form are, as you might expect, designed to bring forth laughter from the audience. Yet this is not the simple, surprised and joyous mirth of the comic form. Compared to the pure, comic form, tragi-comic tales retain (troubling) elements, which, I suggest, invite further reflection on the situation and/or the human condition. This invitation to further reflection, as we shall see, causes the laughter consequent on our recognition of the essential comedy of the tale, quickly, to fall away, replacing this with another gesture (a shuffling of the feet, a sideways glance, a sigh) which while it remains somewhat involuntary suggests in its silence a lesson learned, a regret or empathy for someone ignored or 'othered'.

A single example drawn from *In Search of Excellence* (1982: 6) will serve to illustrate what is, as we shall see, a minor part of Peters' canon:

> Weick suggests that organizations learn and adapt v-e-r-y slowly. They pay obsessive attention to habitual internal cues, long after their practical value has lost all meaning. Important strategic business assumptions (e.g., a control versus a risk-taking bias) are buried deep in the minutiae of management systems and other habitual routines whose origins have long been obscured by time. Our favorite example of the point was provided by a friend who early in his career was receiving instruction as a bank teller. One operation involved hand-sorting 80-column punched cards, and the woman teaching him could do it as fast as lightning. "Bzzzzzt" went the deck of cards in her hands, and they were all sorted and neatly stacked. Our friend was all thumbs. "How long have you been doing this?" he asked her.
> "About ten years," she estimated.
> "Well," said he, anxious to learn, "what's that operation for?"
> "To tell you the truth" - Bzzzzzzt, another deck sorted – "I really don't know."

Ambiguous tales

Before we move on to chart the presence of the common story-types (outlined above) in the work of Peters we must acknowledge that some of the stories relayed within the excellence project have been classed as 'ambiguous'. This classification arises because there are examples of stories within the work of Peters which have defied my attempts to locate them within the poetic modes. Thus, there are tales within Peters' narratives of business, whose meaning and intent remain ambiguous. All tales are, of course, subject to what we might term 'the law of perspective': David's victory is, simultaneously Goliath's tragedy! Yet there is, within our mapping of Tom Peters' storyworld, a small number of tales that defy classification because there is, for example, no clear signal as to the identity of the hero, and so, no clear indication as to the moral of the tale. The majority of those tales classified as 'ambiguous', it is worth noting, occur early in the life of the excellence project, and so, support the suggestion that Peters and his, then co-authors struggled to adjust to the demands of the new literary genre that is popular management.

To illustrate these 'ambiguous' tales I will offer three stories drawn from A Passion for Excellence (Peters and Austin, 1985). I have chosen this text because while A Passion for Excellence contains just a handful of 'ambiguous' stories (see Figure 5.2) it does have more of this type of tale than any other of Peters' texts.

The first of these ambiguous tales is concerned with Management by Wandering Around (MBWA) which is, of course, a key feature of A Passion for Excellence. This tale has been classified as 'ambiguous' because, although the narrative is plainly a story in the terms that we have used to define this narrative form, the message (or moral) of the tale remains deeply ambiguous. Is this, for example, a story about the limitations of 'popular management' or is it instead a commentary on the limitations of management-as-practiced in the 1980s?

Both readings are perfectly possible and that is, of course, the problem: Peters and Austin (1985: 34) seem unable to decide and cannot communicate their intentions. Consequently the (sensegiving) potential of the projection is squandered.

> "MBWA: The technology of the Obvious" introduces you to our obsessions with integrity. The issue came clear in mid-1984. Tom read a book he had been asked to comment upon favorably. The words were terrific. They focused on listening, developing empathy for the person on the other side of the table. They emphasized the importance of traveling thousands of miles if necessary to see a person face-to-face, to watch the eyes. Tom, who takes pleasure in giving support for books he likes, demurred in this instance. Why? The book's implicit thrust was that these are tools anyone can use to gain immediate advantage over others. We're at a loss to describe the depth of our dismay. We believe in truly listening to the customer, taking the customer's view as more important than our own. We believe in truly listening to our people, taking their views as more important than our own. But the whole edifice tumbles if one doesn't deal off a base of integrity.

Our second 'ambiguous' tale, drawn again from *A Passion for Excellence* (Peters and Austin, 1985: 71 emphasis in original) deals with a consulting engagement. The extract reproduced below is clearly a story. It builds and depends on the structural mechanisms outlined by Gabriel and has characters whose conduct is structured by the requirements of the plot (to some degree) and an ending. But who is the hero?

Is this a story that celebrates Peters' (epic) courage as a plain-speaker? Or is it a tragic tale of a capital-goods manufacturer simply failing to grasp the credo of excellence?

Both tales (and more) are viable. Both tales (and more) are certainly possible. The problem being that each is latent and in being been laid side-by-side serve only to seed confusion!

> WE SPENT FOUR long days with thirty top managers of a $1.5 billion capital-goods manufacturer. We scrutinized sales problems, marketing problems, people problems. When it came time to summarize, six were thought to merit top-level follow-up. However, in five of the six it was noted that persistently the approach was: "we're OK. It's only a perception problem." Finally, Tom had had enough. Stepping far beyond the bounds of what's good and proper for a visitor, he virtually shouted, "A perception problem is an engineer's way of saying, 'We've got the right solution, if it weren't for the damned people who invariably get in the way of implementation.'"

The third of our ambiguous tales again introduces a number of unsettling and, ultimately, bewildering possibilities. Is this an epic tale of committed consultants, working tirelessly on behalf of the client? Or is this the tragic tale of a leader failing to model the conduct necessary for business excellence?

Again both tales (and more) are viable. The difficulty being that in the absence of clearer plotting and direction both remain latent, and so, persist as contradictory projections of sense.

> We were once called in to work with a company that was having a terrible problem: the chairman was determined to enhance entrepreneurship, but the message was not getting through. As consultants we spent a lot of the chairman's money reanalysing his strategy, checking his structure and job descriptions, and dissecting each one of his business subsystems (capital budgeting and the like). They all looked great, aimed at the right target. Out of sheer desperation, we looked at the only other thing we could think of left to look at – his calendar, the way he spent his time. We looked at the meetings he attended, and did a detailed content analysis of the agenda over a period of several months. We looked at the visits he made and the people he talked to and the order in which he talked to them while at a site. He was even kind enough (or brave enough) to allow us to run a phone log

on him for several months. The net? He was "Mr. Entrepreneurship" – in the speeches he made on the Fourth of July – but he spent barely 3 percent of this total time on his presumed objective. His attention wasn't there. And his people knew it.

270 (parentheses in original)

Mapping Peters' storyworld

Gabriel (2000, 2004) and Boje (1991, 2001) have observed that written accounts of the business of management such as those that appear in the *Harvard Business Review* represent simplistic fabrications of reality and/or self-interested and highly partisan projections of a top management world-view that jars with the everyday stories which people tell one another at, or about, work. Both Boje and Gabriel, of course, do complain that, in their fieldwork activity, they often struggle to unearth good stories and talented storytellers. Nonetheless, they protest that when organizational actors choose to relate tales of working, certain story types tend to dominate. Thus, Boje and Gabriel suggest that employees tend to favour tales that highlight the laughable and/or paradoxical elements of their working experiences and would seldom choose to relay an epic story to a colleague or close acquaintance. In this respect the analyses offered by Boje and Gabriel make it clear that, despite Maidique's (1983) celebration of Peters' storytelling, all of this gurus' narratives of organization – even those richest in poetic resources – are limited and distorted to some degree because epic tales of heroic endeavour predominate.

Epic tales

As Figure 5.2 shows, the epic story-form dominates Peters' storyworld. *Thriving on Chaos* (Peters, 1992) is, we should note, perhaps the least diverse of Peters' texts insofar as 94% of the tales relayed are of the epic form. *The Pursuit of Wow*

Text	Epic Tales (%)	Comic Tales (%)	Tragic Tales (%)	Romantic Tales (%)	Tragi-comic Tales (%)	Ambiguous Tales (%)
In Search..	97 (71)	21 (15)	9 (6.5)	0 (0)	8 (6)	2 (2)
A Passion..	132 (80)	9 (5)	12 (7)	0 (0)	5 (3)	7 (4)
Thriving..	110 (94)	0 (0)	6 (5)	0 (0)	0 (0)	1 (1)
Liberation..	93 (82)	1 (1)	18 (16)	0 (0)	2 (2)	0 (0)
Seminar	33 (81)	2 (5)	3 (7)	0 (0)	2 (5)	1 (2)
Wow	53 (93)	0 (0)	3 (5)	0 (0)	1 (2)	0 (0)
Circle	29 (76)	3 (8)	2 (5)	0 (0)	1 (3)	3 (8)
Re-imagine	30 (68)	2 (5)	7 (16)	0 (0)	5 (11)	0 (0)
LBT	90 (79)	12 (10)	11 (10)	0 (0)	1 (1)	0 (0)
Dividend	87 (83)	7 (7)	9 (9)	0 (0)	2 (1)	0 (0)

FIGURE 5.2 An analysis of the stories recounted by Peters in his key works sorted by narrative type. Relative percentage weightings appear in brackets.

(Peters, 1994) is similar in this regard insofar as 93% of the tales that feature in this text are of the epic-form. *Re-imagine* (Peters, 2003) in contrast has the lowest proportion of epic tales but at 68% of the total, these tales still constitute more than two thirds of the storyworld developed in and through the text.

Comic tales

The comic tales that Boje and Gabriel suggest are more typical of the stories that people actually tell of/at work never amount to more than a minority of the tales recounted by Peters. Combining the comic with the tragically, or darkly, comic form it is clear that comic tales are not a particular feature of Peters' repertoire: For example none of the 118 tales relayed by Peters in *Thriving on Chaos* are comical and only three of the 114 tales relayed in *Liberation Management* have comedy as their central organizing principle.

Comical tales *do* feature a little more prominently in those works that derive most directly from Peters' speaking engagements (see Chapter 2). Thus, it is worth pointing out that 10% of the tales relayed in the *Tom Peters Seminar* and 16% of the stories recounted in *Re-imagine* are of a comic or darkly comic form. Yet having made this observation we must also note that these are texts that remain impoverished in poetic terms such that, in the seminar text, this figure of 10% represents just four of the 41 tales relayed and in *Re-imagine* the figure of 16% accounts for just seven of the 44 stories exhibited.

Tragic tales

Tragic tales are similarly under-represented in Peters' accounts of the business of management. These tales, which rail against organizational failings and/or encourage readers to empathize with, or take pity on, characters who find themselves in unenviable predicaments, typically, account for somewhere between 6% and 8% of the stories recounted by Peters. However, there are exceptions. *Liberation Management* which, as you will recall, was written at a time when Peters experienced a number of personal and professional difficulties (see Chapter 2) has a total of 16 (15%) tragic tales. Similarly *Re-imagine,* perhaps Peters' grumpiest and most disaffected text, has 7 (16%) tragic tales.

Romantic tales

The fourth story type discussed by Gabriel (2000) is the romance. Gabriel (1995) has observed that 'romantic' tales seldom accounted for more than 10% of the stories he and his colleagues collected throughout their research. Reflecting on this finding he implies that romantic tales are products of maturity and organizational immersion.

Romantic tales, as we noted earlier, deal with matters of the heart; they relate stories of love and romantic intrigue. Peters professes a love of business (see for example, Peters, 2003). Indeed, he protests that business excellence is a product of passion and obsession (Peters and Austin, 1985). Yet despite this talk of love, lust, passion and obsession, Peters' storytelling repertoire is devoid of romance.

Had Peters not been, so clearly, a man of conviction and strong belief, had he perhaps just one fewer ex-wife,[2] it might have been tempting to put this lack of romance down to a certain coldness of character. But since Peters is so clearly warm-blooded we must look for another means to account for the absence of romance in his tales of corporate endeavour.

Peters between the mill-stones?

Gabriel's (2000) analysis of organizational storytelling provides, perhaps, the most direct (and the most cutting) means of rationalizing the absence of romantic tales in Peters' narratives of business. Gabriel's analysis, as we have seen, suggests that romantic tales become available to organizational researchers who succeed in associating with mature respondents or who successfully immerse themselves in the day-to-day processes of organization. Given this there is room for the suggestion that the paucity of romantic tales in our catalogue of Peters' work demonstrates one or a number of the following problems:

- That Peters' research lacks depth.
- That Peters and his researchers failed to develop a rapport with their respondents.
- That Peters' respondents lack maturity and/or self-confidence.

David Sims (2003) provides an interesting account of organizational storytelling, which may offer us an alternative (and less cutting) means to rationalize the nature of Peters' storytelling endeavours and the omissions we have observed in this catalogue. Sims argues that middle-managers are under pressure to narrate their experiences of working in ways that will make sense to three distinct constituencies – their superiors, their subordinates and themselves! However, he suggests that the middle-manager's need a) to impress his/her bosses and b) the associated need to organize and orientate his/her juniors causes these individuals to relay tales that undermine their own sense of self.

If we stretch Sims' analysis only slightly, we have a potential explanation for the absence of romantic tales in Peters' story catalogue. Thus, Sims' analysis of managerial narratives suggests that Peters' awareness of the (rational) expectations of his clients (see Peters, 1989) may have caused him to ignore stories that deal with love and romantic passion at work, despite the pain and discomfiture that this may cause him at a personal level. Viewed in these terms the absence of romantic tales in the Peters catalogue of storytelling may represent evidence of Peters' own organizational liminality (Czarniawska and Mazza, 2003) insofar as it suggests that this, perhaps the most famous of the business gurus, still feels the need to pander to the 'hard' approach to management that he claims to defy.

Of course we cannot be sure that in choosing not to speak of romantic matters Peters causes himself pain. But a number of things *are* clear. First, our catalogue demonstrates Peters' preference for and dependence on the epic story-form. Second, our catalogue demonstrates, if not the exclusion of the romantic form then certainly its absence. Third, our catalogue demonstrates a sustained decline in Peters' storytelling, accelerating from the mid-1990s that has only recently reversed. Challenging the analysis developed by Collins (2007, 2008) therefore the revised storytelling catalogue, revealed here, demonstrates that in his most recent books, Peters is once again willing and able to render the world of managing others through stories. Yet the observed increase in Peters' storytelling activity is but a part of the change to report for there is within this increasing *quantity*, I suggest, a shift in the *quality* of Peters' stories which is worthy of further reflection and consideration.

Quantity and quality

Commenting on *Re-imagine* (Peters, 2003), *The Economist* (20/12/2003) complains that Peters' tales of organizational endeavour have become more shrill, his characters less agreeable. Indeed, Collins (2007) has complained that those few stories that were reproduced within *Re-imagine* were too brief, too thin, too hastily rendered to act, reliably as sensegiving devices. This criticism does not, however, apply to the books that Peters has produced since 2003. Indeed, it is worth observing that while epic tales continue to dominate both *The Little BIG Things* (Peters, 2010) and *The Excellence Dividend* (Peters, 2018) these stories are, in comparison to those that feature in earlier works, more complex, more nuanced. Indeed, as we shall see the epic tales, which feature within *The Little BIG Things* and within *The Excellence Dividend* have been leavened with humour and embellished with self-deprecatory asides to generate richer and, ultimately, more pleasing projections of sense.

The first of the tales reproduced to demonstrate this renaissance in Peters' storytelling is from *The Little BIG Things* (Peters, 2010: 190–191 emphasis and ellipses in original). This tale is interesting because it mixes epic and comic forms and in so doing produces a celebration of Richard Branson that, since it lacks the shrillness of earlier tales of managerial endeavour is genuinely worthy of reproduction.

> Richard Branson's idea of fun is going head to head in the ring with someone who has him by a jillion pounds. As Michael Specter wrote in his wonderful *New Yorker* profile ("Branson's Luck"), "Branson likes to enter a market controlled by a giant – British Airways, say, or Coke, or Murdoch. Then he presents himself as the hip alternative."
>
> He allows himself to get pissed off at something stupid (pathetic airline customer "service"), and on the spot, more or less, starts an airline, or whatever. (NB: I happen to believe that ... **all** ... successful innovation,

products or processes, are the … lived-out fantasies of pissed-off people.) With a fortune measured in billions, he commands a payroll of about 55,000 feisty folks in 200 very independent companies. (Think Virgin Atlantic, Virgin Blue of Australia, Virgin Limousines, Virgin Money, Virgin Active health clubs, Virgin Galactic space travel …)

Branson *is* his brand. He enjoys his nutty stunts that personify his brand's hipness and engages in them even when out of camera range; upon discovering the car back to his hotel after a recent party (whose guests include the Google founders, half Branson's age) was full, Sir Richard simply hopped in the trunk. Specter goes so far in his profile as to dub him the "anti-Trump," while, around the office, "Branson's nickname is Dr. Yes, largely because he has never been able to bring himself to fire people, and often has trouble saying no to even the most ridiculous and unsolicited ideas."

As I read the Branson profile I let my mind wander to Howard Schultz, Starbucks founder. I like Schultz *and* his company a lot. But it seems to me that when one hears of its future, it's almost always in terms of Howard's goal of adding thousands upon more thousands of new shops, or some such. Branson is surely happy when his businesses succeed and grow (though not awash with in tears when one fails, as long as it was a spanking good try), but his primary goal truly does seem to be the sheer fun of doing something cool to twit a giant or, more recently, by investing big in biofuels – to save the world.

In short (and long), I wish there were many more like him.

I'm not Branson by a long, long shot; but I understand the guiding impulse. The *only* reason that I take on new stuff, and keep accumulating frequent flyer miles, has long been the unadulterated pleasure I get from always marching "the other way" – and in particular storming after those I think have let us down, from numbers-obsessed execs to health care leaders' lack of patient-safety rigor as measured by hundreds of thousands of preventable deaths in the United States alone.

My advice?

This is *strategic:* **Do your darnedest to "make it fun," "make it a ride to remember," "make it a bloody ball"!**

The second of the more complex and nuanced tales I have chosen to illustrate Peters' renewal as a storyteller might have been rendered as an epic declaration and in this form might well have acquired a hectoring tone. Yet in the example below we find an epic tale that is genuinely engaging because it has been (I suspect) rehearsed, embellished and laced together with genuinely comic asides. And as you will see it has an opening gambit that really hooks the reader!

I cross-dressed for the first time on March 31, 2007. I went to a local (Dorset, Vermont) costume party and tried valiantly to represent Elizabeth

Cady Stanton, rightfully called the Mother of the American Women's Rights/Women's Suffrage Movement.

But that gets ahead of the game ...

The idea animating the party was that you had to dress as someone you admire – *and* be prepared to respond to questions as the admired personage would have responded. I thought it would be great fun and therefore took it seriously. Franklin? Churchill? Lord Nelson? John Paul Jones? John Cleese/Monty Python? No problem, I had them all pegged. And a satisfactory costume would hardly be a challenge (e.g., Churchill, cigar and brandy; Nelson or Jones, folding telescope; and I can do Cleese almost as well as Cleese does Cleese, at least in my own mind).

That was five weeks before the party. And now late in the afternoon on March 31, 2007, following Susan's "sartorial" guidance and that of a close friend, Lola Van Wagenen, and eminent women's historian, I was encased in a white wig and a long black dress, courtesy of a Boston costume shop, and, though tripping over my hems again and again ["Welcome to our world" – Lola], ready to go – and, courtesy a dozen mesmerizing books hastily ingested on a dozen plane trips, ready to respond to questions ...

I was indeed shamefaced – shamed, after almost fifteen years of loudly and doggedly championing change to women's still diminished role in business and government, that I was almost totally ignorant of the astounding history of the American women's rights movement. And worse yet, of the gruesome details of women's status in our society only 100 years ago – that makes use of the loaded word *"slave"* frighteningly appropriate. It was no coincidence that the American women's movement, effectively launched in Seneca Falls, New York, on July 13, 1848, grew in tandem with the abolitionist movement in America.

Peters (2010: 300–301 ellipses in original)

The third tale I have selected is especially interesting, I think, because it shows Peters modelling, within his storytelling and within his own actions, the focus on symbols and symbolism that *In Search of Excellence* advised would be necessary for cultural change. In addition this tale shows Peters reaching for something ... and failing. Yet because these elements of failure and success have been carefully mixed, what might have been a simple epic has become instead a pleasingly honest and genuinely entertaining story of human endeavour:

Lockheed invented the "Skunk Works" as an alias for Advanced Development Programs; while there are conflicting stories about the exact origins of the term, the official story places the birth of the first Skunk Works in the 1940s. It was a small unit, based in Burbank, California, that used a totally unconventional approach to developing essential military aircraft – e.g., the famous SR-71 Blackbird spy plane, a pillar of our Cold War tactical package - in record time at a minimum cost with maximum innovation executed by a group of astonishingly motivated people. (Too good to be true? I agree except for one things: It *was* true.)

I came across the Lockheed Skunk Works in the early 1980s – and immediately fell madly in love. I had long been convinced that "normal pathways" would rarely yield innovation at Big Companies. And I was on the lookout for byways – placed that stunk to the reigning bureaucrats. And Skunk Works, or skunkworks as I prefer, filled the bill perfectly.

In the introduction, I reported that this book as to a large degree a "return to basics." Well, the skunkwork idea is as basic as it gets from me when it comes to innovation. I had adored the skunkworks idea so much in the 1980s that I named my Palo Alto consultancy "Skunkworks Inc." My colleagues and I held, six or seven times a year, "Skunk Camps," five-day intensive innovation-strategy seminars of the edge of the Pacific (fittingly), aimed at regenerating the "Spirit of Skunk" in the bellies of tiring corporations. (Naturally, in retrospect, tired corporations rarely showed – our "Skunks" were largely from midsized companies, like W.L. Gore or Perdue Farms, determined not to calcify.) I even wore an elaborate "Skunk Suit" to conduct "graduation" – given to me by the American Electronics Associations from my help in keeping them "non stuffy."

All this (too much info?) is a long-winded way of saying that somehow, by hook or by crook, you have to figure out how to fool *yourself*. How to run a trick play – that catches *you* off guard. How to run end runs on *yourself*. I won't guarantee much in this world, or in this book. But I will pretty much guarantee – no I *will* guarantee – that standard structures won't do the trick when it comes to innovation and renewal, even in moderate-sized companies, let alone the Bumbling Beasts'

Peters (2010: 313; emphases and ellipses in original)

Our next extract also has a pleasing, confessional tone. It is, I suggest, amusing yet purposeful and memorable precisely because of its self-deprecating humour!

Once (in Helsinki as I recall), I was being interviewed, through an interpreter. It wasn't an aggressive interview, but the interlocutor was trying to dig beneath the surface. And dig she did – after the fact, I was taken aback when I realized how forthcoming I'd been.

Her "weapon"? She was pleasant enough, but not overwhelmingly so. That wasn't it. The weapon was (I finally realized) ... *nodding*. Constantly. And ... taking copious notes. The nodding was obvious and constant, not half-hidden by any means. And the note-taking was also pronounced.

And I was a total sucker for it – doubly amazing because, as I said, there was a translator in between the two of us; and triply amazing because it was, obviously, not exactly my first, or one of my first 5,000, interviews; besides I'm exceptionally well-trained in rat psychology, B.F. Skinner-style.

What was going on? *By nodding and taking notes, regardless of my level of awareness of what was up ["She wants me to blurt something out." "She's nodding like crazy."], she was respecting me and what I was saying so brilliantly that it was worth immortalizing.* No wonder I shared my previously most hidden secrets – that's an exaggeration, but, frankly, not by much.

Here then, are two "tricks" that are guaranteed – *guaranteed* – to keep a person talking:

1   **Nod your head non-stop and frequently.**
2   **Ostentatiously take notes.**

Both tactics/tricks shout at the other, *"You are important and interesting – I must capture for eternity the pearls of wisdom you are imparting."*

Peters (2010: 337 emphasis and parentheses in original)

The Excellence Dividend (Peters, 2018) demonstrates a similar development of Peters' storytelling capabilities. Immediately below you will find three, interconnected stories about *Commerce Bank/Metro Bank*. Taken individually these tales are not particularly remarkable but as a collection they are interesting because they produce an account of Vernon Hill that is, I suggest, altogether more powerful than that which a more conventional epic could ever hope to achieve:

> To observe the Excellence Dividend at work … Let's turn to Vernon Hill, founder of Commerce Bank in the United States and now Metro Bank in the United Kingdom. For years, the retails banking model, as software moved to every desktop and countertop, and then to every pocket has been to abandon bricks-and-mortar branches and compel customers to use ATMs, and now smartphones, and to perform as many transactions as possible online. Hill the contrarian, opened Commerce Bank and said in effect. *"We want 'em in the branches where we can get beyond soulless 'transactions' and turn an inhuman account number into a fully engaged member of our family."* His plan was to build gorgeous, colourful, pulsating "stores" (the Commerce/Metro term for branches); pay good wages; train like crazy; and fill the stores with enthusiastic employees who would provide sterling service and convert customers into "fans" – one of Hill's favourite terms. Very long hours have been one signature of the Commerce/Metro experience – his branches are open a previously unheard-of seven days a week (and until midnight on Fridays!). The most complex transactions are completed in a flash. No problem is too convoluted that it can't be solved autonomously by frontline staffers taught literally never to say "no." (*When a computer glitch occurred at one point, an employee went so far as to put a customer's plane ticket on her personal credit card in order to preserve that customer's deeply discounted, time-sensitive airfare; her imaginative act earned kudos from bank management; let alone the shock and awe of the customer.*)
>
> *Peters (2015: xvii–xviii; parentheses and emphasis in original)*

To top it off, the bank has always advertised itself as "dog friendly." Its ubiquitous mascot, Duffy ("Sir Duffield" in the United Kingdom), is featured in every promotion. Come to the bank and you'll likely leave, as I did in London, with a bright red dog bowl emblazoned with the bank's logo, a pooper scooper (also with logo), and, of course, dog biscuits. The biscuit giveaway count – featured in the annual report a few years ago – totalled two million.

xviii

In 2007, Hill sold Commerce Bank to T D Bank for $8.6 billion, a rousing testament to the effectiveness of his contrarian, fan-generating approach. He rested for a while but couldn't remain idle for long; so he took is "WOW-bank" philosophy, captured in his book *Fans Not Customers,* across the Atlantic. The innovative Metro Bank became the first new, major chartered bank in the United Kingdom in 150 years. Hill put on his version of the Greatest Show on Earth, the British bought the whole act (thousands came out for branch/store openings), joined in the fun, and in short order Metros had more than one million accounts – oh and his UK customers took to "dog friendly" even more avidly than their American counterparts.

xviii (emphasis in original)

My final example concerns what would otherwise be a simple tragic tale (and complaint) about poor product design. Indeed, in *Re-imagine* (2003) we would have received, I suggest, only the capitalized elements of the extract offered below, and so, no story! Yet as we shall see Peters, while still voicing a complaint now offers a complex tale with comical and memorable asides, which enables and effects more meaningful reflections on the manner in which we respond to good design.

MY STORY

ON A LATE FEBRUARY DAY IN 2016, IT RAINED CATS AND DOGS IN TAKAKA NEW ZEALAND ...

I was coming out of the hardware store and had my iPhone, as usual, deep in my pocket when the surprise storm hit. But pocket protection was not enough. The water snuck in somehow. The phone was inoperable, kaput – though I tried every trick to revive it known to man and the Internet.

Gorgeous.

Functional.

And done in by a bit of rain.

Bottom line: bad design.

(Sorry, ghost of Steve.)

Well it ain't gonna happen twice. Now if there's even a single cloud in the sky, I carry my phone safe in a Ziploc bag.

Ziplocs!

How do I love thee!

Let me count the ways.

I do love may any-and-all-purpose Ziplocs so much that I've got a reputation for Wretched Ziploc Excess. For my sixtieth birthday, one of my business partners put together a book of letters he'd collected from my various friends and colleagues wishing me well. The book was touching. Touching and at time hilarious. Those present at the subsequent birthday bash read their contributions.

The partner and pal who pulled all this together had contributed a piece of his own which he read with gusto to the gathered guests. The entire piece – about six hundred words – was about me and my Ziplocs.

There's a whole drawer in my office filled with Ziplocs of every size, from sandwich size (useful in a thousand ways!) to the two-gallon giants, sometimes hard to find, and without which I simply could not exist.

I think my Ziplocs have as much beauty as they do utility. One of my favourite aspects of the bags is that when you seal them up, there is a memorable clicking sound that tells you that you've done it right. No rain will intrude to ruin a several-hundred-dollar iPhone, that's for damn sure.

Why in the world am I relating this story?

Simple!

I LOVE, LOVE, LOVE THINGS THAT ARE BRILLIANTLY DESIGNED.

FEARLESS FUNCTIONALITY.

AESTHETICALLY PLEASING.

EMOTIONALLY IRREPLACEABLE.

(AND I HATE, HATE, HATE THINGS THAT ARE DESIGNED IN A SLOVENLY OR CARELESS FASHION.THEY ARE NOT "PROBLEMATIC." THEY ARE INSULTING.)

Peters (2018: 245; emphasis and parentheses in original)

Concluding comments

This chapter has offered a map of Peters' storytelling and an analysis of the core story-forms (or poetic modes) that Peters has used to convey the excellence project. Our initial charting of Peters' storytelling reveals a peak in activity around 1985, a steady decline from this date until the mid-1990s. a collapse in Peters' storywork between the mid-1990s and 2003, and a subsequent resurgence and renewal in the texts published in 2010 and 2018.

These shifts and movements are interesting but on their own they tell us little. After all Peters (Peters and Waterman, 1982; Peters and Austin, 1985; Peters, 2003) is clear that it is the individual with the best *not* the most stories who will influence the sensemaking of stakeholder. In an attempt to move from a simple consideration of *quantity* therefore we have offered reflection on the types of tales that Peters relates. Noting a preference for the epic story form, the total absence of romantic tales and the relative neglect of comic and tragic story-forms within the excellence project we have raised questions about the *quality* of Peters' storytelling. Indeed, we have suggested that Peters' storyworld, despite its stated desire to initiate and to secure purposeful change within organizations, often lacks an intimate connection to the lived realities of social organization and might therefore be considered limited as a cognitive tool. Yet having made this point I have argued that the most recent books produced by Peters (2010, 2018) offer more complex tales which because they deal in comic asides and self-deprecation retain a seductive quality far in excess of the shrill narratives that typified *Re-imagine*.

In our next chapter we will continue with our analysis of the storyworld of the excellence project as we consider (a) the heroes of the excellence project and (b) the manner in which Peters, himself, comes to be placed within these narratives. As we shall see there has been a significant shift in Peters' position within the storyworld of the excellence project.

Notes

1 Peters it is worth noting lists this text on his homepage and indeed draws on its contents: observing that it is one of three biographies that have been produced on the excellence project.
2 Peters has now been married three times.

6

EXCELLENCE AND THE MANAGEMENT STORYTELLER

Introduction

In Chapters 2 and 3, we noted changes to and continuities within the excellence project. For example we noted a shift in Peters' narratives *from* the east coast *to* the west coast of the United States, and *from* big business *to* smaller enterprises. In this chapter, we will consider these shifts in the context of the storyworld of the excellence project. Confirming the dynamism of the excellence project we will demonstrate that the exemplars of excellence which dominated the storyworld of *In Search of Excellence* (Peters and Waterman, 1982) and to a lesser extent *A Passion for Excellence* (Peters and Austin, 1985) have been supplanted by new heroes with, sometimes surprising biographies. Reviewing these tales, however, we will demonstrate that while the heroes of the excellence project have indeed changed, the essential *heroics* remain the same! In addition we will chart Peters' shift from narrator to hero of the excellence project. I will suggest that this development has done little to advance the excellence project.

The exemplars of excellence?

Using Tom Peters as a cipher to decode the enigma machines that are management consulting and 'popular management', Stewart [2009] (2010) captures the essential ambivalence that many feel towards the excellence project. Exploring the foundations of *In Search of Excellence*, Stewart raises a number of familiar complaints. Some of these complaints are, of course, accurate and pertinent. *In Search of Excellence* is, for example, flawed conceptually and empirically. Other complaints, however, are altogether less persuasive. For example the suggestion that Peters and Waterman are, in retrospect, 'particularly bad stock pickers' (Stewart [2009], 2010: 246) who backed the wrong horses when they named their

DOI: 10.4324/9781003188940-7

excellent organizations is, as we have seen, a hollow critique that is, furthermore, very much dependent on the time-frame selected.

This is not to suggest, of course, that Stewart is wrong to seek a critical engagement with the excellence project. Within liberal democracies it is important that we (and I do mean all of us) exercise our right to subject ideas to critical scrutiny. And this is especially the case when the ideas, in question, claim a mastery over the organized world and carry with them broader ramifications for civic society. Yet critics of the excellence project, too often, misunderstand and/or misrepresent their target, and so, offer complaints, which because they are based on fundamental mis-readings of this project, are largely irrelevant. Stewart, while voicing a normal, scientifically based, critique of the excellence project actually seems to understand this tension. While attacking Peters, the failed organizational scientist, for example, Stewart [2009] (2010: 268) suggests that *the* guru of management truly deserves this (contested) epithet because he is, at root, a 'crypto-evangelist' who trades in hope and fear in order to substantiate his core concerns (see pp. 263–281 for Stewart's reflections on this issue). And yet, having voiced this understanding of the essence of the excellence project, Stewart chooses to ignore his own insight and returns once again to a rather orthodox, scientific critique of the excellence project. Thus, Stewart complains that *In Search of Excellence* offers an unrepresentative account of US business practice that is self-interestedly skewed in favour of just a few company examples. Indeed, while failing to attribute his source – a worrying oversight for someone who would criticise the gurus for transgressing the normal boundaries of scientific discourse – Stewart [2009] (2010: 244) observes that while *In Search of Excellence* builds on a sample of 43 companies it actually fails to discuss 15 of these cases – offers but cursory attention to 20 'or so' (244) more and, in truth, discusses just seven of the sampled companies in any depth.

This summary of the narrative processes which constitute *In Search of Excellence* is we should concede pretty accurate: Peters and Waterman (1982) do neglect the bulk of their sample. And yet this criticism, while accurate within its own frame, largely misses the point because it is based on the assumption that the excellence project is, at root, a scientific endeavour which is to be weighed and valued according to its correspondence with an empirical *truth*. Challenging this line of critique I have argued that the excellence project is, in fact, largely immune to orthodox forms of academic critique because Peters is engaged in a moral (*crypto-evangelical*) project which deploys stories as persuasive examples to forge a connection with normative ideals, with larger human problems, with enduring romantic *truths*. While conceding the essential accuracy of Stewart's complaints therefore I offer a counterpoint. I will argue that the core issue is *not* whether *In Search of Excellence* has arranged and arrayed its case-work representatively. Instead, the pertinent question is: What is it that Peters' tales of excellence represent? In this chapter we will address this issue through a consideration of Peters' storytelling practices.

The storyworld of the excellence project

The storyworld of the excellence project, as we shall see, tends to turn on three tropes variously concerned with:

1   An independent owner-manager who offers exceptional, personal service directly to the customer.

A single example will serve to illustrate:

> Several years ago, my wife and I flew to Chicago for New Year's Eve. We went for the express purpose of having dinner with two good friends. They chose one this great restaurant city's top restaurants. The meal was fabulous as expected. We stayed until just past midnight. Most diners decided to leave at about the same time. It was a bitter cold Chicago night, with wind coming off the lake. We went out to try the difficult pre-Uber task of hailing a cab. Outside in that merciless cold, we saw someone in a beautiful light dress running back and forth practically dragging cabs to the curbside. The someone was none other than the restaurant's owner.
> Wow.
>
> *Peters (2018: 274)*

2   The leader – whether this leader be in a corporate setting, within the military, the school system or indeed within the prison system – who develops and communicates a core sense of vision and purpose that is sufficient to engineer useful and lasting changes in organizational practices that truly benefit the customer.

These stories, while demanding admiration for the leader framed in the tale, generally offer accounts of individuals who are notable because inter alia they:

• model exemplary conduct for others;
• are impatient with rules, with unhelpful bureaucracy and with other (related) forms of obstruction;
• have shown themselves to be reasonable, decent, trusting and trust-worthy individuals;
• remain customer focused;
• focus on design to produce processes and outcomes that serve their customers and their employees.

Again, a single example will suffice as an illustration at this stage:

> In 2009, American Airlines and Southwest Airlines held their annual meetings on the same day in Dallas, headquarters to both. APA, the Allied

Pilots Association picketed American's meeting. The Southwest meeting marked founder **Herb** Kelleher's retirement after 37 years ... Herb was asked to reveal his full set of secrets, ... he severely limited his remarks: "You have to treat your employees like customers."

Peters (2010: xx; emphasis and ellipses in original)

3   Rank-and-file employees who – thanks to the unstinting efforts of their leaders – have been 'empowered' to adopt new working practices that are for customer and employee alike, transformative.

'One of our favourite stories ... is about a Honda worker who, on his way home each evening, straightens up windshield wiper blades on all the Hondas he passes. He just can't stand to see a flaw in a Honda!' (Peters and Waterman, 1982: 37)

In an attempt to demonstrate the presence of these tropes, while charting the changing cast list of the touring company that is the excellence project I will offer a loosely chronological analysis of the excellence project designed to reveal and to examine (a) the heroes of the excellence project and (b) Peters' own transformation from narrator to hero. We begin with an account of the exemplars of the excellence project.

Representing excellence

The storyworld of *In Search of Excellence* as we noted in Chapter 5 is made up of 137 tales and is dominated by the epic story-form. Many of the tales rendered in this text (and throughout the larger excellence project) do not name their heroes (or villains). This preference for anonymity may be explained, in part, as a product of the practices, which McKinsey demands of its employees (see Collins, 2007; McDonald [2013], 2020: 44–45). In addition we should concede that anonymity generally helps to protect tales from unhelpful revision within contexts marked by plurality (see Collins, 2018, 2021d for an elaboration of this point).

Analysing those tales which do identify the heroes of the drama it is apparent that the storyworld of Peters' first major work is dominated by the 14 exemplars of excellence, which Peters and Waterman choose to highlight as beacons for change. Thus, of the 137 tales rendered within *In Search of Excellence* 54 relate to the exemplars chosen by Peters and Waterman. That said the pattern is uneven. There are, for example, no tales associated with six of these exemplars – *Bechtel, Boeing, Emerson Electrical, Fluor, Johnson and Johnson* and *McDonald's*. Furthermore, just four companies – *Dana* (eight stories), *Hewlett-Packard* (eight stories), *IBM* (17 stories) and *3M* (seven stories) – dominate the storyworld and, together, account for close to 75% of the exemplary tales rendered (see Figure 6.1). Given this, we should concede that our headline analysis of the heroes of *In Search of Excellence* does seem to confirm the accuracy of Stewart's complaint. Thus, it is clear that the storyworld of *In Search of Excellence,* like the broader narrative of this text,

Text and story count	Key Actors 1-6. (Story count in brackets)
In Search of Excellence (137)	1. Anonymous (31) 2. IBM (17) 3=. Dana (8)/ Hewlett Packard (8) 5. 3M (7) 6. Authors (5)
A Passion for Excellence (165)	1. Anonymous (30) 2. Authors (19) 3. IBM (6) 4=. GE (5)/ HP (5) 6. Domino's (4)
Thriving on Chaos (117)	1. Anonymous (32) 2. Author (11) 3. Tenant (5) 4=. Domino's (4)/ 'The Japanese' (4) 6. 'Imagined You' (3)/ Worthington (3)/ SAS (3)
Liberation Management (114)	1. Anonymous (45) 2. Author (26) 3. Ingersoll-Rand (6) 4=. Union Pacific Rail Road (5)/ Titeflex (5) 6. Imagination (4)
The Tom Peters Seminar (41)	1. Author (14) 2. Anonymous (12) 3. Union Pacific Rail Road (2) 4=. Remaining stories each feature different actors
The Pursuit of Wow (57)	1=. Author (22)/ Anonymous (22) 3. Fed Ex (4) 4=. Bank of Boston (3)/ Verifone (3) 6=. De-mar (2)/ Imagined You (2)
The Circle of Innovation (38)	1. Author (27) 2. Anonymous (22) 3=. Bob Waterman (2)/ Southwest Airlines (2) 5. No other actor features more than once
Re-imagine (44)	1=. Author (19)/ Anonymous (19) 3. No other actor features more than once
Little BIG Things (114)	1. Author (63) 2. Anonymous (30) 3. Author's family (7) 4. Bob Waterman/ McKinsey (5) 5=. Starbucks (3)/ Delaware delegates (3)
The Excellence Dividend (105)	1. Author (54) 2. Anonymous (34) 3=. Bob Waterman/ McKinsey (3)/ Author's family (3) 5=. IBM (2)/ Pat Carrigan (2)/ Herb Kelleher (2)/ Peter Drucker. No other actor features more than once.

FIGURE 6.1   Main actors ranked 1 to 6 featuring in stories appearing in key works of Tom Peters.

is skewed in favour of a very few organizations whose structure and conduct reflect not so much the objective reality of the situation as the authors' broader concerns, complaints and predilections. Yet if we accept that Peters is and has always been an evangelist – whether cryptic or otherwise – our analytical priorities shift. Thus, the question becomes *not* whether Peters' narratives and stories are truly representative of practice *but* what Peters seeks to represent, to project, to change through the tales of excellence that are rendered in his work. Given this shift in priorities, I will offer critical reflections on the storyworld developed and advanced by Peters to substantiate the excellence project. Mindful, however, of the need to offer an analysis that reflects Peters' priorities rather than, say, my own personal preferences I have chosen to reproduce a selection of tales, which mirrors the manner in which the storyworld of the excellence project has been constructed and arrayed.

Given IBM's dominant position in the storyworld of *In Search of Excellence* it seems appropriate to begin with reflections on the manner in which Peters and Waterman use stories related to this organization to demonstrate/to advance the core requirements of business excellence. The first story selected for analysis, as we shall see, is typical of the tales, which Peters and Waterman have developed to outline and to project the leadership qualities of those who lead their excellent organizations. Thus, our first tale suggests that those who drive business excellence must be customer-focused, decisive *and* impatient with those who simply dither over decisions and in so doing delay purposeful action.

> "I was at a meeting of sales managers with Mr. Watson (Senior) one time," says Gordon Smith, recently retired from Memorex. "The purpose was to assess some customer problems. On the front table there were eight or ten piles of papers, identifying the source of problems: 'manufacturing problems,' 'engineering problems,' and the like. After much discussion, Mr. Watson, a big man, walked slowly to the front of the room and, with a flash of his hand, swept the table clean and sent papers flying all over the room. He said, 'There aren't any categories of problems here. There's just one problem. Some of us aren't paying enough attention to our customers.' He turned crisply on his heel and walked out, leaving twenty fellows wondering whether or not they still had jobs."
>
> *Peters and Waterman (1982: 159)*

Our second tale of IBM again addresses the issue of customer service.

> A Lanier data-processing executive in Atlanta, a competitor in some areas, swears by IBM mainframes: "I remember the last time we had trouble. In hours the horde descended, from everywhere. They called in about eight experts on my problem. At least four were from Europe, one came from Canada, one from Latin Amercia. That's just where they happened to be."
>
> *159*

Warming to their theme Peters and Waterman offer further reassurance on IBM and its commitment to customer service:

> The eerie part of the IBM story on service is the absence of chinks in the armor. Recently, in a one-week period, one of us (1) sat next to a twenty-five-year-old Oakland-based IBM sales person on a flight from New York to San Francisco, (2) talked to a senior AT&T executive with an IBM background, (3) talked to a Memorex executive who had been an IBM manufacturing executive, (4) discussed an IBM sales decision with a hospital administrator, and (5) talked with a young ex-IBM sales man in a classroom setting. They didn't look alike; they ranged from an attractive young black woman to a grizzled fifty-year-old. But they did talk alike. All these people agreed that IBM has had problems - software, even quality sometimes. But all also agreed, using practically the same words, that IBM's service and reliability are unmatched. What's so impressive is the depth and consistency of their belief that IBM really cares about service.
>
> *160*

The second and third tales reproduced above, in comparison to the first, lack the visible presence of a senior manager calling the shots. And this may be why there seems to be no visible chinks in the armour of IBM's customer service narrative. Yet, since all tales turn on position and perspective, we must wonder about the unaccounted costs (birthdays missed, weekend plans cancelled) which it seems IBM staff must accept if they are to deliver IBM's over-reaction to customer problems!

The tales which relate to *Dana* are perhaps more robust, less prone to revision. Here we have a decisive leader, impatient with bureaucracy but, and this is I think crucial, someone disinclined to throw papers to the floor or to imply the termination of employment as a response to perceived failure.

> Dana did away with time clocks. "Everybody complained," McPherson says. "'What do we do without time clocks?' I said, 'How do you manage any ten people? If you see them come in late regularly, you talk to them. Why do you need time clocks to know if the people who work for you are coming in late?'" He also reinforces the focus on starting from positive assumptions about people's behavior as he elaborates on the story: "My staff said, 'You can't get rid of the time clocks. The government requires a record of every person's attendance and time worked.' I said 'Fine. As of now, everyone comes to work on time and leaves on time. That's what the record will say. Where there are big individual exceptions, we will deal with them on a case by case basis.'"
>
> *Peters and Waterman (1982: 250)*

> McPherson is a bug on face-to-face communication and on discussing all the results with all of the people. He required that there be a monthly face-to-face meeting between division management and every member of the division to discuss directly and specifically all of the detailed corporate individual results. (We see that time and again in the excellent companies. They are obsessed about widely sharing information and preventing secrecy. They willingly trade any marginal loss of competitive information for the added commitment.) McPherson even stressed face-to-face contact in institutional advertisements. He ran ads that, as he says, "made my middle managers very nervous at first." One said: "Talk Back to the Boss," another "Ask Dumb Questions." McPherson deplores management's unwillingness to listen: "I wanted a picture, for a slide presentation, of a worker talking to his foreman. We had fourteen thousand photos in the file, but not one of a supervisor listening to a worker."
>
> *250*

Highlighting the extent to which 'management' should be understood as both problem and solution for American business, Peters and Waterman offer a contrast between *Dana's* management and that which had prevailed, it seems, within *General Motors*:

> The McPherson philosophy comes down to the value of everyone's contributing ideas, not just keeping up the pace on the line. "The way you stay fresh," stresses McPherson, "is you never stop traveling, you never stop listening. You never stop asking people what they think." Contrast that with the following comment from a General Motors worker, recently laid off after sixteen years in the Pontiac division: "I guess I got laid off because I make poor-quality cars. But in sixteen years, not once was I ever asked for a suggestion as to how to do my job better. Not once."
>
> *252*

The tales associated with *IBM* tend to be clustered in those chapters that deal with customer service and with productivity through people. The *Dana* tales in contrast deal with what is now termed 'empowerment'. Furthermore, the tales drawn from *IBM* and from *Dana* deal with general *truths*, and so, stand the test of time pretty well. The stories drawn from the *Hewlett-Packard* experience, in contrast, seem somewhat dated now because they signal the birth of the quality movement and in so doing treat 'the Japanese' as a major challenge to the US economy. It is, however, worth observing that common across all of the stories rendered so far is the understanding that managers must show commitment to change, must model the conduct they expect in others and – from time to time – may need to engage in memorable public demonstrations of commitment that are highly symbolic.

> Anderson introduced the latest quality campaign a year ago. He made the announcement, as is typical with major new HP programs, at "morning coffee break" in the cafeteria, where most of the division's 1,400 employees meet every week to talk about business. He asked his staff to start defining and measuring quality. He used the Japanese encroachment in the industry as an example and a reason for urgency. And as the year progressed, a variety of quality programs permeated the division. By the end of the first year, as measured by such vital standards as mean-time-between-failures, the already superb quality had improved fully 100 percent. Anderson is shooting for another 100 percent improvement this year from a basis that already beats the industry by a wide margin. Division management signaled early and dramatically that the quality drive was real. During one notable "morning coffee break," five pallets of defective circuit boards were hauled in and dumped on the floor. Management explained to the astonished onlookers that those boards, and some less visible software bugs, were the equivalent of $250,000 in lost profit sharing (most employees at HP are stock owners and part of the profit-sharing program). This act was

to characterize the way the division punishes and rewards performance. For quality failures, everyone shares the blame. For achievement, individuals are singled out.

176 (parentheses in original)

The company is seldom first into the market with its new products – Xerox and IBM, for example, were first with high-priced laser printers. The company's marketing strategy is normally that of a counterpuncher. A competitor's new product comes on the market and HP engineers, when making service calls on HP equipment, ask their customers what they like or dislike about the new product, what features the customer would like to have …. And pretty soon HP sales men are calling on customers again with a new product that answer their needs and wants. The result: happy and loyal customers."

178 (ellipses in original)

Unlike the tales of *Hewlett-Packard*, which focus on the vision and conduct of a very visible leader, *3M* is represented as a curious and rather fabulous collective that all-but defies description. Analytically this is probably unacceptable … but as poetry it works fairly well. And that surely is the point! Peters and Waterman are not natural scientists nor are they, truthfully, social scientists operating in the field of management education. They are instead, activists engaged in the (dark) arts of business of edification. The extent to which the tales rendered by Peters and Waterman are, in truth, representative of the practices developed within their sample of excellence therefore is largely irrelevant. All that really matters, within this branch of evangelism is (a) that management is represented as driven, customer-focused and decisive, and (b) that employees and customers are portrayed as responding positively to the symbolic interactions that management has developed to communicate its sense of purpose.

There's an excitement about being in the game parks of East Africa that's impossible to describe. The books don't do it. The slides and movies don't do it. The trophies most of all don't do it. When you're there, you feel it. People who've been there can hold one another in rapt conversation for hours about it; people who haven't been there can't quite imagine it. We experience some of the same helplessness in describing an excellent company attribute that seems to underpin the rest: action orientation, a bias for getting things done. For example, we were trying to depict to an executive responsible for project management coordination how it might be possible radically to simplify the forms, procedures, paperwork, and interlocking directorates of committees that had overrun his system. We said, quite off-handedly, "Well, at 3M and TI they don't seem to have these problems. People simply talk to each other on a regular basis." He looked at us blankly. Our words hardly sounded like exotic advice - or even helpful advice. So we said, "You're not competing with 3M. Let's go to St. Paul for a day and take a look. You'll be surprised." Our friends at 3M were tolerant of the excursion, and we observed all sorts of strange goings-on. There were a score or more casual meetings in progress with sales people, marketing people, manufacturing people, engineering people, R&D people - even accounting people - sitting around, chattering about new-product problems. We happened in on a session where a 3M customer had come to talk informally with about fifteen people from four divisions on how better to serve his company. None of it seemed rehearsed. We didn't see a single structured presentation. It went on all day -people meeting in a seemingly random way to get things done. But at the end of the day our friend agreed that our descriptions had been fairly accurate. Now his problem was the same as ours: he didn't know how to describe the situation to anyone else.

119

A Passion for Excellence (Peters and Austin, 1985) introduces a new collection of heroes – Bill Creech, Stew Leonard, *Domino's* and *Milliken* – to the cast list of the excellence project. It is worth noting however that *IBM* and *HP* both remain prominent in this storyworld occupying third and fourth places respectively in the tally of tales (see Figure 6.1).

A Passion for Excellence unlike *In Search of Excellence* does not build on a sample of companies. Complaints as to the representativeness (or otherwise) of the story-world developed by Peters and Austin (1985) therefore simply do not apply to this text. Nonetheless, it is plain that – with varying levels of toe-curling *shenanigans* – the individuals and companies who feature within the storyworld of *A Passion for Excellence* have been selected and arrayed to demonstrate what individuals may be moved to achieve given the effective communication of managerial vision, trust and commitment. Our first meeting with Bill Creech, for example, establishes his track-record as a manager albeit within a military context whereas the second tale featuring this individual invites us to celebrate the manner in which he has brought renewed purpose to his command through 'empowerment':

> General Bill Creech led a remarkable turnaround of the U.S. Air Force's Tactical Air Command. TAC has a clear peacetime "product," the sortie, in which the weapon system (plane) and its pilot and support group are tested as a unit in simulated combat conditions, and a peacetime "bottom line," the sortie rate. When General Creech arrived at TAC in 1978, the sortie rate had been falling for ten years at a compound annual rate of 7.8 percent. From 1978 through 1983, it rose at a compound annual rate of 11.2 percent. It used to take about four hours on average to get a part to a temporarily inoperable plane. In 1984 the average was eight minutes. Since the budget for spare parts actually decreased along the way, and other "external" factors became more adverse, the turnaround was a product of management, nothing else.
>
> *Peters and Austin (1985: 48)*

Does the ownership stuff count for much? Well, you have the over-whelming statistics from TAC, Kollmorgen et al., to support the point. But perhaps the last word, and the best, comes from one of Bill Creech's non-commissioned officers. The general asked him what the difference was between the old, specialist organization and the new organization, in which the plane and the sortie are the "customer," where the supervisor ("designated crew chief," remember) "owned" the plane. The NCO's to-the-point reply: "General, when's the last time you washed a rental car?" We think that may say it all. None of us washes our rental cars. There's no ownership. And there's no ownership if you're a specialist, no matter how well trained, if you're responsible only for two square feet of the right wing of a hundred planes. Only whole planes fly. Only "owners," especially in competition and with flags flying, will go all out to make a whole plane fly. Creech had, pure and simple, made that NCO a proud owner – with (and this is vital, too) the wherewithal to get the job done.

Peters and Austin (1985: 239; parentheses in original)

Milliken is offered to us in order to highlight the importance of commitment to the customer. Indeed, the unnamed 'marketing director' in the tale below is offered as an exemplar of/for the 'naïve listening' that, we are assured, generates real customer intelligence:

In February 1984 Tom spent four days with Milliken's 450 principal of-ficers at their annual top-management retreat. The sole subject was getting close to the customer-with Tom's connivance, not just listening, but "naïve listening." About a month after the meeting was over, he received a letter from the marketing director (let's get it straight- marketing director, not born-again accountant or lawyer) of the division that manufactures carpets for institutions such as schools and hospitals. In it he described how he is repositioning his product line, focusing on new features, adding some new products. The reason: right after the February meeting and making his commitment to "naïve listening," he had gone out and worked two weeks, on the swing shift, in a customer's hospital. As he said, "Getting close to the customer is a winner!! [his emphasis]. I just got back from my second week working in a major hospital as part of the housekeeping staff. What an experience... to actually maintain your products (and competi-tive products) in the environment where they are used. Plus, it gave me an opportunity to do a lot of naive listening while at this hospital. I worked the second shift (3:00pm until midnight) and actually cleaned carpeting as well as hard-surface floors. I operated all the machinery they used daily, plus handled the same housekeeping problems that our customers face daily. I cleaned every stain from blood to urine, plus a few that I cannot even spell. To be honest, I was stiff and sore and worn out at the end of the two weeks, but I plan to do it again at least every six months. What did I learn? [At this point he goes for about half a page talking about the features that really had come through in the "naïve" setting in which he had placed himself.] Now I can put together my trade advertising as well as my entire merchandising program based directly upon the needs of my customers as I observed them. No more SWAG (Scientific Wild Ass Guess) on what the market needs. I'm learning–from new-product introduction to maintenance of existing products–exactly what our health care customers require. We can now design products and programs that have a differential advantage for our customer plus get a fair profit for Milliken…. I guess if we will just follow the Golden Rule-'Do unto others as you would have them do unto you'-we will become more efficient in our dealings with all people, including our customers!! I know I'm on the road to answering 'Where's the beef?' for the health care market."

Peters and Austin (1985: 16; parentheses in original)

In a similar fashion Stew Leonard is portrayed as a demanding but essentially decent boss who in seeking the best for his customers is plainly willing to invest in his staff.

Stew Leonard, Jr., of Stew Leonard's, describes an apropos experience, which surfaced at one of Leonard's many customer-focus group meetings, as shown in Sam Tyler and John Nathan's 1985 PBS film, In Search of Excellence: "One of the ladies stood up and she said, 'I'll tell you what I don't like.' She said, 'I don't like your fish,' and we said, 'What do you mean, you don't like our fish? 'She said, 'Well, it's not fresh. I like to go to a fish market and buy fresh fish.' The fish guy was there, and he stood up and said, 'What do you mean it's not fresh? We get it fresh every morning from Fulton Fish Market, and we get it fresh from the Boston piers every morning.' He said, 'I guarantee you it's fresh!' She said, 'But it's packaged. It's in a [plastic wrapped] supermarket package.' So what we did was to set up a fish bar with ice in it. And we did that right after that meeting. Now there's wrapped fish in one place, but some people like to buy it fresh right off the ice, so it's available across the aisle at the same price off the ice. Our packaged fish sales didn't decrease at all, but we doubled our total fish sales. We were doing about fifteen thousand pounds a week; now we're doing thirty thousand pounds a week." (Peters and Austin, 1985: 75 parentheses in original).

Stew Leonard's, as we noted, is Frank Perdue's biggest single-store customer. Stew wanted to change his chicken packaging technology a while back, and Frank's people were the only ones expert in the new techniques. So Frank, without a second though, (*sic*) sent two Lear jets up to Connecticut to fetch fifteen of Stew's chicken packers down to Salisbury, Maryland, for schooling at Perdue Farms' headquarters

(276)

Stew Leonard (of Stew Leonard's dairy store) solicits his people's ideas regularly. One unique way is via regular visits to competitors. There aren't many stores that compete with Stew across the board, but sometimes he will come across an interesting department like one of his (e.g., bakery goods), or an interesting store in another business (e.g., a florist). When he does, even if it's three hundred or four hundred miles away, he's likely to grab fifteen of his people (including hourly people, even very recent hires) and hop into the 15-person van that he uses for just such occasions. Off they go to Stew's challenge to join the One-Idea club. The issue? Who will be first to come up with one new idea for Stew's gleaned from the competitor's outfit? Next, can everyone come up with at least one new idea? (It must be implementable immediately upon returning home.) That's almost all there is to it – but not quite. Even though Stew Leonard's is at the top of the heap, none of his travelers is allowed to talk about anything that Stew's does better than the competitor they're visiting. The point is for each person to find at least one thing that the competitor does better than Stew's. "It's so darned easy to fall into the trap," Stew says, "and grouse that 'Those guys don't know what they're doing with this, or that.' We have a rule. We just don't allow that. You should be able to find at least one thing that the competitor does better. Often as not it'll be a tiny thing. But that's the way you get better." The new ideas gleaned are communicated throughout the store in the company newsletter, Stew's News

334 (parentheses in original)

Domino's is offered to us as an organization with a culture which teaches its people that they must do whatever it takes to honour the company's commitment to the customer:

Domino's Pizza lives by and owes its phenomenal success to its 30-minute (maximum) "We deliver anywhere" pledge. Domino's Pizza Distribution, therefore and logically enough, must never allow a franchise to run out of dough. "Shutting a store down" is the number one sin. It nearly happened a while back, and Distribution President Don Vlcek [*sic*] got a call telling him about the probable disaster. His ready response (in a low-margin business): "Charter a plane. Get it there!" Charter they did, get it there they did. In another instance, Vleck's lieutenant, irrepressible young Jeff Smith, did have a store shut down for lack of dough. He went out and bought a thousand black arm bands and his whole team wore them in mourning for quite a time afterwards. The message, at Domino's, is clear – and memorable.

276

William Donald Schaefer is, similarly, offered to the reader as a maverick leader who will demand the best from employees in order to serve his customers/

constituents. Elements of this tale work pretty well: The mayor's warning about abandoned cars and pot-holes in unspecified locations is amusing and memorable. Yet the more we hear of the mayor's conduct the less agreeable he appears. Indeed, there is, despite Peters' celebration, more than enough here to suggest (a) that the good people of Baltimore have elected a bully and (b) that Peters is comfortable with Schaefer's conduct!

> Mayor William Donald Schaefer of Baltimore has wandered with his constituents for years. Maintaining a feel for his city has long been at the top of his list of priorities. Richard Ben Cramer reported in Esquire (October 1984):"I'm not pleased with this," he'd scolded them [members of the cabinet] many times. "That is NOT ... GOOD ... ENOUGH." PEOPLE, he'd write on his easel. He picked the easel thing up a few years ago, thought it might get the message across. For greater weight, he'd write: PEE-PULL. Or: WHAT IF YOU LIVED THERE? He wanted the cabinet to have a feel for the citizens they governed. Sometimes he'd decide the problem was they just couldn't goddam see. He'd be riding around like he does on weekends, with his driver and a cop riding shotgun, and he'd see the potholes, and broken streetlights, caved-in trash cans, dirty parks, housing violations, abandoned cars, crooked traffic signs, dead trees, a missing bus stop, trash at the curb. "What are the bastards, doing with the money?" he'd mutter aloud in the Buick. Then he'd get out his pen and his Mayor's Action Memos and tear into the thing: Get the g----m trash off East Lombard Street .... Broken pavement at 1700 Carey for TWO MONTHS .... Abandoned car at 2900 Remington. Why? Then the memos would be on their desks Monday morning, and the trash, the pothole, the abandoned car had better be gone when he drove by again. How'd it get there in the first place? One time he popped them an Action memo: "There is an abandoned car ... but I'm not telling you where it is." City crews ran around like hungry gerbils for a week. Must have towed five hundred cars. That was NOT ... GOOD ... ENOUGH: Schaefer called in his cabinet, the best municipal government in America. The mayor held two fingers up, and he poked them at his own glittery eyes. "Do you know what these are? Do you? These are eyes." The mayor was jabbing at his face now. They thought he might hurt himself. "I GOT TWO. AND YOU GOT TWO." Then he grabbed a cabinet member and started menacing him with the fingers in the eyes. The cabinet guy's head was burrowing between his shoulders. "So how come my eyes can see and a smart young fella like you can't see a damn thing huh? HOW COME?" But today it's worse. He won't look at them. He is staring down at the table. His head, in his hands, rocks back and forth in sorrow. At his shoulder is the easel with the single work he'd written: ERR-JEN-C.

> *11 (emphasis and ellipses in original)*

The storyworld of *Thriving on Chaos* continues to celebrate the manner in which *Domino's* (placed in fourth position within the storyworld of this text) directs its staff to ensure customer service. Importantly however it is made clear that this direction is constructed in and through empowerment.

> The last word is reserved for Domino's Bressler: "At the crew meetings, I get the crew together and ask each one of them, 'What have you done for the customer today?' We put all the stories, what they've done, and then we vote. I give the manager who's done the best deed for the customer an award. And then I tell him to go give one to one of his people. So they hold the same contest at their store. That gets your people to think about what the customer is." In a way, it is that simple; this final vignette speaks a thousand words about the underlying mind-set of the customer -obsessed organization— and leader.
>
> *Peters (1987: 291)*

> Consider the case of janitor, the sole person on duty at a commissary of Domino's Pizza Distribution Company. He took an off-hours call from a franchisee about to run out of pepperoni. (Having a franchisee run out of anything is the cardinal sin at Domino's Distribution.) On his own initiative, he located keys to a truck, loaded the vehicle with one small box of pepperoni, and drove hundreds of miles to keep the franchisee from closing down. It never occurred to him that Distribution, as the subsidiary is called, would want him to do anything else-and he was right.
>
> *Peters (1987: 291)*

The *Tennant Company* (sitting in third place within the storyworld developed by *Thriving on Chaos*) is also praised for the manner in which it empowers employees and (in the second tale reproduced below) for its own capacity for learning.

> Frank Smith is a good example of an employee who takes quality seriously. Frank is one of the people responsible for making sure the Tennant Company factory has the reputation of being one of the cleanest in the country. A painter in the maintenance department, he has been painting interior and exterior walls and ceilings at Tennant company for years. Frank has applied hundreds of gallons of white paint each year at the request of department managers, who remembered once in a while to thank him for the good job. Nevertheless, Frank knew he was doing an important job. And there is no doubt in our minds that a clean plant is one of the highest priority objectives in any quality process. When people take pride in work areas, they will also take pride in their work. About six years ago, as part of the quality emphasis, Frank decided to put a little extra into his job. He began creating wall murals – pictures of fish, grouse, or deer, paintings of Tennant company products, slogans about quality, or whatever the people

who work in the area requested. Every year, requests for his work increase, along with the positive comments on what a great job he is doing. Frank proves that quality can be achieved in more ways than assembling products. He achieves quality with a brush, a ladder, a bucket of paint, and a fertile imagination.

Peters (1987: 384)

Tennant Company was known for producing top-quality floor maintenance equipment. But during my visits with our Japanese joint-venture partner in the late 1970s, I had been hearing complaints – sometimes bitter – about hydraulic leaks in our most successful machines. Back home, I began asking questions: Why were the hydraulic leaks happening only in the machines we sent to Japan, and not in those were selling in the U.S., where, in fact, we were selling many more of the same machines?

As it turned out, the leaks weren't just happening, in Japan. The machines we sold here at home were leaking too. The difference was that U.S. customers accepted the leaks. If a drop of oil appeared on a freshly polished floor, they simply wiped it up. In Japan, the leak was cause for complaint. Japanese customers expected better quality.

Peters (1987: 65)

Within *Thriving on Chaos* (and, indeed, within *The Pursuit of Wow*) Peters chooses to frame some of his stories from the perspective of the reader. These tales are, I suggest, designed to place the reader directly within the narrative and since they, simultaneously, pose questions and tender solutions may be read as attempts to *give* sense directly to the audience that Peters has framed. The heroes of these tales I have labelled as 'Imagined You' insofar as they invite the reader to place his/ herself, directly, within the predicament. A single example, drawn from *Thriving on Chaos* (Peters, 1987: 222 parentheses in original) will suffice to illustrate these imagined heroes/heroics:

You are the head of training in a $15 million firm, which urgently needs a spanking-new, high-visibility international management program. The president has been after you to get going for six months. What is the fastest and most effective way to move toward development and large-scale implementation?

You've been chatting about the subject around the office. Now a vigorous young woman comes to you with her strongly held idea for such a program. What do you do? One course is to ask her to write a proposal to float with the executive committee. Another is to bring it up casually at a meeting with your peers or seniors to see how it flies. The second approach is better than the first, but it's still dumb. There's a much better answer.

First, forget the international headquarters staff three doors down. They've fought this idea for years on the pretext that "if it ain't entirely broke, why try to fix it" – in other words, hands off! Instead, sit down with your young would be champion and go through a list of the international line managers whom you know best, or better yet, whom she knows. Pick out a couple. The persons you've identified should not be sceptical about trying something new. They probably should not even be very senior. They should be people who you or your champion know will be excited about this topic. They must be line managers.

Find some pretext to send the young champion off on a brief field trip to visit with the foreign managers you've identified – to gather live, raw, far-away-from-headquarters input from them at the outset. And then the proposal? Not yet. When your eager champion gets back, have her write up three or four pages of rough notes. Fewer and rougher is better; high polish puts people off. Then, the next time you're meeting with international managers (perhaps you could stop in for lunch or coffee during a training session), pull out those unimposing notes. Chat about a couple of the key points with several of the managers-once again, those most likely to be friends instead of foes. Have your champion do the same sort of thing as opportunities present themselves. Then gather a little more data. Perhaps send your champion off to a couple of companies you've heard about that a have interesting new international training programs. Circulate notes from those visits to the people you've both talked with.

And so on. The objective is to strike some sparks-to get several committed champions to own the idea. Not you or even your senior international counterparts, but your young champion and a few enthusiastic mid-level line person in the field.

Liberation Management (Peters, 1992) introduces the reader to *Ingersoll-Rand* (which holds third position within its storyworld, to *Titeflex* and to the *Union Pacific Railroad* (which jointly hold fourth position). In a departure from previous practice this text offers tales drawn from contexts that acknowledge, explicitly, the presence of unions within the workplace. Yet the heroics remain familiar being, as before, built on notions of trust, vision and empowerment. The tales associated with *Ingersoll-Rand,* for example focus on the manner in which this organization, belatedly but well ahead of its competitors, (a) took steps to discover the manner in which users had been obliged to compensate for the limitations of their own product design and (b) altered its designs and standard practices to reflect user-needs:

> The findings that resulted from these visits sound almost trivial in retrospect. In fact, they were "revolutionary" by normal standards. Team members visiting Sikorsky Aircraft observed, for one thing, that many workers wrapped mounds of tape around the business end of the grinder, to prevent their hands from sliding into the dangerous spinning grinding pad. Subsequently, working with an industrial designer (see below), the creators of the

new tool incorporated a simple guard piece which prevents the hand from slipping. This "insignificant" feature was completely new to the industry.

Peters (1992: 76; parentheses in original)

There were other stories. McNeil, visiting a Boeing supplier in Everett, Washington, noticed that the hands of one young woman, who was using a competitor's aluminum-cased tool, were blue with cold. "Doesn't that bother you?" he asked her. "She didn't seem to understand my question," he told me. "She assumed it was normal to have ice-cold hands." McNeill gave her a prototype. Two weeks later, when the IR salesperson came back to collect it, she has hidden it, and refused to give it up.

Peters (1992: 80)

The stories associated with *Union Pacific* are similarly focused on employees and on the manner in which employees have, in truth, settled for systems, processes and design practices that do little more than honour some out-dated convention or tradition:

"So one day, I had three keys made to the terminal," he continued. "The morning shift came in and I put the keys down on the table. 'What's that for?' they said.

"'So that you can unlock the door in the morning,' I said.

"'What? You aren't going to be there?'

"I said, 'No, I can't keep coming in at four a.m. You guys work four-thirty a.m. to one 1pm, but I have to stay until six and it's killing me.' And they said, 'What if we have a problem?'

"'Solve it,' I said.

"'What if we can't?'

"I said, 'Here's my number at home, call and wake me up.'

"'You trust us?' they said.

"'I wouldn't have made these keys if I didn't.' They couldn't believe it."

Now the workers do believe—and so does union leadership. "Preston is the post unique trucking company I've handled," we were told by Sonny Musso, then president of Merchandise Local Union #641 in New Jersey. "They don't just tell [drivers] 'You can do that.' They explain why, or why not. [The driver] can talk to the president or chairman of the board if he wants to." In fact, Musso became an unabashed salesman. "When I see a good account, I'll give them a cal, suggest they should give the business to Preston," he said. "Preston pays attention to the people who do the work, which few companies do."

While hundreds of less-than-truckload haulers shut their doors following industry deregulation in 1980, Preston's fortunes have soared: Revenue has more than tripled … and accident and grievance rates have tumbled. Tough customers like Charlie Corace, executive director for quality at

McNeil Pharmaceutical, told us that the Johnson & Johnson subsidiary is looking at Preston "as a company to model ourselves after. I've become one of their biggest salespeople. I called the company I used to work for and told them about Preston, that it's the company they should be doing business with ...

"I now have a Preston truck on my credenza. People walk into my office and ask why. I tell them about what can be accomplished when you support your people. When I look at that Preston truck, I don't see the truck, I see five thousand people pulling together."

Peters (1992: 256; ellipses and parentheses in original)

Mike Walsh comes from a modest job at Cummins Engine to the chairmanship of the Union Pacific Railroad. He lays off 10,000 people, yet the unions admire him, old-line managers change their ways, 100 years' worth of bureaucratic excess is erased in 5 years. The "trick": trust and respect. After a misbegotten drug raid in Louisiana, Walsh hops in the company plane, dragging his top officers with him, hightails it to the scene—and publicly apologizes to the assembled railroaders for management's despicable act of mistrust. Claiming that most fellow CEOs "badly underestimate" the amount of change the workforce can handle, Walsh turns over responsibility to the front line almost overnight—and opens the books to everyone. One long-time railroader, now a UPRR exec, says: "We're letting people do what they wanted to do, and were capable of doing all along."

Peters (1992: 460)

In another Teamster stronghold, at the birthplace of the industrial revolution in America, another miracle of trust and respect occurs. Jon Simpson arrives at the limping hose maker Titeflex. Customers are screaming. He unplugs the fancy computer system, drags the furious customers down to the front line, and instructs his front-line workers to "do it"--fix the problem for the customer as they see fit. He opens the books, confers with the unions, dumps first-line supervisors, installs self-managing teams in short order—and achieves a spectacular turnaorund in 90 days.

Peters (1992: 460)

Titeflex was an early adopter of the touted MRP I computer/software system. Unfortunately, as was true for so many pioneer MRP I users in the 1980s, the system was superimposed directly upon antiquated processes. We "automated chaos," Simpson told me. "The computer governed our lives." But that didn't last for long in the new regime. Simpson, on a business trip to Boston right after he came aboard, called back to the office and was informed that the computer was down. Customer orders could not be shipped. He recalls commanding one of his senior managers to "Go down to the local five-and-dime and get a box of crayons, then write the customer's address on the box and ship the product." The manager did. It worked. MRP I, R.I.P.

Peters (1992: 66)

Ralph Stayer is also highlighted as a very special individual who has demonstrated a very clear and personal capacity for learning, which allows him to lead and to change his organization:

> Ralph Stayer joined the family-owned sausage-making company located in Sheboygan, Wisconsin, upon graduation from college in 1965 and took the reins from his father in 1978. "The business was growing very rapidly," he recalled when we spoke with him in 1988. "Yet my gut told me we weren't really special. When I looked around, people weren't having fun." He recalled an incident in 1980 that mad a big impression. "I'd hired one employee early on, who was very competent," he told us. "Then one day it struck me that he was just a soldier, carrying out my orders. I tried to get him to take more responsibility, but he couldn't. I'd ruined him! A few years of my style had beaten the independence out of him." That's a harsh diagnosis, especially when self-administered—but Stayer was serious. "It wasn't because our employees were bad people," he added. "If anything needed fixing, it was me."
>
> *Peters (1992: 238)*

> "The watershed for me was about two and a half years ago. I was still wearing some of my habits from my old career, and made the mistake of standing in front of this group of men and women and saying, 'Thou shalt not take vacations during this critical shipping period.' At which point my workers came back and said, 'Thou shalt not tell us when we can take vacations. We're adults, treat us as adults.' That was a critical moment for the organization. It was the day they stepped up to owning the business. And I backed off. Ever since then, they not only have been responsible for their own vacations, they've been responsible for structuring their own work, structuring their own budgets, for deciding, literally, every single significant aspect of their working life.
>
> *Peters (1992: 240)*

Liberation Management extends once more the reach of the excellence project by choosing to highlight developing practices within the US prison system. Yet while we have new heroes to applaud, the heroics remain largely the same.

"We could beat prisoners and build up hostility between the keeper and the kept," associate warden Wayne Smith told us, "but here we allow inmates to somewhat manage themselves." Establishing this new ethos hasn't been easy. Conservative staff members fought Luther under the generally unassailable banner of "compromising security." For example, when he decided to allow popcorn at special events like movies, some guards objected. The Inmates would stuff the popcorn in the locks, they claimed. The popcorn was distributed. The locks stayed popcorn-free. (Not all staff can come to grips with the McKean approach. Luther eased out two associate wardens whose resistance persisted.) (Peters, 1992: 250 parentheses in original)

Another inmate, Steve Monsanto [offers similar testimony]: Shakedowns take place in every federal prison. In other facilities, the guards usually tear the con's cell apart. At McKean [prison], though, after a shakedown guards must place everything exactly as they found it. Monsanto remembered returning to his cell once, to find it torn apart by a new officer. He told a lieutenant, who told Monsanto to leave the cell alone. "The new officer will put it back," he said. (Peters, 1992: 250 parentheses in original)

The Tom Peters Seminar perhaps surprisingly given that it builds directly on Peters' live seminar performances, offers less than one half of the tales developed within *Liberation Management* (and less than one quarter of the tales rendered by *A Passion for Excellence*). Yet *The Tom Peters Seminar* does signal a significant shift in the storyworld of the excellence project: It is within this text that Peters comes to occupy first place in his own storyworld – moving up one position from the slot he had occupied since the publication of *A Passion for Excellence* (Figure 6.2). Indeed, it is worth observing that tales, which place Peters at the centre of the drama, dominate *The Tom Peters Seminar. Union Pacific,* for example, occupies third place in this storyworld but holds this position, we should note, despite featuring in just two stories!

A number of the tales, which place Peters at the centre of the excellence drama, concern events and interactions that have taken place during his seminar

Text and story count	Author(s) as key character – number of stories and rank ordering	% of total stories where author appears as key character
In Search of Excellence (137)	5 stories – 6th in total story count	4%
A Passion for Excellence (165)	19 stories – 2nd	12%
Thriving on Chaos (118)	11 stories – 2nd	9%
Liberation Management (112)	26 stories – 2nd	23%
The Tom Peters Seminar (41)	14 stories – 1st	34%
The Pursuit of Wow (57)	22 stories – 1[st] =	39%
The Circle of Innovation (38)	27 stories – 1st	71%
Re-imagine (44)	19 stories – 1[st] =	43%
Big Little Things (114)	63 stories – 1st	55%
Excellence Dividend (105)	54 stories – 1st	51%

FIGURE 6.2   An analysis of the growing prominence of the author as a key character appearing in stories relayed by Tom Peters in his key works since 1982.

events. Some of these tales we should note honour the core precepts of the excellence project insofar as they applaud exceptional customer service:

> My own epiphany came a couple of years ago when I gave a speech at a Marriott hotel in Orange County, California. The valets did a bang-up job of parking almost 1,000 cars. They were well-dressed, courteous to a fault, and actually ran back and forth from the cars. Some show! During my speech, I mentioned this and said, "Hats off to Marriott!" There was sustained applause, suggesting others had also enjoyed this spectacle of excellence. After the talk, Paul Paliska came up and introduced himself. Turned out he was the founder of Professional Parking Services, Inc.-- valet-parking specialists who subcontracted to Marriott.
>
> *Peters (1993: 138)*

The Pursuit of Wow is, again, dominated by tales which place Peters within the narrative but there is, at least, room for a larger supporting cast. The characterization labelled earlier as 'Imagined You' is, for example, present and prominent within the storyworld of *The Pursuit of Wow.*

> You're a partner in a consulting company. Your four-person team is making a presentation to the client tomorrow. You've got a fabulous team leader, and you want to give her all the autonomy in the world. Fine, don't interfere with the "substance" – but do show up at the office at 1 A.M. to drop off pizza. Your trivial yet noble act will become lore, or something close to it, for moths to come—if not years.
>
> *Peters (1994: 32)*

FedEx holds the third place in the storyworld of *The Pursuit of Wow* (with four tales) while the *Bank of Boston* and *Verifone* share fourth spot (with three tales apiece).

> Five years ago you would have characterized retail banking at the Bank of Boston as third-class citizenship, low on prestige, compensation, and fun. The lowest tier was the inner city in Roxbury – that was Siberia.
>
> But we woke up one day and realized we had to do more in the inner city – not in the pursuit of fun but as a business opportunity/obligation. We rediscovered our roots – our old branch in Roxbury. We decided the only way we could do good and do well simultaneously was not through the large, monolithic culture that we had, but by giving autonomy to somebody to run our inner-city branches as a stand-alone business.
>
> We found a very talented African-American woman who grew up in the neighborhood, and she started First community Bank within Bank of Boston. From third-class citizenship in Siberia, today that's the most energized and successful start-up business we have. And we have lots of successful

startups. They're visited by scores of businesses every year, mostly other banks, to see how we do it.

Is innovation possible? Yes! And it had nothing to do with R&D in a conventional sense, but with purpose. And commitment.

Peters (1994: 148)

The Chief Executive of *Verifone* is similarly rendered as an individual prepared to challenge others who, nonetheless, remains open to learning:

I remember introducing myself to a new employee at *one of our Asian locations. He was surprised that I would talk to him – at his previous job he had never even seen the CEO. I encouraged him to send me e-mail and let me know what was happening. I left, figuring he agreed with me. Turned out he was just giving me lip service. About six months later, his superior told me he had developed an attitude problem. I decided to have a talk with him.

So next time I was in his region, I took him out to lunch, which blew him way. He couldn't believe the CEO would have the time, let alone the interest. I listened to his point of view and told him I was glad he was unhappy, because it meant he cared. Then I asked how he expected to get anything changed if he kept his gripes to himself. I said, 'You're creating a self-fulfilling prophecy. If you tell me your concerns and nothing gets done, then you have every reason to be pessimistic. If you choose not to say anything to anybody, then screw you. Nobody can help you.'

He appreciated my honesty and understood exactly what I was saying. After our lunch, I had a changed person on my hands. But that's not the end of the story. During the course of lunch, he told me that we were fouling up. We were shipping products from our factory in Taiwan to other Asian factories, where we would modify them to fit each country's specific needs. We were then shipping the product to the customers. This was the wrong thing to do, he said, because there were strict quality controls in the Taiwan factory, and by opening the products up and modifying them on site we were potentially compromising that quality.

He went on to say that he had designed a process that would enable us to make the modifications – not just for those countries but for most of the world – right at the factory.

Well, I listened and I realized he was on to something. We implemented his plan, and it led to a profound change in the way we work. Our build-to-order time fell from three months to about 15 days!

Peters (1994: 254)

★ ★ ★ ★ ★

Peters is often less agreeable in the tales within which he occupies the centre stage. Commenting on Peters' narratives, Stewart [2009] (2010: 279) suggests that 'Peters' books are a litany of confrontations with infuriating local phone companies, snooty airlines, and all the other horrifying bureaucratic monsters that populate the nightmares of the modern consumer. He is a permanently dissatisfied customer, the screeching spokesman for the little guy against the machine'. This may be a little strong. Peters, as we have seen, does not spend all of his time complaining and as we shall see he does retain the capacity to secure the affiliation of the reader through humour and through positive exemplars. Nonetheless, Stewart, while perhaps exaggerating the position, is correct to point out that those tales which feature Peters as a central character do, often, focus on his very personal experiences and complaints:

> Looking for a Boboli pizza shell. (They're s-o-o good; does anybody make their own anymore?) Not where they usually are. There's a clerk at hand (from the butcher's counter, next to where the Boboli used to be). 'Could you tell me where the Bololis are?' I ask.
>
> 'They moved 'em,' he replies, then walks away.
>
> Ok, it had been a stressful day. And I'm not that keen on the store. (His is the standard scintillating response.) So … so I pretty much lost it.
>
> They. They … 'They' moved it? Who be they? What be they? What be they? Where be they? Can w-e ask t-h-e-y?
>
> *Peters (1994: 70).*

> On New Year's Day, 1994, I was staying at the Radisson Hotel in Burlington, Vermont, after attending a friend's 50th birthday party. Wanting to catch the last half of the Orange Bowl, I switched the cable TV in my room to the local NBC station. The reception was unwatchable fuzzy. I called the front desk, and the clerk said she'd send up an engineer.
>
> None came.
>
> Early the next afternoon, I wanted to watch another football game on NBC. Turned on the TV. Same trouble.
>
> I called downstairs, and, after I explained the previous night's snafu and its continuation, the desk clerk apologized. Said she'd send an engineer 'right up.' By the time I checked out, two hours later, he hadn't made it to the sixth floor.
>
> *Peters (1994: 105)*

The Circle of Innovation is similarly dominated by Peters and, once again, features a narrow cast-list. Only *Southwest Airlines,* we should note, features more than once in the storyworld of this text. Peters, a late convert it seems to the virtues of this distinctive and dynamic organization (see Freiberg and Freiberg, 1997) offers generous applause:

> Southwest Airlines has the best baggage-handling record around. The best safety record. The best on-time record. The fewest customer complaints.

And it seems to pull it off year after year, invariably ranking at the top of the Department of Transportation's lists of the best.

A buttoned-down, tidy place. I have no doubt. On the other hand, what allows Southwest to keep this extraordinarily tidy company going ... and add spunk to flying for customers ... is the extraordinarily spirited gang of over 20,000 who staff the airline—from flight attendants and pilots to accountants and mechanics.

While doing some interviewing for a PBS show, Service with Soul, we asked Executive Vice President for Customers (Nice title, eh? Have you got one like it!?) Colleen Barrett what Southwest's employment criteria were. Her ready answer: "We look for ... listening, caring, smiling, saying 'thank you,' and being warm."

Peters (1997: 468; parentheses and ellipses in original)

There's a wonderful story told at Southwest about a pilot-applicant. Upon walking into the Dallas headquarters, he as not as friendly as he might have been to the receptionist ... not realizing that the reception- ist had a potentially decisive role in his subsequent hiring. When the company chose not to offer him a job, CEO Herb Kelleher commented, "There are a lot of people who can fly airplanes, not so many with great attitudes."

Peters (1997: 470; ellipses in original)

Re-imagine is again dominated by Tom Peters. Indeed, in the absence of a sup- porting cast the 44 tales that constitute the storyworld of this text amount to a one-man show – albeit as we will see in a later chapter – a one-man show that has become keener (a) to highlight the role of women within and beyond the workplace and (b) the indignities that are routinely visited on what are, we are assured, these dynamos of the economy.

Recently, when an Irish journalist asked me to state my view of the current state of (corporate) play, I replied: 'Twenty years ago we honored those who didn't 'rock the boat.' Ten years ago we started begging everyone to become a 'change agent.' And, now, in the midst of full-blown madness, I'm asking ... begging ... 'everyone' to become no less than ... patently disrespectful.'

I think he thought I was nuts. But, then, these are kind of nuts-y times.

Peters (2003: 328)

A very large corporation once brought me in to introduce its leadership team to –'radical' points of view. So I rolled out the old projector and re- galed members of the team with a scintillating PowerPoint presentation, right?

No!

Instead, I introduced them to ... WEIRD. They wanted to 'get serious about branding.' So I introduced them to the best branding freaks I know: Jean-Marie Dru of TBWA/Chiat/Day. Mickey Drexler, formerly of Gap. Rich Teerlink of Harley-Davidson. And so on.

For every opportunity, there is ... Someone(s) Weird.

Weird rules. (In weird times.) (Duh.)

Peters (2003: 329; ellipses and emphasis in original)

The Little BIG Things and *The Excellence Dividend* signal, as we have seen, a reversal in the decline of Peters' storytelling that has been evident since the peak of 1985. That said it is also the case that Peters continues to dominate the storyworlds of both of these texts. Indeed, he features prominently in no fewer than 63 (of the 114) tales rendered by *The Little BIG Things* and in 54 (of the 105) tales rendered by *The Excellence Dividend*. Both of these texts we should note are also heavy on nostalgia. Characters from the 1970s and 1980s – McKinsey and Bob Waterman for example – and Peters' own extended family feature prominently in these texts. Indeed, these works often simply reproduce tales that will be familiar to any reader who has continued to follow the work of Peters.

Only *Starbucks* features more than once in the storyworld of *The Little BIG Things*. A similar situation prevails in *The Excellence Dividend* where only *Commerce Bank* (three tales) *IBM* and *Southwest Airlines* (two tales apiece) merit more than a passing glance.

> My local Starbucks stayed open a few minutes late – and the barista fetched something he had already put away - to fill my order.
>
> When I handed the barista at my *other* local Starbucks my thermos, she filled it up without question, even though at the time it was a non-standard order (I think they undercharged me – a two large-cups price for what doubtless was three large cups in quantity. On and they thoroughly...**washed the thermos before filling it, without my asking or even imagining!**)

Peters (2010: 389; emphasis and ellipses in original)

A tale is told about the fabled IBM founding chairman Thomas Watson:

> **"Mr. Watson, how long does it take to achieve excellence?"**
>
> **Watson: "One minute. You make up your mind to never again consciously do something that is less than excellent."**

Peters (2018: 45; emphasis in original)

Take Southwest Airlines. It remains a low-price airline with a high-value "people culture" that delivers top-rated customer service and experiences. It begins from pilots and mechanics to flight attendants with a distinctive hiring approach. Per former Southwest president Colleen Barrett:

> **We look for...listening, caring, smiling, saying "Thank you," being warm.**

Is Barrett's list for public consumption? Or is it real?

An example: I'm about to board a Southwest flight from Albany, New York, to Baltimore. The plane is ready for boarding. As is typical, three or four wheelchairs are lined up at the gate. The crew makes their appearance, obviously rushing from a flight that arrived late, and heads for the jetway. The pilot stops, turns to the older woman in the first wheelchair in the line, and says, *"May I help you down the jetway?"*

She says, "Thank you, yes."

Off she goes with the pilot conveying her to the aircraft.

I've chalked up about ten thousand flights, yet this experience was a first. (I actually think I gasped: airlines are frequently entry #1 on the "customer unfriendly" lists.)

I contend that the pilot's courtesy – and courtesy while under pressure to boot – was no accident, that in fact it was a direct by-product of "We look for listening, caring, smiling, saying 'Thank you,' being warm."

Peters (2018: 127; emphasis and ellipses in original)

Perhaps Peters should have shared this thought with Mayor Schaefer!

Concluding comments

This chapter has offered further reflections on the storytelling practices that Peters has employed to advance and to substantiate the excellence project. Noting that *In Search of Excellence* has been identified and critiqued as a form of 'bad science' I have, nonetheless, rejected the suggestion that this text may be dismissed because it is dominated by a few case examples that are within the context of the larger narrative, statistically unrepresentative. Instead I have suggested that we should take *In Search of Excellence* seriously for what it, in truth, represents. To this end I have examined the storyworld of this text (and that of the larger excellence project) to understand just what it is that Peters would project as (a) the core tasks of management and (b) the core challenges of business. To illustrate the manner in which Peters has represented these concerns throughout the life of the excellence project I have reproduced a range of stories which in reflecting the broad dimensions of Peters' storyworld offer an account that is, I believe, reliably representative of his core concerns.

Peters' storyworld, of course, draws on a variety of organizational examples and settings, but is, I have argued, built on three (sometimes overlapping) core tropes:

- The independent business-person who takes care to offer a service experience that is truly remarkable.
- The leader who treats employees like customers so that they, in turn, will do whatever it takes to delight the customer.
- The empowered employee moved to deliver small commercial miracles.

While offering concrete examples of these tropes I have also charted Peters' transition from narrator to hero. Peters, as I have shown, has changed from the guide on the side of the excellence project to become instead its hero – the sage on the stage with all the answers necessary for future change and prosperity. Viewed as a continuation of the design stories that Peters has offered in the context of the work of *Ingersoll-Rand* this transition from narrator to hero *could* be read, positively as signalling Peters' growing and very personal impatience with poor service and with the shoddy design practices that place employees at risk and which cause genuine harm. Yet this may be a kindness too far. Indeed, we might suggest that those tales that place Peters, front-and-centre, are dominated by rants and tirades concerning the small inconveniences and the tiny indignities that he has experienced, personally, in his daily life. In this respect, Peters' transition to the hero of his storyworld signals not so much his concern for the rank-and-file as his growing distance from the cut and thrust of contemporary management practice. Furthermore, this shift from narrator to hero raises questions as to the efficacy of Peters' storytelling practices.

John Steinbeck [1959] (1990) captures this dynamic rather well. During Second World War John Steinbeck worked as a war correspondent in the European theatre of operations. He was it seems to me, a rather problematic correspondent insofar as he was just a little too keen to become personally involved in combat. This proclivity makes Steinbeck's war-time experience unusual.

The nature of modern warfare dictates that most soldiers work some way behind the frontline and consequently see very little 'action' because front-line combatants depend on the existence of a huge logistical operation that is designed around the need to feed, house, arm, transport, pay and, where necessary, nurse the soldier sent to 'the front'. Most of those who wear uniforms therefore tend to be involved in driving, cooking, cleaning and building rather than shooting.[1] In contrast, however, war correspondents tend always to be 'in the thick of it' and tend always to be 'at the front' (even if most do not fight) because their editors demand good stories *and* 'good stories' tend to be defined as being 'where the fighting is'. Yet despite the fact that Steinbeck had 'been where the action is' and despite the fact that he had actively participated in night raids on the enemy he chose not to place himself within his text. Introducing an edited collection of his war reporting Steinbeck ([1959], 1990: 7–8) explains this narrative choice and in so doing offers us very clear guidance on the art of the managerial storyteller. He confides:

> All of us developed our coy little tricks with copy. Reading these old pieces I recognize one of mine. I never admitted having seen anything myself. In describing a scene I invariably put it in the mouth of someone else…It was the style to indicate that you were afraid all the time. I guess I was really afraid, but the style was there too. I think this was also designed to prove how brave the soldiers were. And the stories were just exactly as brave and as cowardly as anyone else.

Steinbeck, I believe, offers two rather important lessons here. First he reminds us that as we attempt to change how people think, feel and act we are seldom usefully cast as 'the heroes'. It is, he reminds us, easier to wax lyrical on the endeavours of others in a manner that the audience will find agreeable, and so, edifying! Second Steinbeck reminds us that stories are not reports. Indeed, he makes it clear that, as a 'war reporter' he was not a simple chronicler of events. Instead it is apparent that Steinbeck regarded himself as a storyteller, and so, felt able – within practical and ethical limits – to change and to embellish events to produce a desired outcome or effect.

Looking in detail at the tales used to project the excellence project I suggest that Peters tends to fail in his endeavours (a) when he places himself as hero (especially one wronged by shoddy service) and (b) when he fails to think through the characteristics of those whom he would have us believe represent exemplars of excellence. Indeed, the presence of exemplary tales, which appear to condone threats and bullying suggests to me that the culture of excellence and, indeed, the culture of US business continues to exhibit the core dysfunctions that were familiar to (and lamented by) Pascale and Athos [1981] (1986).

In our next chapters we will seek out, as it were, the edges of Peters' narrative projections. Indeed, I will set out to bump your shins against these, as yet, hidden dangers so that together we might reflect on (a) the authenticity of Peters' preferred worldview and (b) the position of women workers in the excellence project.

Notes

1 Gibbs (1967: 71) while reflecting on the haphazard nature of Britain's military planning in 1940 captures the need for a complex logistical operation dedicated to support the front-line but uses this as an opportunity for humour:
   'Didn't they teach you at school that every man in the line wants at least three behind the line?'
   'Doing what?'
   'Oh' – said the conducting officer vaguely, 'Having lunch, dashing about on motor bicycles, telephoning, being a general, filling up forms, cutting hair, walking about with stretchers, sorting letters, pushing guns about, putting washers on taps, and doing all the thousand and one jobs that chaps do do.'

7

HIERARCHY AND ANXIETY IN MANAGEMENT STORIES

Introduction

This chapter offers further reflections on the storyworld of Tom Peters and on the manner in which the excellence project represents its core concerns. In an earlier chapter we highlighted the divisions between sensegiving and sensemaking perspectives on storytelling. Building on these reflections we have argued that while the excellence project calls on stories to substantiate its core concerns, it proceeds from a cognitivist base and so fails to commit to narratology. Building on a critical appreciation of narratology we have argued that while excellence project is plainly a moral project, it is nonetheless a projection that may be challenged by more local forms of sensemaking, which in welling up from within the organization offer a challenge to the top-down, epic narratives that are preferred by Peters. In short we have suggested that Peters' storytelling often lacks an authentic connection to the lived experience of social organization. This chapter pursues this intuition. It will demonstrate that Tom Peters' storyworld, too often, fails to communicate an appreciation of the insecurities of the modern workplace and of the anxieties that this context precipitates. Accordingly this chapter will offer a review of the tales that frame the excellence project, which is refracted through the lens offered by Martin et al. (1983). To this end our chapter is structured as follows: We begin, as we must, with an account of the analysis of organizational storytelling developed by Martin and her colleagues. Here we will consider 'the uniqueness paradox' in organizational storytelling and the schema, which Martin and her colleagues have developed to examine and to account for this paradox. Contrasting Peters' storytelling, with the practices revealed by Martin et al. (1983), I will show that the storyworld of the excellence project is in some sense bogus because it fails to recognise, and so cannot address, the tensions and anxieties associated with paid employment.

DOI: 10.4324/9781003188940-8

The uniqueness paradox

Martin et al. (1983) observe that most organizational cultures make a claim to
uniqueness and would seek to substantiate this by reference to cultural manifestations such as shared stories. Yet the authors point out that these organizational
stories; these artefacts of cultural distinctiveness 'exhibit a remarkable similarity
in content and structure' (439). Consequently, they advise, there exists a 'uniqueness paradox' (439) in the sense that *a culture's claim to uniqueness is expressed through
cultural manifestations that are not in fact unique*' (439; original emphasis).

Examining these common organizational stories as cultural manifestations, as
vital elements of our organized existence, Martin et al. argue that 'seven stories
that make tacit claims to uniqueness ... occur, in virtually identical form, in a
wide variety of organizations' (439). To aid the analysis of these projections, the
authors identify the commonly encountered stories as a series of questions. These
questions, as we shall see, highlight core anxieties in relation to the experience
of work and in so doing narrate the experience of organization 'from below':

1   Do senior organizational members abide by the rules that they have set
    down?
2   Is the big boss human?
3   Is the organization meritocratic?
4   Will I get fired?
5   Will the organization assist me to relocate?
6   How does the organization deal with mistakes?
7   How does the organization deal with obstacles?

Commenting on the presence and persistence of these common organizational story-forms, Martin et al. concede that while these seven questions are
not exhaustive of narrative possibilities, the stories they spawn are, nonetheless,
widespread and enduring within organizational contexts because they 'express
tensions that arise from a conflict between organizational exigencies and the
values of employees, which are, in turn, reflective of the values of the larger
society' (447). Thus, Martin et al. suggest that the narratives which are developed as responses to the seven questions outlined above are, in fact, related to
concerns which organizational members have with respect to equality, security
and control.

The authors argue that story-themes one, two and three (above) address concerns related to equality and inequality at work while story-types four, five and
six relate to tensions formed around a security-insecurity duality. Story-type
seven, they advise, is different insofar as this reflects concerns that arise with
respect to control and autonomy in this context.

Figure 7.1 reflects our attempt to allocate Peters' tales of business excellence
to one of the seven story themes outlined by Martin et al. (1983). There is, we
should acknowledge, a very clear potential for overlap between these story-forms.

In Search of Excellence Story Count (%)	A Passion for Excellence	Thriving on Chaos	Liberation Management	Tom Peters Seminar	The Pursuit of Wow	The Circle of Innovation	Re-imagine	Little BIG Things	Excellence Dividend
Type 1	71 (52)	38 (23)	38 (33)	40 (35)	14 (34)	23 (40)	22 (58)	4 (9)	4 (3)	0 (0)
Type 2	29 (21)	103 (62)	66 (56)	43 (38)	15 (37)	23 (40)	8 (21)	24 (55)	44 (39)	32 (30)
Type 3	0 (0)	0 (0)	0 (0)	3 (3)	0 (0)	0 (0)	0 (0)	0 (0)	1 (1)	0 (0)
Type 4	1 (1)	0 (0)	0 (0)	1 (1)	0 (0)	0 (0)	0 (0)	0 (0)	0 (0)	0 (0)
Type 5	0 (0)	0 (0)	0 (0)	0 (0)	0 (0)	0 (0)	0 (0)	0 (0)	0 (0)	0 (0)
Type 6	3 (2)	0 (0)	2 (2)	0 (0)	0 (0)	0 (0)	0 (0)	1 (2)	2 (2)	0 (0)
Type 7	10 (7)	24 (14)	11 (9)	26 (23)	12 (29)	11 (19)	5 (13)	15 (34)	58 (51)	70 (67)
N/C	23 (17)	0 (0)	0 (0)	1 (1)	0 (0)	0 (0)	3 (8)	0 (0)	5 (4)	3 (3)

FIGURE 7.1 An analysis of Tom Peters' storywork in the context of Martin et al.'s (1983) account of recurrent organizational stories.

Yet, despite this potential for overlap, it proved relatively easy to assign Peters' tales to one of the seven 'scriptal types' outlined by Martin et al. It was, for example, generally easy to distinguish those stories that dealt, centrally, with the immediate fear of dismissal (type four) from those tales that chose to highlight the essential decency and humanity of a senior figure (type two).

As an illustration of this point it may be useful to observe that within *Liberation Management* Peters (1992: 578) offers a tale that deals with a Research Assistant who accidentally breaks a piece of expensive equipment and is forgiven. This tale, we should acknowledge, might have been classified as one dealing with the essential humanity (or otherwise) of the boss (type two) and might, I accept, have been classified as a tale dealing with the organization's posture towards honest mistakes (type six) or to 'obstacles' to progress (type seven). Given this potential fluidity, it will be worth taking a moment to examine these alternative scriptal types before offering an explanation of the manner in which I have assigned the tale of our unfortunate Research Assistant.

★ ★ ★ ★ ★

In *A Passion for Excellence,* Peters and Austin (1985) offer numerous tales that testify to the essential humanity of those who steward their excellent organizations. Since these tales, which invite us to accept that the excellent organizations are invariably led by fine, noble and upstanding specimens of humanity have featured heavily throughout this book I offer but one (further) example of this story-form as an illustration of a 'type two story'. In the tale reproduced below we encounter Gavin Herbert – that rare thing (it seems) – a boss with ears as well as a mouth who regards managing as a hands-on form of work:

> 'Naïve listening' is a term we ran across when talking with the chairman of Allergan, a highly profitable Irvine, California, subsidiary of SmithKline Beckman. About $100 million of the company's $200 million in revenues comes from a product family of ointments and the like aimed at helping contact-lens users. Chairman Gavin Herbert described the breakthrough

that led to development of the product: 'I've repeatedly argued that reading the data and talking to the ophthalmologists is not enough. In the pharmaceutical industry we're overwhelmed by data. All the prescription information comes in by the bushel, rapidly and neatly summarized. We have more than you need. But we miss the basic customer. I've always insisted that our people stay in touch with the users, the patients. In the process of talking with contact-lens wearers, we kept coming across, in one form or another, the same problem: 'itchy-scratchy eyes.' Now you know and I know that no ophthalmologist, after twenty years of professional training, is going to write down as his diagnosis 'itchy-scratchy eyes.' It's just not professional language. Yet it was the problem. We started working on coming up with something to deal with the itchy-scratchy eyes. That, plain and simple, was the genesis of this immensely successful product line.' (We find it interesting that the company was founded by the current chairman's father, a practising pharmacist. The family, in fact, lived right over the pharmacy, and the current chairman put in his time behind the computer too. Time and again we discover that the hands–on companies are led by people who got their start in hands–on jobs.)

Peters and Austin (1985: 13; parentheses in original)

The Little BIG Things (Peters, 2010) reproduces many examples of what might be termed 'type six stories' – tales that offer guidance on the manner in which 'mistakes' should be addressed. I will offer but two examples as illustrations. The first of these comes from Max Kraus:

> ... some years ago when I was running Electro-Nite Company. We sold some equipment to a Chinese steel mill that would help to improve their steel quality. This was just after the opening of trade with China, an we had to plow through massive red tape with the U.S. government, get a letter of credit, etc. But we finally made the shipment; it went by air and we waited to hear if all was well.
>
> Unfortunately the next word, in those days by teletype, was that it did not work. As a believer in 'walking around' sales as well as management and also intrigued by the possibility of a trip to China, I sent a reply saying that we guaranteed our equipment and that if they would provide a visa for me and an engineer we would come to see the problem. In those days visas were completely non-existent, but within twenty-four hours we had a reply accepting our offer. Again, paperwork took a couple of weeks, but off to China we went.
>
> We were met at the Beijing airport, escorted to our hotel, and offered a car, guide and interpreter for three days to see the Wall, Summer Palace etc. – and then flown to Wuhan. The steel mill was massive, with over 100,000 workers, and of course a crowd gathered to see us work on the equipment. Much to my dismay and embarrassment, the problem turned

out to be two long screws that were causing a short circuit. I removed the screws and told the group that while I was embarrassed, I hoped that I had demonstrated our commitment to service and satisfaction.

Peters (2010: 140–141)

The second example is perhaps less positive and certainly less edifying. Indeed, as we shall see this is a tale that allows Peters to rant against what Perrow (1979) would call 'normal accidents'. This story it is worth noting also seems to suggest that the excellence project remains an endeavour that, even today, has only a partial take-up across the United States:

> My wife recently waited five hours in an ER with a broken ankle – she described the pain as "second only to labor." But she isn't even pissed off – it's what happened to all her friends, it's "what you expect". As I write I've been to a "Top 10" hospital three times in the last ten days for tests. No, I was not left for hours upon more hours on a gurney in a hallway as Susan was. Nonetheless, there was a major error, two errors in one case, associated with each visit. One snafu could have had dangerous consequences for my beloved pacemaker. Yup, they batted a thousand. Three-for-three, an error **100%** of the time.
>
> *(Peters, 2010: 210–211 emphasis in original)*

The Excellence Dividend (Peters, 2018) is a text focused on 'implementation' and is consequently rich in those story-types that deal with organizational obstacles (type seven tales). I will offer but two tales as illustrations. The first of these tales concerns Linda Kaplan Thaler the founder of the *Kaplan Thaler Advertising Agency*. This tale, as we shall see, offers advice on the necessary ingredients for business success, which contrary to most business school teaching suggests that the goals associated with long-term strategic planning might be considered to be an obstacle!

> Linda said the reason her agency grew so fast was because "We never concentrated one minute on the future. We always focused on what we can do today. I always tell people don't spend one second thinking about a vision, forget about it. Don't dream your way to success…We never thought about becoming too big or hugely successful, we just did the best we could every day.
>
> *Peters (2018: 45; ellipses in original)*

Our second example of a tale that deals directly with 'obstacles' features Tom Peters (reporting good customer service) and a local business, whose employees simply would not allow themselves to be bested by an unexpected (and uninvited) obstacle.

> My grand-daughter, age four at the time, came with her parents to visit us on the South Coast of Massachusetts. We are about five minutes from

Buzzards Bay. Among other things, I got Zoe a cute dragon float to play with at the beach. When it came time to inflate it I was out of luck. The toy had a weird valve, and my bike pump wouldn't fit. I decided to try the local service station, about ten miles away. Well their air hose coupling device wouldn't work either. It's a longish story, but the short version is that a station mechanic I knew jury-rigged a fitting, but the job wasn't easy. At one point there were no fewer than three of them working to inflate Zoe's dragon float. Eventually the job was done, and back I went to the beach.

I took a picture of the three guys at work on Zoe's float. Among other things, I put the picture on a slide and used it in a speech to car dealers. Also, just a little bit later we had a car problem and should have taken our vehicle to the dealership. Instead we took it to that local service station for what amounted to an $800 job.

Peters (2018: 276)

Returning now to our hapless Research Assistant, it is worth reiterating that the tale reproduced below, *might* have been classified as an organizational example of the management of 'mistakes' and/or 'obstacles'. And it *might* have been classified as a response to the question: Is the big boss human? Yet since the tale in question takes the fear of dismissal as the key point of focus (and anxiety) I have chosen to classify it as, that rare thing within our corpus of Peters' storytelling, a 'type four' tale, which responds to the question: Will I get fired?

I was helping another graduate student, Dennis Smith, mount a large photomultiplier tube in the Cerenkov detector, and I dropped it. It imploded just like a TV picture tube, with a loud and sickening crash. I had just destroyed $15,000 worth of hardware. Dennis consoled me. It could happen to anybody, he said. I thought it might be the end of my career. Fifteen thousand dollars was twice what I earned in a year as a research assistant. Some of the money would be recovered by firing me.

A short time later I saw … Alvarez, and confessed what had happened. 'Grrrrrreat …!' he roared, and put out his hand as if to congratulate me. He shook my hand vigorously, but I protested. 'Welcome to the club,' he continued. 'Now I know you're becoming an experimental physicist.' To become a real member of the Mafia, you have to murder someone. To become an experimental physicist, Alvarez seemed to feel, you had to destroy some expensive equipment. It was a rite of passage. 'Don't do anything differently,' he advised. 'Keep it up.'

Peters (1992: 578; ellipses in original)

★ ★ ★ ★ ★

Unclassified tales

It is important to observe that a minority of Peters' tales (see Figure 7.1) – 35 in total or 4% of the 932 tales that constitute our corpus – could not be accommodated within the Martin schema. This outcome was, of course, anticipated. Martin and her colleagues, after all, do not pretend that their seven story types are, in any sense, comprehensive or exhaustive of narrative possibilities either within or beyond the workplace. What was unexpected was that the majority of these unclassified tales (66%) were to be found in just one publication, *In Search of Excellence*. The presence and preponderance of these unclassified tales within *In Search of Excellence*, is I suggest significant for at least a couple of reasons. First, the presence and predominance of these tales within *In Search of Excellence* might be taken as demonstrating the extent to which Peters and Waterman felt obliged to justify the development of a business narrative that was so firmly rooted in and dependent on stories. Thus, a number of the tales, unclassified within what I have termed the Martin schema do not address the tensions and anxieties offered by Martin et al., but are instead offered as testimonials to the organizing potential of stories. A tale reproduced in an earlier chapter offers an illustration of this process and is therefore worthy of further reproduction:

> As we worked on research of our excellent companies, we were struck by the dominant use of story, slogan and legend as people tried to explain the characteristics of their own great institutions. All the companies we interviewed, from Boeing to McDonald's were quite simply rich tapestries of anecdote, myth and fairy tale. And we do mean fairy tale. The vast majority of people who tell stories about TJ Watson of IBM have never met the man or had direct experience of the original more mundane reality. Two HP engineers regaled us with an hour's worth of "Bill and Dave" (Hewlett and Packard) stories. We were subsequently astonished to find that neither had seen, let alone talked to, the founders.
>
> *Peters and Waterman (1982: 75; parentheses in original)*

Second, the discovery that the majority of unclassified tales are to be found within *In Search of Excellence* makes space for the suggestion that the authors struggled, initially at least, to weave sensegiving tales of management endeavour into the core narrative of the excellence project. Indeed, a proportion of the tales unclassified within the Martin schema signal but fail, properly, to precipitate the persistent organizational dualities identified by Martin et al. (1983). For example Peters and Waterman offer a tale that appears to demonstrate some awareness of the tensions that arise around the autonomy-control duality and yet this narrative projection fails to offer, either, orientation or animation to the reader (see Collins, 2018) because, as rendered, it declines to provide concrete examples of the ways in which the aspirant business leader might manage this tension to produce business excellence:

> Adult subjects were given some complex tasks to solve and a proofreading chore. In the background was a loud, randomly occurring distracting note; to be specific it was "a combination of two people speaking Spanish, one speaking Armenian, a mimeograph machine running, a desk calculator, and a typewriter, and street noise – producing a composite nondistinguishable roar". The subjects were split into two groups. Individuals in one set were just told to work at the task. Individuals in the other were provided with a button to turn off the noise, "a modern analog of control – the off switch". The group with the off switch solved five times the number of puzzles as their cohorts and made but a tiny fraction of the number of proofreading errors. Now for the kicker: "... none of the subjects in the off switch group ever used the switch. The mere knowledge that one can exert control made the difference".
>
> *Peters and Waterman (1982: xxiii)*

Similarly Peters and Waterman reproduce a tale which, while noting a link between perception and action (Peters and Waterman, 1982: 74) misfires as a sensegiving device because it fails to signal what managers might actually do to reshape the perceptions, and so, the actions of their subordinates within this workplace context.

> what's called 'foot-in-the-door research' demonstrates the importance of incrementally acting our way into major commitment. For instance, in one experiment, in Palo Alto, California, most subjects who initially agreed to put a tiny sign in their front window supporting a cause (traffic safety) subsequently agreed to display a billboard in their front yard, which required letting outsiders dig sizable holes in the lawn. On the other hand, those not asked to take the first small step turned down the larger one in ninety-five cases out of a hundred.

The predominance of these unclassified (and misfiring) tales within *In Search of Excellence* suggests that, at the birth of the excellence project, Peters and Waterman were – in their terms – still acting themselves into the form of thinking, which would allow stories to be used, not as examples of organizational life, but as sensegiving exemplars for a new form of organized existence.

Commenting on the birth pangs of the excellence project, Hyatt (1999) provides support for this speculation. He notes that the earliest iterations of the excellence project – conveyed in the form of a lengthy presentation to McKinsey's clients – actually employed a rather orthodox (expositional) academic narrative, which left most audiences cold. Indeed, Hyatt suggests that the excellence project only began to acquire a more receptive audience when stories and more anecdotal forms of analysis were given their, now familiar, place within the narrative. Hyatt (1999), therefore, provides support to those like Maidique (1983) and McConkie and Bass (1986) who have asserted that the excellence project is at root, a moral-political endeavour, which deploys and depends on the arts of the storyteller to achieve its effects. And yet Hyatt's intervention reminds us that the narrative approach, which we now regard as central to 'popular management', remained a 'work in progress' even as *In Search of Excellence* went to press.

Classified tales

The tales classified in our catalogue are, as we shall see, significant both for what they say and for what they fail to speak of. Yet we must concede that in seeking to classify Peters' tales within the framework outlined by Martin et al., I have been obliged to make minor adjustments to the schema.

In Martin et al.'s (1983) analysis, story type 1 reflects the question: *Do senior organizational members abide by the rules that they have set down?* and is said to reflect a duality focused on equality-inequality. In Peters' storytelling, however, questions in relation to leaders and rules surface within a dynamic that is more focused on 'control' and on the nature of managerial working that has been fostered within the excellent organizations. Figure 7.2 modifies the catalogue of Peters' storytelling to acknowledge the distinctive manner in which the excellence project construes managerial work and, in so doing, seeks to document the orientations that shape the excellence project.

Control

Martin et al. (1983) suggest that stories of managerial control arise and are commonly relayed within organizations as employees attempt to manage the organization's disciplinary demands in the context of their own desire for autonomy.

	Duality	In Search of Excellence Story Count (%)	A Passion for Excellence	Thriving on Chaos	Liberation Management	Tom Peters Seminar	The Pursuit of Wow	The Circle of Innovation	Re-imagine	Little BIG Things	Excellence Dividend
Type 2	Equality-Inequality	29 (21)	103 (62)	66 (56)	43 (38)	15 (37)	23 (40)	8 (21)	24 (55)	44 (39)	32 (30)
Type 3	Equality-Inequality	0 (0)	0 (0)	0 (0)	3 (3)	0 (0)	0 (0)	0 (0)	0 (0)	1 (1)	0 (0)
Type 4	Security-Insecurity	1 (1)	0 (0)	0 (0)	1 (1)	0 (0)	0 (0)	0 (0)	0 (0)	0 (0)	0 (0)
Type 5	Security-Insecurity	0 (0)	0 (0)	0 (0)	0 (0)	0 (0)	0 (0)	0 (0)	0 (0)	0 (0)	0 (0)
Type 6	Security-Insecurity	3 (2)	0 (0)	2 (2)	0 (0)	0 (0)	0 (0)	0 (0)	1 (2)	2 (2)	1 (2)
Type 7	Control	10 (7)	24 (14)	11 (9)	26 (23)	12 (29)	11 (19)	5 (13)	15 (34)	58 (51)	70 (67)
Type 1	Control	71 (52)	38 (23)	38 (33)	40 (35)	14 (34)	23 (40)	22 (58)	4 (9)	4 (3)	0 (0)
N/C	---	23 (17)	0 (0)	0 (0)	1 (1)	0 (0)	0 (0)	3 (8%)	0 (0)	5 (4)	3 (3)

FIGURE 7.2   An analysis of the organizational dualities expressed by Tom Peters' stories.

Our analysis of Peters' storytelling practices, however, suggests that the architect of the excellence project actually manages this duality by collapsing it! In Peters' sensegiving tales, therefore, we are assured that no one need forfeit their autonomy at work. Indeed, we are given to understand that for excellent companies there is no necessary trade-off between autonomy and control in the workplace. The anxiety that is characteristic of Martin et al.'s storyworld is, therefore, absent from these tales of the technology of management because the excellent organizations, we are assured, have demonstrated (to Peters' satisfaction at least) that the conventions of command and control have been rendered redundant by social, by market and by technological developments that demand empowerment. Gerald Mitchell is presented as a role model for managers within this context:

> During our first round of interviews we could "feel it". The language used in talking about people was different. The expectation of regular contributions was different. The love of the product and customers was palpable. And we felt different ourselves, walking around an HP or 3M facility watching groups at work and play, from the way we had in most of the more bureaucratic institutions we have had experience with. It was watching busy bands of engineers, salesmen and manufacturers casually hammering out problems in a conference room in St. Paul in February; even a customer was there. It was seeing an HP division manager's office ($100 million unit), tiny, wall-less on the factory floor, shared with a secretary. It was seeing Dana's new chairman, Gerald Mitchell, bearhugging a colleague in the hall after lunch in the Toledo headquarters. It was very far removed from silent board rooms marked by dim lights, somber presentations, rows of staffers lined up along the walls with calculators glowing, and the endless click of the slide projector as analysis after analysis lit up the screen.
>
> *Peters and Waterman (1982: 16)*

Similar praise is offered for Rene McPherson. Although it is worth noting that Peters cannot resist the opportunity, here, to demonstrate that the conduct of managers such as Gerald Mitchell and Rene McPherson actually highlight the manifest failings of the US Business School curriculum:

> When Dana's Rene McPherson, who made his mark with sparkling accomplishment in that most difficult of areas, productivity in a slow-moving, unionized industry, became dean of the Stanford Graduate School of Business, one of our colleagues, who had just become associate dean, anxiously took us aside. "We've got to talk", he insisted. "I've just had my first long meeting with Rene. He talked to me about his Dana experience. Do you know that not one thing he did there is even mentioned in the MBA curriculum?".
>
> *Peters and Waterman (1982: 36).*

Equality

The equality-inequality duality is, similarly, raised and resolved – again to Peters' satisfaction. The response to the question: *Is the big boss human?* is for the excellent organizations at least, plainly and straightforwardly, *yes.*

> …we visited Northrop, where we were doing some consulting, and where our friend Marv Elkin runs the purchasing organization. He's done a remarkable job of changing vendor-producer relationships for the better in the course of the past two or three years. We sat down to chat with him about it a bit, and mentioned Lord Sieff's comment about visits. Now, Marv's an animated fellow, and he leaped up halfway through our description: 'That's it! That's it!' Yes, it was. It turned out to be exactly what Marv had been doing. He stated that over the past two years, in a program that departed remarkably from the company's previous adversarial relationship with vendors, he had visited over 150 suppliers. Equally important, his visits weren't thinly disguised opportunities to take whacks at the suppliers. They were open-ended, with no set agenda. He asked them to make a presentation on their company's history, their strategy, their work force, their quality programs: 'It was just a chance to get acquainted, to learn about them, to show interest (which I desperately had) in them as a whole.' It's a program that he's kept up, and gotten others of his own people thoroughly involved in as well. It's been a long first step toward reversing decades of adversarial and negative relationships, where the only senior contact came in the heat of battle and in responses to pressing problems. And it came none too soon, because the quality programs that Northrop is having shoved down its throat by the Air Force are now requiring Marv to turn up the heat on his vendors. The groundwork, however, has been clearly - and expensively (in terms of time) – laid by his visits. Now all of them are in a position to work together.
>
> *Peters and Austin (1985: 21; parentheses in original)*

The response to the question: *Is the organization meritocratic?* is perhaps, more muted insofar as few stories are devoted to this issue. Yet we might counter that this minimization actually signals Peters' taken-for-granted assumption that, in a business context shaped by hyper-competition and by the whim of sovereign consumers, modern organizations simply cannot afford to be anything other than meritocratic.

The tale reproduced below is taken from *Liberation Management* (Peters, 1992: 162 parentheses in original) and offers a very clear confirmation of this assertion:

> A career at Imagination means anything but climbing a ladder. Horizontal movement is the norm, fluidity the key. 'One of our best video guys came out board as a bookkeeper,' Shepherd explained. 'Gary [Withers] came

across him one night working on his own in the editing suit. The fellow was petrified that he'd been caught. But Gary said, 'Let me see what you're up to.' The next day Gary told the finance head that the bookkeeper was now working on video.'

Security

Peters' treatment of the security-insecurity duality contrasts starkly with the stories rendered by Martin et al. (1983). Indeed, Peters' scant treatment of this dynamic suggests that the new technology of management – embodied in Gerald Mitchell's post-prandial embrace – might be viewed as a violation.

Martin et al. (1983) argue that, for workers, the threat of dismissal is a reasonable fear, and so, a recurrent storytelling theme. Yet Peters' storyworld pays little mind to such anxieties. In a corpus of more than 900 stories there are just 11 tales that deal with (in)security. Nine of these tales reflect story-type six, and so, deal with the manner in which organizations deal with 'mistakes' whereas just two of these tales of (in)security deal with the threat of dismissal. We have already reproduced one of these stories in our initial reflections on classification. The remaining tale, reproduced below, is interesting insofar as it offers a direct contrast to the account developed by Martin et al. (1983). Thus, where the storyworld of Martin and her colleagues suggests that tales of dismissal arise in the context of a reasonable and persistent anxiety about the capricious nature of social organization (and managerial conduct), the storyworld of the excellence project seems to suggest that summary termination, deservedly awaits those who confine themselves to their contractual obligations:

> … one of us remembers Cat [the manufacturer of construction equipment] from our days ordering construction equipment for the Navy in Vietnam. We would go to almost any ends, stretching the procurement regulations to the limit, to specify the always more expensive Cat equipment. We had to, for we knew our field commanders would string us up if we didn't find a way to get them Cat. When you're airlifting bulldozers into unfriendly territory for the purpose of building short airstrips behind enemy lines, you want machinery that works – all the time.
>
> *Peters and Waterman (1982: 171–172)*

Questions related to the management of relocation (story type 5) and the consequent, need to ease such transitions are, entirely, absent from Peters' storyworld. This finding is particularly revealing for it suggests that issues associated with economic dislocation and organizational insecurity – concerns which, for workers within the 'gig economy', retained on 'zero hours contracts' are very real and persistent – are simply irrelevant.

Peters' cavalier treatment of this issue is, no doubt, a reflection of his own – chaotic and peripatetic – employment experiences with McKinsey and Co.

(Crainer, 1997) and his preference for the 'professional service firm' as a template for all forms of modern organization (Peters, 2003). The concept of the professional service firm is, however, disturbingly amorphous and ambiguous in Peters' work, and so, offers a very limited template for policy. For Peters, it seems, professional service firms are united by a preference for 'project working' and a disdain for key customs and practices that are labelled as 'bureaucracy'. Yet while the precise conceptualization of the professional service firm remains vague the changes in working practices associated with this new form are plain enough. Thus, Peters, himself, informs us that professional service firms cannot promise employees a traditional career. Instead they promise to provide a stream of new challenges and rewarding experiences that will, we are assured, enhance future employability within a project working environment (Peters, 2003).

Boltanski and Chiapello (2007) have sought to intrude on the cult of anti-bureaucracy that has shaped this account of the professional service firm. They argue that corporate attempts to redefine 'the career' in terms of employability represent nothing less than the crystallization of a new spirit of capitalism. However, they argue that this new spirited existence short-changes employees since it obliges workers to trade the security that is associated with a career and with an occupational pension for the insubstantial *promise* of autonomy.

Commenting on the 'scissors crisis' which has intensified working practices while reducing security both in employment and in retirement, Bunting (2005) argues that 'popular management' cheats its subjects. Indeed, she scoffs at the suggestion that employees should refashion their career security in an age of employability by converting themselves into 'brands'. Observing that most, heavily bank-rolled branding efforts are outright failures (*new Coke anyone?*), Bunting invites us to consider the extent to which employees might actually brand their activities in any lasting or meaningful sense!

Noting the volatility of modern employment practices and the reduction in social reciprocity which popular management has sought to excuse, therefore, Bunting is downcast. She argues that guru theory has constructed the foundations for a world of work staffed by 'willing slaves' who fail to comprehend the extent to which their autonomous working practices are, in truth, driven by managerial demands and – more insidiously – by unvoiced but wholly unreasonable expectations.

Bunting is, of course, correct to highlight the manner in which the excellence project and popular management more generally offer a promise that is self-serving, and singularly lacking in reciprocity. Yet Mitchell's (1985) analysis of business excellence suggests that Bunting may be just too pessimistic.

Mitchell (1985) compares those organizations celebrated as 'excellent' with those organizations which have been praised for offering their employers good working conditions. He observes that those organizations vaunted as 'excellent' in the 1980s fail to feature on the contemporaneous listings that have celebrated 'the best companies to work for'. And through this stark comparison Mitchell suggests that employees remain sceptical of managerial attempts to refashion the rhetoric and practice of organization and are, when allowed a voice within this public discourse, inclined to reject the sensegiving stories of the excellence project. Mitchell's review therefore suggests that Bunting has been too willing to cast employees as drones who have been duped by the blandishments of popular management. Indeed, our critical review of Peters' storytelling practices suggests that the sensegiving endeavours of the excellence project lack an authentic connection to the day-to-day experiences and anxieties of employment and have little real appeal for those who are obliged to manage the day-to-day anxieties and the increasing insecurities of modern employment.

Concluding comments

This chapter has embedded Peters' storywork within the schema outlined by Martin et al. (1983) and in so doing has offered a distinctive appreciation of Peters' preferences and orientations. My reflections on the common storytelling practices reviewed by Martin and her colleagues offer insights on the making of the excellence project and suggest that Peters struggled, initially, to accommodate sensegiving tales of organizational endeavour within his narratives of business excellence. Yet, beyond this historical concern, and perhaps more significantly, the work of Martin and her colleagues demonstrates a disjuncture between the sensemaking processes of everyday life, which attend to the anxieties consequent on employment, and the sensegiving ambition of the excellence project, which seems to be deaf to these very human concerns. Thus, my analytical re-view of the storyworld of the excellence project suggests that Peters' storytelling practices lack an authentic connection to the world of work and should be regarded as an attempt to diminish or to deny the organizational frictions, stresses and dislocations that are consequent on the pursuit of the sovereign consumer and the search for business excellence.

In the next chapter I will turn my attention to the position of women within the storyworld of the excellence project. As we shall see women workers have, in any sense, a marginal presence within the excellence project.

8

WOMEN IN MANAGEMENT STORIES

Introduction

The conventions of critical management scholarship demand that 'popular management' should be challenged and must be debunked. As a leading and unapologetically pro-business commentator, Tom Peters has been attacked and has often been ridiculed by more critical scholars (see Gabriel, 2008). Such attacks make for good sport, of course (Collins, 2001), but they have a tendency to descend into misrepresentation and caricature. Indeed, commentaries on the excellence project, as we have seen, often contain fundamental errors of fact which suggest that Peters belongs to that category of writers who should be attacked but need not be read! This attitude can make it difficult to legitimate any more sustained engagement with guru literature. Indeed, experience suggests that academic colleagues are, often, dismissive of the excellence project *and* disdainful of any attempt to explain why this might be made the subject of serious academic scrutiny. Mindful of this prejudice I will nonetheless build on the analysis developed in Collins (2012) to offer an analysis of Tom Peters' storywork that, as we shall see, has been designed to consider the role, status and position of women in the storyworld of the excellence project.

Accordingly, the chapter is structured as follows: We begin by acknowledging the emergence of, what Peters has referred to as the 'women's thing' (Peters, 2018, n/d). This 'women's thing', as we will learn, builds on Peters' quite sudden realization that he and the business world more generally have, together, failed to appreciate the market power and potential of women. To counter what is, we are assured, a deep-rooted and persistent form of organized stupidity, Peters has developed a narrative, which advises women to *roar* their discontents. In this chapter we will (re)consider this narrative. Reflecting Peters' conviction that stories can provide key insights into personal orientations and organizational priorities (see

DOI: 10.4324/9781003188940-9

Peters and Waterman, 1982; Peters and Austin, 1985; Peters, 2003, 2018) we will review the tales that shape Peters' narratives of business. Building on an analysis of the key texts that constitute the excellence project we will consider the position of women within the storyworld of the excellence project and we will assess the extent to which Peters' public conversion to the 'women's thing' has altered, meaningfully, his narratives of business excellence. Finally our concluding section will reflect on the extent of Peters' conversion and in so doing will suggest a response to his *thing* that builds on the transgressive potential of humour.

The women's thing

Tom Peters dates the development of 'the women's thing' quite precisely. It occurred, he reports, at 9am on December 18, 1996 in the offices of *Wordworks* 'one of America's nine *million* women-owned businesses' (Peters, n/d: 3 emphasis in original) when thirty female entrepreneurs made him, painfully, aware that he, in common with much of the rest of the business world, had been blind (and deaf) to the needs, power and potential of women. Since that day in December 1996 Peters has, he tells us, worked to incorporate 'the women's thing' within his narratives of business excellence so that organizations, the world over, will hear when women *roar* their discontents.

Returning to this moment some years later Peters (2018: 324–325 emphasis and parentheses in original) builds a story around what he had previously reported:

> Heather Shea Schultz called me while I was on the road. She was CEO of my Palo-Alto-based training and consulting company. Heather said she'd organized a meeting to enlighten me on women's issues. (Presumably she thought that I had a deficit that needed addressing.) She pretty much ordered me to attend – and respecting her (and her tenacity) as I did, I dutifully agreed to show up.
>
> The group she'd assembled and I met in Boston.
> **My life was never again the same.**
> **(That is not an exaggeration.)**
> At the appointed moment, I walked into the conference room at Wordworks, a superb editorial-talent organization run by my longtime colleague Donna Carpenter LeBaron. About fifteen women were having coffee and conversing.
>
> Heather introduced me around, and I was, frankly, overwhelmed. One of the women owned a wildly successful home furnishings company. There was an Indy race car driver, the first woman to race at Indy as I recall. And a senior Disney executive. A college president. And on it went.
>
> Heather called us together and said something like the following: "Tom has become one of the most prominent people in the business world, and he is a very okay guy. He believes in dramatically increasing the proportion of

women in leadership roles and so on. And he appointed me to lead his training company – the appointment, moreover, was made while I was on maternity leave; points for that. As well as a colleague, he is also a friend; hence, I feel comfortable saying in the de facto privacy of this room, that like most of his species, he is more or less clueless about what it's like to be a woman in business – both in our professional roles and as consumers. And you all have agreed to join me in providing him with a speed-learning experience."

These were powerful women, and they were unemotional as they recounted tale after tale of misunderstandings and indirect (and sometimes direct) snubs, from the boardroom to the car dealer's showroom and the doctor's examining room.

Thus is 1996, began my now twenty-two-year-old "women's campaign."

Rhetoric and poetry

Analysing organizational rhetoric, Höpfl (1995) offers an account of popular management, which in considering the manner in which gurus advance and substantiate their core concerns explores the divisions between rhetoric and poetry; between the sensegiving perspectives evident in the excellence project and the sensemaking perspectives we have used to question and to condition Peters' projections. She argues that we should separate those rhetorical texts that seek to advance the corporate management of identity from those, which in seeking a more intimate connection with the complex and contested nature of identity might be considered to be poetic.

Höpfl concedes that rhetoric and poetry have often been considered as equivalents. Indeed, she acknowledges that these narrative forms have often aroused suspicion and in being jointly associated with manipulation, self-advance and trickery have attracted condemnation. Nonetheless, she protests that rhetoric and poetry exhibit different orientations and in so doing trace quite different trajectories. Pursuing these differences in orientation, Höpfl (1995: 178 emphasis in original) argues that rhetoric is a masculine projection defined by its *directedness*. Rhetoric, she argues, has a trajectory towards its intent and is fulfilled by its outcome. It is directed to an audience (present or absent) and achieves its objective by provoking a response. Rhetoric is therefore completed by 'the Other'. It is 'concerned with the skills and strategies of manipulation and [so] offers a repertoire of stylistic devices which are to be developed to this end' (176). Poetry on the other hand seeks a relationship with the complexity and connectedness of a lived experience that extends beyond the workplace. Reflecting on this distinction, Höpfl argues that poetry restores voice to the text and in so doing threatens the ordered, but manipulative rationality of corporate rhetorics. Poetry is, therefore, separate from and disruptive of organizational rhetoric: Its narrative speaks from within movements, processes and biographies and in highlighting organizational ambivalence invites employees to withdraw their consent to corporate plans.

Commenting further on the experience of organizational rhetoric and on the tensions between the life-narratives of the poetic and the templates-for-performance promulgated by guru theorizing, Höpfl places gender – explicitly – within the debates on popular management and organizational storytelling. She argues that women, in particular, have difficulties with guru rhetoric. Guru theory and popular management are, she warns, predicated on the existence of a self-identity that is simple, singular, stable and saturated by the world of work whereas the identity of women workers is complex, multiple, moving and – more so than for their male counterparts – divided between any number of competing dimensions and orientations. Viewed from within the masculine perspective of guru theory, therefore, women represent a disruptive presence that must be dominated. Remarking on this process of domination, Höpfl suggests that guru literature manages women by acting to deny their organizational membership.

It might be countered, of course, that Höpfl's work tends to downplay the extent to which all narrative forms – including 'the poetic' – depend on rhetorical flourishes to secure their meaning and effect (Schön, 1979; Collins, Dewing and Russell, 2009). Equally it might be argued that Höpfl's own separation of 'the rhetorical' from 'the poetic' is, itself, evidence of a highly masculinist projection. Indeed, the works of Tyler (2005) and Bendl (2008), for example, suggest that Höpfl has produced an account of work, management and organization which fails to concede the difficulties that men have in the performance of masculinity. This is fair criticism, of course. And yet Höpfl's work remains useful for our purposes because it appreciates the limits which local sensemaking processes place on public sensegiving and in exploring this limitation *does*, at least, invite us to make gender an explicit element in the analysis of guru theory. In this regard Höpfl's reflections are productive for they prompt us to consider the manner in which Tom Peters' stories locate and account for the position of women within his excellence project and in so doing invite us to consider the reality of his conversion to the women's thing.

Women in Tom Peters' storyworld

Figure 8.1 tabulates those tales from Peters' storyworld, which feature female characters, or otherwise signal the presence of women (at work). It shows that women feature in just 80 of the 932 tales (9%) that constitute our corpus. Women are by any calculation, therefore, very seriously under-represented in the storyworld of the excellence project. Indeed, it is worth noting that *In Search of Excellence* offers but three tales from a total of 137 stories (2%) which feature women and that, together, the first four books that constitute the excellence project offer just 23 tales which acknowledge the presence of women. That said we should concede that women have become slightly more visible in the narratives of business excellence that Peters has published since the mid-1990s. In this regard there is some evidence to suggest that Peters' epiphany of 1996 has, in fact, led to a more substantive change in his conduct.

Text	Total story count	No. of Stories featuring women (%)
(1982) *In Search of Excellence* (joint with Robert Waterman)	137	3 (2)
(1985) *A Passion for Excellence* (joint with Nancy Austin)	165	11 (7)
(1987) *Thriving on Chaos*	117	6 (5)
(1992) *Liberation Management*	114	3 (3)
(1993) *The Tom Peters Seminar*	41	4 (10)
(1994) *The Pursuit of Wow*	57	6 (11)
(1997) *The Circle of Innovation*	38	6 (16)
(2003) *Re-imagine*	44	11 (25)
(2010) The Little BIG Things	114	16 (14)
(2018) The Excellence Dividend	105	14 (16)
Total	932	80 (9)

FIGURE 8.1 Women in Tom Peters' storyworld.

Yet when we subject Peters' tales of women to more detailed scrutiny it soon becomes apparent that, while women are, now, increasingly present in Peters' storyworld, they remain marginal to and, largely, silent within a world of work that is overwhelmingly masculine in its orientation and trajectory. In an attempt to explore these storytelling preferences and practices we will offer an analysis of Peters' texts pre- and post-revelation.

1982–1996

In Search of Excellence is Peters' most famous and most lauded text. This is, we have argued, the text that established the basic structure of popular management and in so doing opened the flood-gates for guru theory. Yet when we examine the tales that Peters and Waterman use to advance their analysis of business excellence it quickly becomes apparent that in this political project women will serve the revolution by making the tea. Thus, in a corpus of 137 tales women appear in just three stories and then indirectly and never in the context of the workplace itself. Indeed, in the first of these stories (reproduced below) 'the woman' is an adjunct to the main action and is, consequently, mentioned as an aside:

> LaPiere, a white professor, toured the United States in 1934 with a young Chinese student and his wife. They stopped at 66 hotels or motels and at 184 restaurants. All but one of the hotels or motels gave them space, and they were never refused service at a restaurant. Sometime later a letter was sent to the establishments asking whether they would accept Chinese as guests. [There was a strong anti-Chinese bias in the United States at the time.] Ninety-two per cent said they would not. LaPiere, and many after him, interpreted these findings as reflecting a major inconsistency between behaviour and attitudes. Almost all the proprietors *behaved* in a tolerant fashion, but they expressed an *intolerant* attitude when questioned by letter.
>
> *Peters and Waterman (1982: 73–74; parentheses and emphasis in original)*

In the second story we have not one but a number of women present. This tale, however, deals with its characters en bloc. Thus, we have saleswomen, who parade and are rewarded with trinkets, and management – unlabelled in gender terms, and so, male – who orchestrate the actions of their female employees. The saleswomen, we should note, do rather a lot in this narrative. They are always on the move. Yet it is the managers who are the heroes of this drama. Thus, the saleswomen have (literally) walk-on parts in a larger pageant, which has been designed to reveal their past conduct and in so doing to shape their future behaviour. Consequently the women present in this tale do not appear as characters in their own right. They have no names; no biographies; no real identities beyond the blanket of being 'saleswomen'. In short they lack full organizational membership. They are but *variables* within a very public system of management control:

> Tupperware makes about $200 million in pre-tax earnings on about $800 million in sales of simple plastic bowls. The key management task is motivating the more than 80,000 salespeople, and a prime ingredient is "Rally". Every Monday night all the saleswomen attend a Rally for their distributorship. At Rally, everyone marches up on stage – in the reverse order of last week's sales – during a process known as Count Up (while their peers celebrate them by joining in All Rise). Almost everyone, if she's done anything at all, receives a pin or badge – or several pins and badges. Then they repeat the entire process with small units marching up. On the one hand, this is a fairly punishing drill – straight head-on-head competition that can't be avoided. On the other hand, it is cast with a positive tone: everybody wins; applause and hoopla surround the entire event; and the evaluation technique is informal rather than paper-laden. In fact, the entire Tupperware system is aimed at generating good news opportunities and celebration. Every week there is an array of new contests. Take any three moribund distributorships: management will give a prize to whichever one has the best sales increase in the next eight weeks. Then there are the thirty days of Jubilee each year in which *15,000* are feted (3,000 at a time in week-long events) with awards, prizes and ceremonies of all kinds. The entire environment is one that utilizes, in the extreme, positive reinforcement.
>
> *Peters and Waterman (1982: 123–124; emphasis*
> *and parentheses in original)*

The third tale of women and work reproduced by Peters and Waterman (1982) is similar to the first insofar as it casts 'the woman' in a supporting role and places her in a domestic setting. Indeed, in this third tale the presence of the woman is merely implied and arises only insofar as we are willing to assume that a family is composed of a husband, a wife and (some) child(ren). Thus, the woman's identity is entirely constituted by her position within a family that is surprised by, but (we are assured) eternally grateful to, a generous corporate benefactor. Indeed, the real hero of this, second-hand, tale is *Proctor & Gamble,* which appears in the guise of a 'good Scrooge'[1]:

> One of our colleagues was in the brand-management program at P&G for three months as a summer hire. He recalls that his family still received a Thanksgiving turkey from P&G five years later.
>
> *Peters and Waterman (1982: 261–262)*

In fairness to Peters, however, we should point out that there are some tales in his pre-1996 texts where women do feature more prominently. Indeed, there are, we should note, a small number of stories in the key texts produced between 1982 and 1996 which feature women as senior employees or as organizational decision-takers of some significance.

In total there are 11 tales which allow women to occupy such privileged roles in Peters'. Four of these tales are found in *A Passion for Excellence* (Peters and Austin, 1985), which was co-authored with Nancy Austin and four more are to be found in *Thriving on Chaos* (Peters, 1987). *Liberation Management* (Peters, 1992) offers just one tale of female achievement in the workplace.

The tales reproduced below offer an indication of the manner in which Peters tends to represent women at/in work. The first of the tales selected for consideration features an interaction between 'Sarah' and 'Bill'. Sarah, it seems, began working for Bill in a junior, and gendered, position. Yet despite the modesty of her entry-level Sarah has prospered. Her present position in *WL Gore* is unclear because, we are told, Bill 'doesn't stand on formality' and does not encourage the use of rank and title. However, it is clear that Sarah is trusted as an employee and can, in fact, be entrusted with the good name and reputation of *WL Gore.* Yet it is Bill who is the hero of this tale. When all is said and done it is Bill who owns *WL Gore* and it is he who has caused and allowed Sarah to do whatever it is she must do for the company:

> Sarah worked for W. L. Gore & Associates. She began as a secretary-bookkeeper in one of Gore's twenty-eight factories. Bill Gore doesn't stand on formality. There are no titles whatsoever in the company. Sarah was to go to a meeting in Phoenix to talk about W. L. Gore. She ran into Bill, on one of his many visits, a couple of weeks before going to the event. "I'm going to this meeting, Billy," she said, "and they're going to want to know who I am. What do I do?"
>
> "Well Sarah, that's up to you," Gore replied. "What do you want to be?"
> "Beats me."
>
> "Well how about 'Supreme Commander'?" Sarah agreed. Sarah is an "owner" of W. L. Gore & Associates in the deepest sense of that word.
>
> *Peters and Austin (1985: 218)*

Our next tale of women at work – pre-epiphany – features Laurie Schwartz. Laurie, we learn, has a career. Laurie is in charge. Indeed, Laurie has secured a turnaround in the fortunes of a commercial district whose success is, we are assured, central to the vitality of the City of Baltimore. Yet it is Mayor Don Schaefer who is the hero of this tale. It is Don who is the real agent of change. Thus, the story, below, makes it clear that Laurie is in charge of Charles Street because the mayor, as a full member of the organization, told others 'to do whatever [Laurie] says'. So while Laurie has been allowed to give orders, it is Don who pulls the strings. Indeed, we learn that Laurie is in charge of Charles Street because the mayor deftly manoeuvred her, stirring her desires…to return to the public sector. Laurie's task is, therefore, Don's mission. She is a success because Don willed it so!

> Laurie Schwartz had worked for Mayor Don Schaefer but had taken off to pursue a career in the private sector. After a chance get-together at a Christmas party, he once again tapped her. She had indicated that she might be available for one of his famous "special projects". Without another word, he invited her to a meeting. He didn't tell her what it was about, even after she joined a confab of senior business people from Charles Street.
>
> With amenities quickly out of the way, the mayor got down to business. "I want you to meet Laurie Schwartz. She," he declared, "is now Ms. Charles Street. She's going to get us here." (Baltimore's main business street was not being transformed at a pace that was up to Schafer's soaring standards). And that was that. Charles Street was Schwartz's. The mayor dragged her back down to City Hall, where the city's department heads were assembled. "Laurie's back," the mayor announced. "She's running Charles Street, and you're to do whatever she says"
>
> The charge was about that simple, though the execution obviously was not. A couple of years later Charles Street was fast becoming a gem, with over 100 million new dollars invested in it. Laurie Schwartz was the cheerleader, the quarterback, the de facto chairman of the board.
>
> Did Schaefer really believe that she could pull off this miracle? One suspects he did. It is clear that he delegated the responsibility to her unequivocally. She was out on a limb. She had said she was somewhat interested in doing something for him; in return he had lobbed a key part of the city her way.
>
> Schaefer had done a frightening thing to her. She believed in him, believed in his compelling vision, believed in his track record of making the impossible seem almost routine. Moreover, she believed that he believed in her, and that he wouldn't have done this "to her" unless he thought she *could* pull it off. So she now had the monkey on her back for a piece of his – their – vision. It was her ball, in her court. Deliver or else, her psyche said; and that's precisely what His Honor had intended.
>
> *Peters (1987: 456–457; original emphasis)*

Those few women allowed access to the executive cadre who are not, obviously, in debt to a male sponsor exhibit a distinctive approach to management in Peters' storyworld. This approach, which is lauded by Peters, suggests a style of managing that retains a rather masculine psychology. Thus, in the tale below Mary Kay Ash demonstrates that she has, perhaps uniquely, a proven ability to snap people out of depression:

> Mary Kay Ash, in her book Mary Kay on *People Management,* reprises that "stretching" theme with her account of a telephone call from a "consultant" (her term for May Kay field people) in Michigan, who was not doing well in her business
>
> We talked for a while, and I finally told her. "Here's what we're going to do. We're going to have a special contest just for you. I want you to book ten beauty shows for next week, and after you've held ten, I want you to call me back and tell me how you did."
>
> "Ten shows?"
>
> "That's right," I answered. "I want you to call each hostess in your datebook, and say that you just talked to Mary Kay. Tell her that I've established a contest for you, and then let her know how much you want to win it. Finally ask her to be a hostess for next week." Based on what she told me, I knew her problem: she was giving only one or two beauty shows a month. I also knew that former hostesses would be the most receptive, giving her a better chance to book more beauty shows. With enough exposure, I felt she would do well. She just needed to gain confidence.
>
> At the end of the following week she called me to back to report $748 in sales. Although it was not among the highest sales recorded that week it was by far a record for her. Even though she hadn't booked all ten shows, she was elated and seemed to have snapped out of her depression.
>
> *Peters and Austin (1985: 363)*

Such accounts of female, managerial, achievement are, however, rare in the storyworld of the excellence project. More typically those women who do make an appearance within Peters' tales of workplace endeavour are cast as low-ranking employees. Of course, this casting process is not in itself problematic. Women are, after all, under-represented in the senior ranks of management and are, furthermore, comparatively rare in the upper reaches of professional organizations. What is problematic, however, is Peters' suggestion that an absence of creativity explains women's subordination. Thus, the story reproduced below relates the manner in which an heroic male manager precipitated an outbreak of creativity among a group of women workers whose passivity and lethargy, it seems, had made them contemptible:

> A tough industrial enterprise in Ireland has a couple of dozen facilities, each with about seventy-five to two hundred employees. One of the managers proposed that once every several months each facility should have an

"open house," featuring a garden-variety cafeteria meal for each of their people and members of their families. It was to be held in the canteen at the factory "the people in the canteen [the work force there] are not exactly looked upon as the most creative people in the world. They're held in some contempt, frankly. But you wouldn't have believed how they responded to this. I remember, in place after place, seeing an out-pouring the likes of which I wouldn't have dreamt. It was more like coming to dinner at a fine hotel in Dublin. Massive, beautiful, extremely elaborate butter sculptures were created. It was a delight to behold." And he is further amazed by the reactions of the families: "It was astonishing. In some cases it was the *first* time in over a dozen years of employment that families had ever been to the facility, had ever seen where their husband or wife or son or daughter worked." He adds that the goodwill (and productivity) that have been garnered is substantial. Such small things, such big payoffs!

Peters and Austin (1985: 223–224; original emphasis and parentheses)

Elli Parnelli, the female character in our next tale fares a little better than these Irish employees. At least she is granted a name! But then pets, performing chimps and all manner of compliant children are also named by their keepers. On reflection it may have been better for Elli had she remained nameless because, in this account of a meeting that took place between Peters' co-author (Nancy Austin) and a company chairman, poor Elli is cast as a *good girl* whose clever master has taught her a trick!

Successful North American Tool & Die's chairman, Tom Melohn, talks with Nancy. She asks him what he looks for in a prospective employee. Melohn scribbles something on a table napkin, hides it momentarily, and asks Elli Parnelli, the office manager who makes the hiring decisions along with Melohn, what she looks for. She answers without hesitation: "Someone who's a caring person." Nancy adds that as Melohn looks at Parrnelli and nods his agreement, his eyes are filled with tears.

Peters and Austin (1985: 289)

But at least Elli is a good girl. Such is her grace, in fact, that she can move grown men to tears. Pity the bad girls. Pity the drones, the servants of bureaucracy, the harrumphing heralds of consumer dissatisfaction. Pity those women who for the want of a good man(ager) bring customers to the brink of another form of emotional outburst:

The 8 A.M. request seemed simple enough. I was arriving at the Washington, D.C., hotel at 1P.M., and needed a room for the night.

Night? Try night*mare*. The reservation person said my "early" arrival (4 P.M. is standard check-in time) meant I need a "day room," then a regular room for the night. "Same room, though?" I asked.

"Probably. First you'll need to check with the front desk on the day room."

"You can't do that for me?" I asked.

"No you need to set up the day room first, then get transferred back to me."

"Seems strange," I said.

"Well," she almost huffed, "it's two departments." (As if I give a tinker's dam about the hotel's org. chart!) "But," she added, sensing my frustration, "you *could* ask the front desk for the 'day room,' then after you check in, call down and extend it for the night."

"But I wouldn't be assured of a place to sleep tonight that way, would I?"

"No but the chances are good."

Peters (1994: 175–176; original emphasis)

"Hey-heggggggggggggggggghhhhhhhhhhhhhhh!"

So goes the sixth line of dialogue in Tom Wolfe's *The Bonfire of the Vanities.*

And so go I. And you too, I bet, when you have to deal with an unresponsive behemoth of a company. But let me start the story at the beginning.

Several years ago my wife, Kate, and I built a guest house on our Vermont farm. The phone lines were installed when we were away, and we returned to find two open switch boxes inside the house, with a spaghetti tangle of loose wires dangling from each. I called to get the wiring job done. The approximate conversation with GTE in abbreviated form, adds new meaning to the concept of Catch-22 (and to the word hey-heggggggggggggggggghhhhhhhhhhhhhhh):

ME: I'd like to have some phone work completed. Could you send a service person out?

SHE: Exactly what do you want done?

ME: I'm not sure, because I don't know what was installed. I'd like a service person to help me sort it out.

SHE: You'll have to tell me exactly what you want done.

ME: But I can't I don't know

SHE: Then I can't initiate an order.

ME: Why can't you send a service person out?

SHE: It would be inefficient.

ME: OK, I'll make something up to get us started.

SHE: You're being sarcastic.

ME: No, just desperate.

On it went. I ended up talking to a supervisor and placing a "pretend" order for something I didn't want. Then it was time to schedule the visit (a.k.a adding insult to the injury already sustained).

ME (ON A THURSDAY): Can you get someone out here on Friday or Monday?
I leave for the Far East on Tuesday, and a guest is arriving for a long stay as
soon as I get back.

SHE: I think we can send someone out on Monday or Tuesday.

ME: Tuesday won't help.

SHE: We can try for Monday.

ME: OK what time?

SHE: Excuse me?

ME: What time?

SHE: Monday.

ME: But what time on Monday?

SHE: I could put down morning, but I certainly can't guarantee anything.

ME: My wife and I work and we can't hang around all day.

SHE: I can't help that.

ME: But we can't give up 16 combined hours of working time on the off chance
that the service person will show up.

SHE: Sorry.

ME (TO MYSELF): Hey hegggggggggggggggggghhhhhhhhhhhhhh!

Peters (1994: 9–10; emphasis and
parentheses in original)

Texts post-1996

Peters has produced six books since his conversion to the 'women's thing' in
1996. The first of these, *The Circle of Innovation* (Peters, 1997), offers six tales that
feature female characters to some degree. In absolute terms this figure matches
the number of stories of women and work that featured in *The Pursuit of Wow*
(Peters, 1994) and in *Thriving on Chaos* (Peters, 1987). In percentage terms, however, these six tales represent a significant increase in the tales told of women and
work (see Figure 8.1).

In crude terms *The Little BIG Things* is Peters' most feminized text, offering
16 tales that feature women. That said we should note that these 16 tales account
for just 14% of the tales rendered within this text. *The Excellence Dividend* produces similar outcomes – 14 tales accounting for some 16% of tales reproduced
within this text. In percentage terms, however, *Re-imagine* remains Peters' most
feminized text since its 11 tales of female endeavour account for 25% of the tales
rendered in this text. Such quantitative changes, however, tend to mask thematic
continuities in Tom Peter's storytelling. Indeed, further analysis suggests that
Peters' post-epiphany texts retain the services of the casting director who was
employed between 1982 and 1996. For example two of the six tales featured in
The Circle of Innovation (Peters, 1997: 106 emphasis, parentheses and ellipses in
original) mention women merely as an aside. In the first of these Donna Karan

is mentioned as 'a maverick' in a tale that actually discusses the reward policies of retailers.

> I was giving a speech to, mostly, youngish retail buyers … at Atlanta's Americas-Mart manufacturers' showroom. I was asked a question by an old pro (read … tired/jaded?): 'How do you deal with the conservative incentive systems that buyers face, the ones that punish failure … and barely reward success?'
>
> I felt an immediate surge of anger. I wanted to tell him that wise folks … WOULD-BE VISIONARIES … ignore the damn incentive systems. And then someone else made the point for me: "If you play by the rules there's no chance that your name will enter the list with Stanley Marcus, Richard Branson, Wayne Huizenga, and Donna Karan." I could have hugged him … kissed him.

In the second, Tom Peters' spouse – Susan Sargent – gets an honourable mention as the co-founder of their textile business (282; emphasis and ellipses in original).

> I recently co-founded a textile firm. We're trying to do a log of things right. VERY RIGHT. One big item is … SYSTEMS/POLICIES/PROCE-DURES. That is … I THINK THAT SYSTEMS/POLICIES/PROCE-DURES can be HUMANE/FRIENDLY/ENTICING … and.. a (BIG) plus.
>
> I got a draft of an advertising policy from a member of the firm. It was punishing in its tone. That is … the subtext seemed to suggest that our average customer was a crook … who needed to be kept on a tight leash.
>
> I disagree.
>
> So I insisted on a complete rewrite.
>
> I wanted the language to be friendly. I wanted to explain why we were doing what we were doing. I wanted it to have few technical clauses and sub-clauses and sub-sub-clauses (UNREADABLE BULLSHIT). If getting rid of a little fine print means that the 1 percent (or less!) of bad guys may screw us now and then … SO BE IT. I'm interested in our real customers. And interested in their repeat business. I'M INTERESTED IN MAKING FRIENDS … FOR LIFE!

Indeed, two of the remaining four tales reproduced within *The Circle of Innovation* (1997: 470 ellipses in original) are feminized only insofar as they offer praise for managers who have allowed a consideration of feminine attributes to impinge on their recruitment and selection decisions. In the first of these Herb Kelleher is praised for rejecting an employment application from a pilot who was off-hand in his dealings with a nameless, female, receptionist:

> There's a wonderful story told at Southwest about a pilot-applicant. Upon walking into the Dallas headquarters, he was not as friendly as he might

have been to the receptionist ... not realizing that the receptionist had a potentially decisive role in his subsequent hiring. When the company chose not to offer him a job, CEO Herb Kelleher commented, 'There are a lot of people who can fly airplanes, not so many with great attitudes.'

In the second Colleen Barrett is praised for prosecuting a hiring policy that values the qualities of 'warmth' and 'smiling' (Peters, 1997: 468; ellipses and parentheses in original).

Southwest Airlines has the best baggage-handling record around. The best safety record. The best on-time record. The fewest customer complaints. And it seems to pull it off year after year, invariably ranking at the top of the Department of Transportation's lists of the best.

A buttoned-down, tidy place. I have no doubt. On the other hand, what allows Southwest to keep this extraordinarily tidy company going ... and add spunk to flying for customers ... is the extraordinarily spirited gang of over 20,000 who staff the airline-from flight attendants and pilots to accountants and mechanics.

While doing some interviewing for a PBS show, Service with Soul, we asked Executive Vice President for Customers (Nice title, eh? Have you got one like it!?) Colleen Barrett what Southwest's employment criteria were. Her ready answer: 'We look for ... listening, caring, smiling, saying 'thank you,' and being warm.'

Reflecting on the impact of such narratives, Tyler (2005) argues that even the more positive accounts of women at work that have been crafted by Peters do little, either, to challenge gender stereotypes or to advance the cause of women workers. Indeed, Tyler's analysis suggests that stories which centre on the, supposed, emotional awareness of women workers tend to reinforce those processes that marginalize women in the workplace insofar as they construct men as agents who effect change while type-casting women as the emotional maintenance crew who must manage the affective consequences of economic and technological dislocation. That said, we should concede that two of the 11 tales reproduced in *Re-imagine* (Peters, 2003) do deal with the obstacles to career advancement, routinely, encountered by women. The first of these is credited to Robert Reich who details the trials of a female academic seeking tenure (Peters, 2003: 273). The second of these tales is, however, more positive insofar as it recounts *Deloitte's* efforts to remove those organizational impediments that had prevented women becoming partners in the firm (Peters, 2003: 275; ellipses in original).

Elevating women into the positions where they deserve to be ... and where they will add real bottom-line value ... isn't easy. One organization that has made big strides in this direction is Deloitte & Touche. Douglas McCracken, Deloitte's former big boss, brilliantly described his firm's 'epiphany' in a Harvard Business Review article titled 'Winning the Talent War for Women: Sometimes It Takes a Revolution.'

Deloitte was doing pretty well in that 'war.' It was working hard to hire Great Women. It was giving them very high marks-higher than men!-in their early years. (No surprise: They deserved it.) And then ... the women left.

Ah, you say: The Great Baby Problem strikes!

Not so fast, amigos.

'Deloitte was doing a great job of hiring high-performing women, 'Mc-Cracken writes.' In fact, women often earned higher performance rating than men in their first years with the firm. Yet the percentage of women decreased with each step up the career ladder.

'Most women weren't leaving to raise families; they had weighed their options in Deloitte's male-dominated culture and found them wanting. Many, dissatisfied with the culture they perceived as endemic to profes-sional service firms, switched professions.'Deloitte then did a 'Deloitte' on Deloitte. It carefully examined what was driving women to leave the firm. And it found assumption after assumption that inadvertently blocked women's progress within Deloitte. For example, writes McCracken: 'The process of assigning plum accounts was largely unexamined. Male partners made assumptions: 'I wouldn't put her on that kind of company because it's a tough manufacturing environment.' 'Travel puts too much pressure on women.'

So Deloitte went to work on banishing those assumptions. The firm has not transformed itself overnight, but it has made a decade-long strategic commitment to move women—in much higher numbers than before—into its top leadership ranks.

There is only one story in *Re-imagine*, however, which features a woman in a senior management position and in this tale Carly Fiorina, the CEO of *Hewlett-Packard* (HP), earns her organizational membership by displaying an openly ag-gressive (and masculine) approach to business (Peters, 2003: 86). Thus Fiorina is praised for the manner in which she *sets about* her competitors: Noting that *IBM* and *Sun Microsystems* made extensive use of *Pricewaterhouse Coopers* (PwC), the CEO of *Hewlett-Packard* confides that she made a bid to purchase PwC, solely to prevent her key competitors from gaining access to her trusted advisors!

The Little BIG Things offers perhaps a more positive picture insofar as seven of the 16 tales, which feature women in the workplace place these actors in sen-ior positions. Although it is also worth noting that of the remaining nine tales, one features Tom Peters' mother, four feature his spouse and another grants a role to an aunt. Indeed, it is worth observing that the three tales, as yet unac-counted, feature a waitress (unnamed); nameless parents at an airport and a final figure marked only by her gender. Similar casting protocols structure *The Excel-lence Dividend* where three of the 14 tales are concerned with Peters' mother and spouse, with only eight participants earning the privilege of a name.

In a departure from the pre-1996 texts, five of the 11 tales of women and work that feature in *Re-imagine* (46%) and one of the six tales recounted in *The Circle of Innovation* (17%) feature characters, who despite their professional achievements, are subjected to petty indignities when they encounter car salesman, physicians, auctioneers, and hoteliers. These tales, we should note, seem to have emerged as a direct result of Peters' meeting on December 18, 1996:

> Open your ears (I recently did) and the stories just keep coming at you. During a break in one of my seminars, I was buttonholed by a female banking executive (E-X-E-C-U-T-I-V-E) who told me her version of this too-often-told tale.
>
> She and her husband went into a car dealership. During the 20 minutes that they were there, she reports, the salesperson ignored her…"except at the very end, to explain a feature that would help me when I 'lost my key.'" He (salesman) missed something…the sale. (and I bet he was surprised!?)
>
> *Peters (1997: 419; emphasis, parentheses and ellipses in original)*

> A California State Senator with severe back and neck problems visits a renowned physician, and brings along her husband for moral support. Ten minutes into the conversation with the doc, she is forced to interrupt: "Excuse me, Doctor, but it's my neck that's in pain (the doc had been talking exclusively to the husband about her problem)
>
> *Peters (2003: 169; parentheses in original)*

Such accounts of the perils of the service encounter work well as anecdotes because they entertain and appal in equal measure. Indeed, we should note that, quite unlike Peters' other tales, it is the male characters that appear as contemptible in these stories. The extent to which this approach is sufficient to secure meaningful change we will consider in our concluding comments.

Concluding comments

Tom Peters has – whether we like it or not – made a significant contribution to the business of management. Scholars attempting to come to terms with his mission and legacy have cast his work as a foil for their more reasoned concerns and orientations and in so doing have made broad claims as to the organizing potential of the stories that feature in his texts. In this chapter I have set out to gauge the extent to which Peters' conversion to 'the women's thing' is evident in his own storytelling practices.

Yet before we turn to this it is, perhaps worth acknowledging that in my experience, few adults truly demonstrate reflexivity. Fewer still do so publicly. So Peters should be given credit, I think, for acknowledging – in print – the sexist nature of his early writings. Furthermore, he should be rewarded for taking steps to address this chauvinism. But in calculating Peters' 'reward' we should, first, pause to count the steps taken and the distance travelled.

Unfortunately the analysis of Peters' storyworld and storytelling practices offered here suggests that his journey on the 'women's thing' has been a short one. Put plainly, women remain seriously under-represented in Peters' narratives of business. Worse still they are kept in this subordinated position because the philosophy on which Peters' conversion to 'the women's things' has been based is self-limiting. Thus, Peters tells us that his commentary on the 'women's thing' is motivated by a love of business: He wants to make people richer not better. Invoking speech marks in a fashion that seems to dismiss the whole woman's movement, therefore, he states that he is 'Not a champion for "women's rights"' (Peters. n/d: 4). Excusing this (self-imposed) limitation he insists that 'many others have done that much better than I' (4).

This statement is patently accurate. But it does not justify the manner in which Peters appears to suborn the whole rights movement. Thus, Peters (n/d: 4 original emphasis and ellipses) avers that 'OPPORTUNITY' – not rights – is the central motif in his women's thing. Indeed, he confides that he is a champion for the,

> opportunity that exists ... *if* still male-dominated management took advantage of the leadership skills of under-valued women in their ranks. The opportunity that exists – amounting to trillions of dollars in the U.S. alone *if* bankers and car makers and hoteliers and health care providers "got it" ... started to develop the products that women wanted, started to deliver them in ways that women would appreciate.

Is this a philosophy that might make a difference to the working lives of women?

Is this a manifesto that might help a woman to secure a partnership or a tenured professorship? Hardly, because structured inequalities persist and will, despite Peters' conversion, continue to constrain the opportunities for women workers.

So, we must ask is Peters' women's thing an approach that will support women's employment and advance?

Will it offer supports that enable women to take up opportunities available in work?

Will it offer flexible working, affordable child-care or a living wage? No.

Peters' women's thing, however commendable its headline agenda is, and will remain, I fear, a philosophy that traduces women workers, translating them into emotional props and marketing targets.

Taken as a whole, therefore, our review of Peters' storytelling practice suggests that, at the outset, the excellence project simply failed to acknowledge women as economically productive members of society. Furthermore, our analysis of later iterations of this project suggests that – despite his epiphany of 1996 – Tom Peters still doubts the capabilities of women workers, and so, continues to deny all but a very select few, full organizational membership.

How, then, should we respond to Peters' conversion to the women's thing?

Commenting on the nature of humour, Höpfl (2007) provides a (partial) endorsement for Tom Peters' suggestion that women should roar to make their organizational presence widely known. Building on her account of rhetoric, masculinity and exclusion, Höpfl (2007) offers an analysis of humour that moves, artfully, between boardroom and bedroom. Noting the thrusting and overtly masculine nature of popular management she argues that organizational humour should be viewed as a strategy of resistance. Indeed, she reminds us that all manner of masculine projections *including guru theory and popular management* are vulnerable to the mockery of laughter and advises those who are made the Objects of such projections that a well-timed snigger should be enough to reveal or to induce a blustering impotence.

Recognizing the political nature of the excellence project and the subversive potential of humour, therefore, Höpfl's work suggests that those whom Peters has made the Objects of his now feminized excellence project should, indeed, roar – with that form of laughter, which signals opposition to and their derision for those who would suggest that women are simply and meekly a business opportunity.

Note

1 This is, of course, a reference to Ebenezer Scrooge the hero of *A Christmas Carol* (Dickens, [1841] 1992). In this tale, Scrooge, a hard-hearted miser who chooses not to celebrate the birth of Christ is visited one Christmas eve by the ghost of his former business partner and by three spirits. These spirits educate Scrooge on the poverty of his personal philosophy. Having learned that 'mankind is his business' Scrooge resolves to mend his ways and – amongst other charitable acts – buys a prize turkey for the family of his long-suffering employee, Bob Cratchit. Ironically Peters provides a curious echo of Scrooge's failed doctrine whenever he professes his love for business!

9

CONCLUDING COMMENTS

This book has been produced to mark the 40th anniversary of the publication of *In Search of Excellence* (Peters and Waterman, 1982). The central claim advanced by this text should now be quite familiar and in any case may be rendered quite simply: Peters and Waterman claim to have identified a small group of 'excellent' organizations within the US economy. These 'excellent organizations', we are assured, exhibit common traits and practices and are offered to us as examples/ exemplars of transformational performance that may be mimicked.

In Search of Excellence has, of course, been welcomed by some and attacked by others. More critical commentators have established that the text is plagued by conceptual and methodological problems which place question-marks (rather than exclamation marks[1]) after the authors' core claims. And yet while conceding that *In Search of Excellence* does often make claims that are unsubstantiated. And while observing that the text advances a core idea that not even its authors would accept as fully truthful, I have argued that the larger project spawned and sustained by *In Search of Excellence* remains worthy of our attention. Rejecting the suggestion that *In Search of Excellence* is *simply* a flawed and trivial book that may be ignored I have argued that this text really does matter and does deserve to be taken seriously. Indeed, I have demonstrated that *In Search of Excellence* has changed, quite fundamentally the manner in which practitioners of 'management' account for their conduct.

Turning from this text to its author(s) I have acknowledged the contested nature of the term, 'management guru'. Yet I have argued that Peters is most certainly deserving of this honorific. Indeed, where others have charted a normative path across the terrain of this debate I have chosen a different route. I have rejected the suggestion that Peters is 'a guru' *because* he has produced novel ideas that bring lasting benefit to business organizations. Instead I have argued that Peters is quite correctly known as *a guru* because he trades in hope and fear

DOI: 10.4324/9781003188940-10

in order to secure the affiliation of his audience. And I have argued that Tom Peters is properly regarded as *the* guru of management because he has sustained a position within this industry over 40 years – becoming along the way the very archetype of the business evangelist.

Charting Peters' 40 year (and counting) career as *the* guru of management I have offered, not simply an analysis of *In Search of Excellence* but an account of the genesis and subsequent development of the excellence project. Contextualizing this development I have argued that the excellence project developed as a response to competitive problems experienced by McKinsey and Co., during the 1970s and was, even within this organization, a contested and highly political endeavour. Indeed, I have observed that in a very real and meaningful sense this nascent project cost both Peters and Waterman their careers.

History records, of course, that both Tom Peters and Bob Waterman (but especially Tom Peters) have fared pretty well following their defenestration from 'the firm'. Yet in charting the development of the excellence project I have been at pains to demonstrate that this was a very unlikely success story. Accounting for the success of the excellence project I have offered reflections on its architecture. I have therefore detailed the development of the, now famously alliterative '7-S' framework *and* the formation of the eight attributes said to be common to, and literally typical of, 'excellent' organizations. Peters and Waterman (1982), of course, tend to suggest that these core aspects of the excellence project are to be regarded as 'findings' – as dispatches from the field rendered knowable by their careful research. Yet I have demonstrated that the '7-S' framework was not in any normal sense a product of research. Instead this (almost) paradigmatic framework was developed by a small collective as an attempt to communicate, powerfully and memorably, Tom Peters' *intuition* as to the complex realities of organization and management. Furthermore, I have shown that the so-called 'attributes' of excellence emerged, developed and became a component of the excellence project as Peters struggled to convince McKinsey and its sceptical clients that his hunch as to the developing nature of the competitive environment might somehow be codified and commodified.

Mapping the development of the excellence project over its 40-year life-span I have offered an analysis of the ten 'major works' that Peters has published between 1982 and 2018. This analytical tour is important, I have argued, because so many of those who have ventured an opinion as to the nature and standing of the excellence project seem to operate on the assumption that Tom Peters must be critiqued but need not be read! Offering a critical analysis of the excellence project I have, therefore, taken this opportunity to call out and to correct the errors of those who would attack Peters as a failed pseudo-scientist but who have, personally, failed to commit to the most elementary forms of desk-research. This willingness to undertake a more careful reading of Tom Peters does not mean, of course, that I am in any sense an advocate for the excellence project. I *do* continue to regard the endeavour as significant and I do insist that the excellence project is worthy of sustained academic scrutiny. Yet I have been critical of Tom Peters up to *and in the past* beyond the point of rudeness. I do regret this conduct now and in a small act of contrition I have tried to make it plain that Peters' supporters and his detractors have, too often, misunderstood and misrepresented *the* guru's core interests, orientations and concerns.

This realization of the limits of the current debate on Tom Peters is, I think, highly significant. It demonstrates I suggest that any attempt to come to terms with the excellence project must work to develop a productive form of engagement that goes beyond the standard operating procedures applied within academia. And to substantiate this position I have taken care to show that, despite the very obvious methodological and conceptual flaws of *In Search of Excellence* and despite the fact that the remainder of Peters' catalogue of published work is, in truth, devoid of any sustained commitment to method and methodology (or, indeed, any pretence to objectivity), the excellence project is largely immune to orthodox forms of academic critique. Thus I have argued that there is a need to recognise that while Peters is obviously an educated man, and (since these things are not naturally or necessarily equivalents) a smart guy to boot, he is not an academic researcher, nor is he in any sense a critical theorist. Rather, Tom Peters is openly, honestly and unashamedly a pro-business evangelist. And any critique of the excellence project, if is to have value, must proceed from this recognition.

What, then, is central to Peters' pro-business evangelism? The answer by now should be apparent: Central to Peters' philosophy of business and management is the understanding that work is a moral endeavour and that 'to manage' is to be part of a world-building project enabled by the arts of the storyteller.

This is, of course, an alluring philosophy especially for those charged, formally, with the duties of management. Yet it is simultaneously a deeply flawed world-view. It is flawed because Peters refuses to think-through the complex, political realities of this (moral) universe. Indeed, Tom Peters tends to wave away political concerns with the presumption that we (and I do mean you and I – the hewers of wood and the drawers of water) *will* simply accept the existence of (his) competitive reality and *must* commit to his preferred set of 'organizational needs' up to and beyond the point of altruism. Questions related to politics, plurality, difference and diversity are therefore posted as 'absent without leave' within the excellence project. And yet because the headline analysis of the excellence project is now so familiar, and because its abridged philosophy is, so obviously, alluring it cannot be dismissed, simply, as a normative projection. Instead we must seek out and we must prosecute a critical engagement with the excellence project.

And yet to engage meaningfully and productively with the excellence project we must be prepared to meet it not within the terms of normal academic discourse but upon the terrain it has chosen. Recognizing that Peters builds and depends upon storytelling to advance his core concerns I have offered (a) an analysis of the storyworld of the excellence project and (b) critical reflections on its storytelling practices. This approach I have chosen to probe the priorities, the preferences and the patterns of presence/absence that persist just beneath the symbolic facade of the excellence project. And it is to this encounter that I now turn.

★ ★ ★ ★ ★

By his own testimony and by common consent, Peters has built his success as a guru on the power of organizational storytelling. Unlike others, however I have treated this as an assertion rather than an unalloyed and wholly substantiated truth. I have therefore offered an empirical analysis of Peters' storyworld and his storytelling practices designed to probe his *modus operandi*. Unlike many others who write about management storytelling, however, I have prefaced my analysis of Peters' storytelling with critical reflections on the nature of organizational storytelling. These prefacing remarks, we should note, have been designed and located to reveal the (moral) power of storytelling *and* the core debates that should, but often do not, mark out this arena. Contrasting 'behaviourist', 'cognitivist' and 'narrative' perspectives on organization and management (Tsoukas, 2005) I have argued that Peters' very public commitment to storytelling remains limited and, indeed, limiting because it is trapped within the orbit of a cognitivist framework. Thus I have argued that while the excellence project offers rhapsodies on the power of storytelling it simply fails to appreciate the power of narratology, and so, cannot grasp the manner in which organizational stories build from and in so doing advance organizational plurality.

Looking in detail at the storytelling practices that Peters has used to convey and to account for the excellence project I have charted Peters' dependence upon the epic story-form, his relative neglect of the comic form and his apparent and complete rejection of the romantic form. Reflecting upon these findings I have observed that Peters' limited interactions with the complex realities of the organizational (story)world intimates that he has failed to develop the rapport necessary to connect with the lives, experiences and concerns of others...beyond the conference hall and the executive suite. In addition and in a further signal of Peters' growing distance from the day-to-day realities of organized life, I have observed his transition *from* narrator *to* hero of the excellence project.

Noting the dynamism of the excellence project and its developing concerns I have charted the changing cast-list of the excellence project. While others have continued to complain that Peters' texts are arranged and arrayed in a manner that is unrepresentative of his core research base and/or current concerns I have argued that there is a need to consider *not* whether Peters' case examples are representative but what is, in fact, represented by the tales he renders for our education and edification. To this end I have offered an analysis of the storyworld of the excellence project, designed to map Peters' shifting analytical priorities and the developing cast of heroes, which has been arrayed to promote these core concerns. My research demonstrates that the heroes of the excellence project have, indeed, changed during its lifetime. Yet I have also shown that the acts of heroism, laid before us remain stable through time and have become increasingly familiar – up to and beyond the point of cliché. Furthermore, I have suggested that some of these apparently celebratory tales highlight, albeit unwittingly, the costs that are borne by those who must 'interface' with the customer to deliver 'excellence'. Indeed, I have argued that some of those whom Peters would cast as heroes are, on closer examination, and when viewed 'from below', monstrosities.

Taking this sighting of monsters within the excellence project as a cue to offer a more sustained analysis of the tensions and anxieties that shape the experience of work and organization, I have offered an account of the excellence project that is refracted through the lens offered by Martin et al. (1983). Peering through this lens I have argued that Peters' storyworld conforms, broadly, to the account of storytelling developed by Martin and her colleagues but is dominated by tales which, in effect, deny the presence of those persistent anxieties that shape the organizational storyworld from the bottom-up. This failure to consider the normal anxieties of paid employment *and* the routine degradations that await so many employees is highlighted by a glaring omission in Peters' storyworld. Thus I have argued that Peters' failure to render tales of insecurity demonstrates that his storytelling simply lacks empathy and authenticity.

This is not to suggest, of course, that Peters is always and everywhere tin-eared. In December 1996 Peters tells us that he experienced an epiphany. On this date he tells us, he came to realise that his narratives of business had operated in the absence of any detailed appreciation that women work, travel and buy stuff. Since that date in 1996 he tells us that he has made it (quite literally) his business to reveal the folly of this earlier presumption. Given this very public conversion I have offered an analysis of the position and standing of women in the storyworld of the excellence project pre- and post-epiphany. This comparative analysis demonstrates that Peters' early works did, indeed, ignore women in the workplace and shows that there has been, albeit marginally, some change in his storytelling practices subsequent to 1996. And yet I have argued that such change as is evident remains limited. Indeed, I have suggested that women (especially women in junior positions) remain marginal to the excellence project and have, in fact, been marginalized by its storyworld.

So, what are we to make of Tom Peters? What are we to make of his excellence project in its 41st year and in the light of the analysis developed here?

It is, I think, important to reiterate that the excellence project (halting and unlikely at the outset yet visibly successful in hindsight) remains hugely important. While it has often been disparaged by a motley, ill-assorted coalition of managerial insiders and critical scholars, the excellence project has, truly been transformational. To repeat a point I have now made several times: The excellence project planted and propagated the literary genre that is now known as 'popular management' and has changed quite fundamentally the manner in which we think about management, talk about managing and, indeed, conduct ourselves managerially. This much is plain and this much must be conceded as being wrought by Peters. But there is – as I have tried to make clear – a difference between observing and celebrating the anniversary of the excellence project. And while I do demand that we observe this anniversary, I do not in truth find so very much to celebrate.

I am, of course, prepared to accept that Tom Peters has worked hard and, as much as anyone can deserve a financial fortune, has earned his success. I am prepared to concede too that some managers will have built a career on some adherence to the tenets of excellence and I will readily concede that some, now in gainful employment, may well have channelled aspects of the excellence project to ace their selection interview. And yet I am aware that for all Peters' romantic attachments to small courtesies, to good service, to a smile, a nod and (figuratively or otherwise) to a pat on the back, the excellence project remains conservative in nature and offers (to use a phrase preferred by political commentators from an earlier era) a reactionary manifesto that works to maintain the essential status quo even as it seems to voice a challenge to the core practices of managerial work.

Of course, the excellence project does demand change: It exhorts, for example, naïve listening and MBWA. It is, furthermore, impatient with committee-led decision-making and it is wary of those said, always, to demand hard data in support of their actions. And this outline manifesto may be enough for Peters' followers. Yet for all this talk of change the excellence project does seems perfectly content to leave the larger (sexist, bullying and monochromatic) culture of US business – the culture that so shocked Pascale and Athos [1981] (1986) – mostly intact. Indeed, we would do well to remember that the excellence project truly achieved traction within the US economy only when it was pressed into service by financiers and corporate raiders in the mid-1980s. These individuals and corporations, I suggest, cared little for Peters' deeper disaffections with US business, but desperately needed some means to persuade those so raided and merged that what is now required of them – their renewed effort, their (unreciprocated) commitment, the surrender of their pension schemes (for example) – remains reasonable and worthwhile.

Am I suggesting that Peters, in common with so many other would-be revolutionaries has been co-opted by the establishment and/or betrayed by his congregation? Not quite.

The truth is that Peters could not be co-opted by 'the establishment'. He is, of course, very much a part of *it*. Thus, while we may reflect briefly upon the irony that has seen the headline elements of the excellence project appropriated by corporate raiders and conglomerates, it is nonetheless clear that Peters' professed love of business was always, *always* going to produce a manifesto naturally sympathetic to a free-market agenda, and so, hostile to those employees (and concerns) considered to be marginal within this account of our political economy.

Returning then to my earlier inquiry, and to what we might now take as a summary position on the excellence project in its 41st year. My suggestion is that despite Peters' romantic attachment to values (too often) taken to be old-fashioned, despite his stage-presence, despite his very agreeable and highly likeable public persona, despite his courtesy towards me and despite my publicly stated desire to reciprocate in kind, the excellence project is, in the classical sense of the term, 'a tragedy' because its flaws and failings are inherent. In this respect Peters' half-step towards action on women's rights, his subsequent retreat in the name of a love of business and his failure to address in any meaningful sense the persistent anxieties at/of work are, I suggest, part and parcel of the excellence project. The problems and limitations of the excellence project, highlighted throughout this work are, therefore, 'baked-in' and since they act to deny women (and others marginalized by neo-liberalism) full organizational membership they are – oh so very hard to swallow.

And so I leave you with this: If 30 (plus) years of sustained reflection on the excellence project has taught me anything it is what Peters cannot seem to countenance:

- Organizations are marked by plurality, conflicts and difference. Yet my analysis of Peters' storyworld and storytelling practices demonstrates that the excellence project is designed to reflect the needs of a very small mainstream that is, ironically, quite atypical.
- The excellence project is built, ostensibly, upon a love of business. Yet a love of business will not safeguard your needs for healthcare, for decent housing, for education, for security in old-age, or for family-friendly working policies. Indeed, the fact that so many of us are denied what should be the hallmarks of any civilised society is, in large part, due to the fact that the excellence project has been appropriated by interests and concerns that consider such things as good health and dignity in old-age to be excess costs to which corporations need not contribute.
- The customer's needs may be Peters' paramount concern, but it would be folly to cast your identity wholly within this nexus. You cannot secure your rights as a citizen by casting yourself as a customer.
- While the excellence project endeavours to make saints of its 'transformational leaders', history reminds us that empowerment is a consequence of subordinate action, not its cause. In other words, 'change' is not Peters' to give – it is yours to take.

And if you care to listen you can still hear *and be entertained by* organizational stories that will tell you all this – and more besides. *But* be warned: You won't find any of these tales catalogued within 'popular management'.

So if you need to know *more* of the moral project that is management (and I suggest you most certainly do) you must, first, be prepared to know management *differently*!

Peters knows this, of course – deep down. While working to craft the 7-S framework he lobbied his colleagues to include an 's-factor' that would offer a meaningful account of people, power and politics. But somewhere along the way he set this aside. Recognizing the need for a political reading of the excellence project that is nonetheless rooted within an appreciation of its core ideals I have offered a critical re-view of the major works of Peters. My account of Tom Peters and Management demonstrates that the excellence project manages organizational plurality through marginalization and effacement.

More than 40 years ago, Pascale and Athos [1981] (1986) offered reflections on the relative decline of the American economy and on its prospects for renewal. The authors suggested, as we have seen, that American management (*not* American workers) was short-termist, lacking in concrete experience, inclined to mindless machismo and poorly led. In short, Pascale and Athos argued that American management was 'the problem' and was, consequently, in urgent need of (cultural) change.

As we mark the 40th anniversary of the excellence project – *salut* Tom! – I will simply observe that I agree with Pascale and Athos – and will add that I am, despite four decades of guru theorizing, still waiting for some indication that this change process is underway.

Note

1 The exclamation mark has, of course, become a core component of Peters' narrative practice and a feature of his personal branding.

BIBLIOGRAPHY

Ackman D (2002) 'Excellence Sought – And Found', *Forbes*, http://www.forbes. com/2002/10/10/1004excellent.html

Aristotle (1965) *The Politics*, trans. T S Dorsch, Penguin Classics: London.

Aupperle K E, Acar W and Booth D E (1986) 'An Empirical Critique of *In Search of Excellence*: How Excellent Are the Excellent Companies?', *Journal of Management*, 12 (4): 499–512.

Barnard C I [1938] (1968) *The Functions of the Executive*, Harvard University Press: Boston MA.

Barter R F (1994) 'In Search of Excellence in Libraries: The Management Writings of Tom Peters and Their Implications for Library and Information Services', *Library Management*, 15 (8): 4–15.

Baskerville S and Willett R (eds) (1985) *Nothing Else to Fear: New Perspectives on America in the Thirties*, Manchester University Press: Manchester.

Bendl R (2008) 'Gender Subtexts – Reproduction of Exclusion in Organizational Discourse', *British Journal of Management*, 19 (special issue): s50–s64.

Beigi M, Callahan J and Michaelson C (2019) 'A Critical Plot Twist: Changing Characters and Foreshadowing the Future of Organizational Storytelling' *International Journal of Management Reviews*, 21: 447–465.

Berendt J [1994] (2009) *Midnight in the Garden of Good and Evil*, Sceptre: London.

Beynon H (1979) *Working for Ford*, E P Publishing: Wakefield.

Blackhurst C (2003) 'Master of Reinvention', *The Evening Standard* (London), 01/10/2003.

Boje D (1991) 'The Storytelling Organization: A Study of Performance in An Office Supply Firm', *Administrative Science Quarterly*, 36: 106–126.

Boje D (2001) *Narrative Methods for Organizational and Communication Research*, Sage: London.

Boje D, Alvarez R and Schooling B (2001) 'Reclaiming Story in Organization: Narratologies and Action Sciences', in Westwood R and Linstead S (eds) *The Language of Organization*, Sage: London.

Boltanski L and Chiapello E (2007) *The New Spirit of Capitalism*, trans. Gregory Elliot. Verso: London.

Booker C (2007) *The Seven Basic Plots: Why We Tell Stories*, Continuum: London.

Boyce M E (1995) 'Collective Centring and Collective Sense-making in the Stories and Storytelling of One Organization, *Organization Studies*, 16 (1): 107–137.

Brown A (2006) 'A Narrative Approach to Collective Sensemaking', *Journal of Management Studies*, 43 (4): 731–753.

Buchanan D (2003) 'Getting the Story Straight: Illusions and Delusions in the Organizational Change Process', *Tamara: The Journal of Critical Postmodern Organizational Science*, 2 (4): 7–21.

Bunting M (2005) *Willing Slaves: How the Overwork Culture Is Ruling Our Lives*, Harper Perennial: London.

Bunz U K and Maes J D (1998) 'Learning Excellence: Southwest Airlines' Approach', *Managing Service Quality*, 8 (3): 163–169.

Burnes B (2005) 'Complexity Theories and Organizational Change', *International Journal of Management Reviews*, 7 (2): 73–90.

Burrell G (1997) *Pandemonium*, Sage: London.

Burrell G and Morgan G (1979) *Sociological Paradigms and Organisational Analysis*, Heinemann: London.

Business Week (5/11/1984) 'Who's Excellent Now?': 46–54.

Byrne J A (1992a) 'Ever In Search of a New Take on Excellence', *Business Week*, 31/08/1992, http://www.businessweek.com/archives/1992/b328144.arc.htm

Byrne J A (1992b) 'Tom Peters' Mantra for "Nutty Times"', *Business Week*, 16/11/1992, http://businessweek.com/archives/1992/b32939.arc.htm

Carroll D T (1983) 'A Disappointing Search for Excellence', *Harvard Business Review*, Nov-Dec: 78–82.

Clark T and Salaman G (1996) 'The Management Guru as Organizational Witchdoctor', *Organization*, 3 (1): 85–107.

Clark T and Salaman G (1998) 'Telling Tales: Management Gurus and the Construction of Organizational Identity', *Journal of Management Studies*, 35 (2): 137–161.

Collins D (1998) *Organizational Change: Sociological Perspectives*, Routledge: London.

Collins D (2000) *Management Fads and Buzzwords: Critical-Practical Perspectives*, Routledge: London.

Collins D (2001) 'The Fad Motif in Management Scholarship', *Employee Relations*, 23 (1): 26–37.

Collins D (2003) 'Re-imagining Change: Editor's Introduction', *Tamara*, 2 (4): iv–xi.

Collins D (2006) 'Assaying the Advice Industry', *Culture and Organization*, 12 (2): 139–152.

Collins D (2007) *Narrating the Management Guru: In Search of Tom Peters*, Routledge: Abingdon, OX.

Collins D (2008) 'Has Tom Peters Lost the Plot? A Timely Review of a Celebrated Management Guru', *Journal of Organizational Change Management*, 21 (3): 315–334.

Collins D (2012) 'Women Roar: "The Women's Thing" in the Storywork of Tom Peters', *Organization*, 19 (4): 405–424.

Collins D (2013) 'In Search of Popular Management: Sensemaking, Sensegiving and Storytelling in the Excellence Project', *Culture and Organization*, 19 (1): 42–61.

Collins D (2015) 'Foreword', in Örtenblad A (ed) *Handbook of Research on Management Ideas and Panaceas*, Edward Elgar Publishing: Cheltenham, Gloucester.

Collins D (2016) 'Constituting Best Practice in Management Consulting', *Culture and Organization*, 22 (5): 409–429.

Collins D (2018) *Stories for Management Success: The Power of Talk in Organizations*, Taylor and Francis, Routledge: Abingdon, Oxon.

Collins D (2019) 'Management's Gurus', in Sturdy A, Heusinkveld S, Reay T and Strang D (eds) *The Oxford Handbook of Management Ideas*, Oxford University Press: Oxford.

Collins D (2021a) *Management Gurus: A Research Overview*, Taylor & Francis, Routledge: London and New York.

Collins D (2021b) 'Speaking Truth to Power: The Perils of (Scientific) Leadership in the Green Economy', in Taylor A (ed) *Rethinking Leadership in the Green Economy*, Taylor & Francis, Routledge: Abingdon, Oxon and New York.

Collins D (2021c) *Rethinking Organizational Culture: Redeeming Culture Through Stories*, Taylor & Francis, Routledge: Abingdon, Oxon and New York.

Collins D (2021d) *The Organizational Storytelling Workbook: How to Harness this Powerful Management and Communication Tool*, Taylor & Francis, Routledge: Abingdon, Oxon and New York.

Collins D, Dewing I and Russell P (2009) 'Postcards from the Front: Changing Narratives in UK Financial Services', *Critical Perspectives on Accounting*, 20 (8): 884–895.

Collins D, Dewing I and Russell P (2015) 'Between Maxwell and Micawber: Plotting the Failure of the Equitable Life', *Accounting and Business Research*, 45 (6–7): 715–737.

Collins D and Rainwater K (2005) 'Managing Change at Sears: A Sideways Look at a Tale of Corporate Transformation', *Journal of Organizational Change Management*, 18 (1): 16–30.

Cornuelle R C [1965] (1967) *Reclaiming the American Dream*, Vintage Books: New York.

Crainer S (1997) *Corporate Man to Corporate Skunk: The Tom Peters Phenomenon, A Biography*, Capstone: Oxford.

Currie G and Brown A D (2003) 'A Narratological Approach to Understanding Processes of Organizing in a UK Hospital', *Human Relations*, 56 (5): 563–586.

Czarniawska B (1997) *Narrating the Organization: Dramas of Institutional Identity*, The University of Chicago Press: Chicago, IL.

Czarniawska B (1999) *Writing Management: Organization Theory as a Literary Genre*, Oxford University Press: Oxford.

Czarniawska B and Gagliardi P (eds) (2003) *Narratives We Organize By*, John Benjamins Publishing Company: Amsterdam.

Czarniawska B and Mazza C (2003) 'Consulting as a Liminal Space', *Human Relations*, 56 (3): 267–290.

Deal T and Kennedy A (1982) *Corporate Cultures: The Rites and Rituals of Corporate Life*, Addison-Wesley: Reading, MA.

DeLamarter R T [1986] (1988) *Big Blue: IBM's Use and Abuse of Power*, Pan Books: London.

Denning S (2001) *The Springboard: How Storytelling Ignites Action in Knowledge-Era Organizations*, Routledge: Abingdon, Oxon.

Dickens C [1841] (1992) *A Christmas Carol*, Cecil Palmer: London.

Driver M (2009) 'From Loss to Lack: Stories of Organizational Change as Encounters with Failed Fantasies of Self, Work and Organization', *Organization*, 16: 353–369.

Dumaine B and Berlin R K (1993) 'America's Toughest Bosses', *Fortune* 18/10/1993.

Dunford R and Jones D (2000) 'Narrative and Strategic Change', *Human Relations*, 53 (9): 1207–1226.

Durman P (1997) 'Fading Fame of a Management Guru', *The Times* (London) 10/04/1997.

Economist (The) (15/06/1985) 'The Joy of Business'.

Economist (The) (5/12/1992) 'A Mess of Parables'.

Economist (The) (24/09/1994) 'Tom Peters, Performance Artist'.

Economist (The) (20/12/2003) 'Excellence Revisited', 125–126.

Esler G (2012) *Lessons from the Top: How Successful Leaders Tell Stories to Get Ahead and Stay There*, Profile Books: London.

Fear W J (2014) 'What Is the Story? The Uniqueness Paradox and the Patient Story in the Minutes of the Boardroom', *Management Learning*, 45: 317–331.

Ferguson N (ed) (1997) *Virtual History: Alternatives and Counterfactuals*, Papermac: London.

Fiedler F E (1967) *A Theory of Leadership Effectiveness*, McGraw-Hill: New York.

Foltz K and Resener M (1985) 'A Passion for Hype', *Newsweek*, 27/05/1985.

Fox A (1985) *Man Mismanagement*, Hutchinson: London.

Frank T [2000] (2002) *One Market Under God: Extreme Capitalism, Market Populism and the End of Economic Democracy*, Vintage: London.

Freiberg K and Freiberg J (1997) *Nuts! Southwest Airlines' Crazy Recipe for Business and Personal Success*, Orion Business Books: London.

Gabriel Y (1995) 'The Unmanaged Organization: Stories, Fantasies and Subjectivity', *Organization Studies*, 16 (3): 477–501.

Gabriel Y (1998) 'Same Old Story or Changing Stories? Folkloric, Modern and Postmodern Mutations', in Grant D, Keenoy T and Oswick C (eds) *Discourse and Organization*, Sage: London.

Gabriel Y (2000) *Storytelling in Organizations: Facts, Fictions and Fantasies*, Oxford University Press: Oxford.

Gabriel Y (2004) 'Narratives, Stories and Texts', in Grant D, Hardy C, Oswick C and Putnam L (eds).

Gabriel Y (2008) 'Book Review: David Collins, Narrating the Management Guru: In Search of Tom Peters', *Organization Studies*, 29 (7): 1065–1069.

Gagliardi P (eds) (2003) *Narratives We Organize By*, John Benjamins Publishing Co: Amsterdam.

Gallie W B (1968) *Philosophy and the Historical Understanding*, Schocken Books: New York.

Gates B (1985) 'Business Needs Its "Skunks"', *The Financial Post* (Canada), 12/10/1985.

Geneen H S with Moscow A (1986) *Managing*, Grafton Books: London.

Gerstner L V (2002) *Who Says Elephants Can't Dance?* HarperCollins: New York.

Gibbs A (1967) *Gibbs and a Phoney War*, Peter Dawnay: London.

Gioia D A and Chittipeddi K (1991) 'Sensemaking and Sensegiving in Strategic Change Initiation', *Strategic Management Journal*, 12: 433–448.

Giroux H (2006) 'It Was Such a Handy Term: Management Fashions and Pragmatic Ambiguity', *Journal of Management Studies*, 43 (6): 1227–1260.

Goleman D, Boyatzis R E and McKee A (2013) *The Power of Emotional Intelligence: Selected Writings*, Harvard Business Review Press: Cambridge MA.

Grant D, Hardy C, Oswick C and Putnam L (2004) 'Introduction: Organizational Discourse: Exploring the Field', in Grant D, Hardy C, Oswick C and Putnam L (eds) *The Sage Handbook of Organizational Discourse*, Sage: London, 1-36.

Grant D, Michaelson G, Oswick C and Wailes N (eds) (2005a) 'Discourse and Organizational Change', Special Issue of *Journal of Organizational Change Management*, 18 (1): 6–104.

Grant D, Michaelson G, Oswick C and Wailes N (eds) (2005b) 'Discourse and Organizational Change: Part Two', Special Issue of *Journal of Organizational Change Management*, 18 (4): 309–390.

Greatbatch D and Clark T (2005) *Management Speak: Why We Listen to What Management Gurus Tell Us*, Routledge: London and New York.

Grint K (1994) 'Reengineering History: Social Resonances and Business Process Reengineering', *Organization*, 1 (1): 179–201.

Grint K (1997a) 'TQM, BPR, JIT, BSCs and TLAs: Managerial Waves or Drownings? *Management Decision*, 35 (10): 731–738.

Grint K (1997b) *Fuzzy Management*, Oxford University Press: Oxford.

Groß C, Heusinkveld S and Clark T (2015) 'The Active Audience? Gurus, Management Ideas and Consumer Variability', *British Journal of Management*, 26 (2): 273–291.

Guest D (1992) 'Right Enough to be Dangerously Wrong: An Analysis of the *In Search of Excellence* Phenomenon', in Salaman G (ed) *Human Resource Strategies*, Sage: London.

Hammer M (1990) 'Re-engineering Work: Don't Automate Obliterate', *Harvard Business Review* July-August: 104–112.

Hayes R H and Abernathy W J (1980) 'Managing Our Way to Economic Decline', *Harvard Business Review* July-August: 67–77.

Haynes K (2006) 'Linking Narrative and Identity Construction: Using Autobiography in Accounting Research', *Critical Perspectives on Accounting*, 17: 399–418.

Haynes K (2008) '(Re)figuring Accounting and Maternal Bodies: The Gendered Embodiment of Accounting Professionals', *Accounting, Organizations and Society*, 33: 328–348.

Heller R [1994] (1995) *The Fate of IBM*, Warner Books: London.

Heller R (2000) *Tom Peters: The Bestselling Prophet of the Management Revolution*, Dorling Kindersley: London.

Heller R (2002) *In Search of European Excellence: The 10 Key Strategies of Europe's Top Companies*, Profile Books: London.

Hersey P and Blanchard K H (1988) *Management of Organization Behavior: Utilizing Human Resources*, Prentice-Hall: Englewood Cliffs, NJ.

Hilmer F and Donaldson L (1996) *Management Redeemed: Debunking the fads That Undermine Our Corporations*, Free Press: New York.

Hindle T (2008) *Guide to Management Ideas and Gurus*, *The Economist* in association with Profile Books: London.

Hitt M A and Ireland R D (1987) 'Peters and Waterman Revisited: The Unended Quest for Excellence', *Academy of Management Executive*, 1 (2): 91–98.

Höpfl H (1992) 'Death of a Snake-Oil Salesman: The Demise of the Corporate Life-Lie', Paper Presented to British Academy of Management, Cardiff.

Höpfl H (1995) 'Organizational Rhetoric and the Threat of Ambivalence', *Studies in Culture, Organisations and Society*, 1 (2): 175–188.

Hopkinson G C (2003) 'Stories from the Front-Line: How They Construct the Organization', *Journal of Management Studies*, 40 (8): 1943–1969.

Huczynski A A (1993) *Management Gurus: What Makes Them and How to Become One*, Routledge: London.

Hyatt J (1990) 'How to Write a Business Best-Seller, *Inc.com*, http://pf.inc.com/magazine/19900301/5074.html

Hyatt J (1999) 'When Everyone Was Excellent', *Inc.com*, http://pf.inc.com/magazine/19990515/4703.html

Jackson B (1996) 'Re-Engineering the Sense of Self: The Manager and the Management Guru', *Journal of Management Studies*, 33 (5): 571–590.

Jackson B (2001) *Management Gurus and Management Fashions: A Dramatistic Inquiry*, Routledge: London.

Jackson N and Carter P (1998) 'Management Gurus: What Are We to Make of Them?', in Hassard J and Holliday R (eds) *Organization-Representation: Work and Organization in Popular Culture*, Sage: London.

James C H and Minnis W C (2004) 'Organizational Storytelling: It Makes Sense', *Business Horizons*, 47 (4): 23–32.

Jones R V (1978) *Most Secret War: British Scientific Intelligence 1939–1945*, Coronet Books: London.

Kahn H (1970) *The Emerging Japanese Superstate*, Harper and Row: London.

Kahn H and Pepper T (1978) *The Japanese Challenge: The Success and Failure of Economic Success*, Harper and Row: London.

Kamata S (1983) *Japan in the Passing Lane: An Insider's Account of Life in a Japanese Auto Factory*, Pantheon Books: London.

Kanter R M (1989) *When Giants Learnt to Dance*, Simon and Schuster: New York.

Khurana R (2007) *From Higher Aims to Hired Hands: The Social Transformation of American Business Schools and the Unfilled Promise of Management as a Profession*, Princeton University Press: Princeton.

Kiechel W (2010) *The Lords of Strategy: The Secret Intellectual History of the New Corporate World*, Harvard Business Review Press: Boston, MA.

Kieser A (1997) 'Rhetoric and Myth in Management Fashion', *Organization*, 4 (1): 49–74.

Latour B (1987) *Science in Action*, Harvard University Press: Cambridge, MA.

Latour B (1999) *Pandora's Hope: Essays on the Reality of Science*, Harvard University Press: Cambridge, MA.

Leonard C (1992) 'Millionaire Marketing Guru Who Reigns Supreme', *The Times* (London), 5/12/1992.

Letiche H (2000) 'Phenomenal Complexity Theory as Informed by Bergson', *Journal of Organizational Change Management*, 13 (6): 545–557.

Levi P [1986] (1995) *If Not Now, When?* Abacus Books: London.

Lewis J (ed) (1992) *The Chatto Book of Office Life or Love Among the Filing Cabinets*, Chatto and Windus: London.

Llewellyn S (1999) 'Narratives in Accounting and Management Research', *Accounting, Auditing and Accountability Journal*, 12 (2): 220–236.

Lischinsky A (2008) 'Examples as Persuasive Argument in Popular Management Literature', *Discourse and Communication*, 2 (3): 243–269.

Lorenz C (1986a) 'The Guru Factor', *The Financial Times* (London), 02/07/1986.

Lorenz C (1986b) 'The Passionate and Unrepentant Crusader', *The Financial Times* (London), 18/08/1986.

Lorenz C (1992) Untitled, *The Financial Times* (London), 06/11/1992.

Lutz B (2011) *Car Guys Vs Bean Counters: The Battle for the Soul of American Business*, Portfolio/Penguin: London.

Maidique M A (1983) 'Point of View: The New Management Thinkers', *California Management Review*, 26 (1): 151–161.

Martin J, Feldman M S, Hatch M J and Sitkin S B (1983) 'The Uniqueness Paradox in Organizational Stories', *Administrative Science Quarterly*, 28: 438–453.

Maxwell J C (2011) *The 5 Levels of Leadership: Proven Steps to Maximise Your Potential*, Faith Words: Nashville, TN.

McBeth M, Jones M and Shannon E (2014) 'The Narrative Policy Framework', in Sabatier P and Weible C (eds) *Theories of the Policy Process*, Westview Press: Boulder CO, 3e.

McConkie M L and Bass R W (1986) 'Organizational Stories: One Means of Moving the Informal Organization during Change Efforts', *Public Administration Quarterly*, Summer, 10: 189–205.

McDonald D [2013] (2020) *The Firm: The World's Most Controversial Management Consultancy*, Oneworld Publications: London.

Micklethwait J and Wooldridge A (1997): *The Witch Doctors: What the Management Gurus Are Saying and How to Make Sense Of It*, Mandarin: London.

Middlebrook M (1980) *The Battle of Hamburg: Allied Bomber Forces against a German City in 1943*, Allen Lane: London.

Miller W C (1993) 'Still Searching for Excellence: Using Past Performance to Predict Future Success, *Executive Research Project S95*, The Industrial College of the Armed Forces, Fort McNair: Washington, DC.

Mintzberg H (1973) *The Nature of Managerial Work*, Harper and Row: New York.

Mitchell T R (1985) 'In Search of Excellence Versus the 100 Best Companies to Work for in America: A Question of Perspective and Values', *The Academy of Management Review*, 10 (2): 350–355.

Monin N and Monin J (2005) 'Hijacking the Fairy Tale: Genre Blurring and Allegorical Breaching in Management Literature', *Organization*, 12 (4): 511–528.

Moore R and Benson D (eds) (2013) *The Racing Bicycle: Design, Function, Speed*, Universe Books: London.

Moriguchi C and Ono H (2006) 'Japanese Lifetime Employment: A Century's Perspective' in Blomström M and La Croix S (eds) *Institutional Change in Japan*, Taylor & Francis, Routledge: London and New York.

Musson G and Duberley (2007) 'Change or be Exchanged: The Discourse of Participation and the Manufacture of Identity', *Journal of Management Studies*, 44 (1): 143–164.

Orwell G (1988) *Decline of the English Murder and Other Essays*, Penguin: Harmondsworth, Middlesex.

Pagel S and Westerfelhaus R (2005) 'Charting Managerial Reading Preferences in Relation to Popular Management Theory Books: A Semiotic Analysis', *Journal of Business Communication*, 42: 420–448.

Pascale R T and Athos A G [1981] (1986) *The Art of Japanese Management*, Sidgwick and Jackson: London.

Pattison S (1997) *The Faith of the Managers: When Management Becomes Religion*, Cassell: London.

Perrow C (1979) *Complex Organizations: A Critical Essay*, Scott Foresman: Northbrook, IL.

Peter P J and Hull R (1969) *The Peter Principle*, Souvenir: London.

Peters T (1980) 'The Planning Fetish', *Manager's Journal: The Wall Street Journal* June 1980.

Peters T (1987) *Thriving on Chaos: A Handbook for a Management Revolution*, Guild Publishing: London.

Peters T (1989) 'Doubting Thomas', *Inc.com*, http://pf.inc.com/magazine/19890401/5599.html

Peters T (1992) *Liberation Management: Necessary Disorganization for the Nanosecond Nineties*, MacMillan: London.

Peters T (1993) *The Tom Peters Seminar: Crazy Times Call for Crazy Organizations*, MacMillan: London.

Peters T (1994) *The Pursuit of Wow! Every Person's Guide to Topsy Turvy Times*, MacMillan: London.

Peters T (1997) *The Circle of Innovation: You Can't Shrink Your Way to Greatness*, Hodder and Stoughton: London.

Peters T (1999a) *Reinventing Work: The Project 50*, Alfred A Knopf: New York.

Peters T (1999b) *Reinventing Work: The Professional Service Firm 50*, Alfred A Knopf: New York.

Peters T (1999c) *Reinventing Work: The Brand You 50*, Alfred A Knopf: New York.

Peters T (2001) 'Tom Peters's True Confessions', *Fast Company*, Issue 53. www.fastcompany.com/magazine/53/peters.html

Peters T (2003) *Re-imagine: Business Excellence in a Disruptive Age*, Dorling Kindersley: London.

Peters T (2005) *Sixty*, Skunkworks Publications.

Peters T (2010) *The Little BIG Things: 163 Ways to Pursue Excellence*, Harper Business: New York.

Peters T (2018) *The Excellence Dividend: Meeting the Tech Tide with Work that Wows and Jobs that Last*, Vintage: New York.

Peters T (2021) *Excellence Now: Extreme Humanism*, Net World Publishing.

Peters T (not dated) *Women Roar: The New Economy's Hidden Imperatives*, Tom Peters Group: Boston, MA.

Peters T and Austin N (1985) *A Passion for Excellence: The Leadership Difference*, Fontana: London.

Peters T and Barletta M (2005a) *Tom Peters Essentials. Innovate, Differentiate, Communicate*, Dorling Kindersley: London.

Peters T and Barletta M (2005b) *Tom Peters Essentials. Develop It, Sell It, Be It*, Dorling Kindersley: London.

Peters T and Barletta M (2005c) *Tom Peters Essentials. Inspire, Liberate, Achieve*, Dorling Kindersley: London.

Peters T and Barletta M (2005d) *Tom Peters Essentials. Recognize, Analyze, Capitalize*, Dorling Kindersley: London.

Peters T and Waterman R (1982) *In Search of Excellence: Lessons from America's Best Run Companies*, Harper and Row: New York.

Pettigrew A M (1985) *Awakening Giant: Continuity and Change in ICI*, Blackwell: Oxford.

Pio E (2007) 'Gurus and Indian Epistemologies: Parables of Labour-Intensive Organizations', *Journal of Management Inquiry*, 16 (2): 180–192.

Postrel V I (1997) 'The Peters Principle', *reason online*, www.reason.com/9710/int.peters.shtml

Price R (2019) *The Politics of Organizational Change*, Taylor & Francis, Routledge: Abingdon, Oxon and New York.

Private Eye 1535: 18.

Purves L (2006) 'Reader You're A Dimwit', *The Times* (London) 30/05/2006.

Reingold (2003) 'Still Angry After All These Years', *FastCompany*, 75 http://pf.fastcompany.com/magazine/75/angry.html

Rhodes C and Brown A (2005) 'Narratives, Organization and Research', *International Journal of Management Reviews*, 7 (3): 167–188.

Roberts J (2005)'The Ritzerization of Knowledge', *Critical Perspectives on International Business*, 1 (1): 56–63.

Roethlisberger F J and Dickson W J with Wright H A [1939] (1964) *Management and the Worker: An Account of a Research Program Conducted by Western Electric Company, Hawthorne Works*, John Wiley and Sons: New York.

Rosenzweig P (2007) *The Halo Effect and Eight Other Business Delusions that Deceive Managers*, Free Press: New York.

Roy K [2013] (2014) *The Invisible Spirit: A Life of Post-War Scotland 1945–75*, Birlinn: Edinburgh.

Rüling C C (2005) 'Popular Concepts and the Business Management Press', *Scandinavian Journal of Management*, 21: 177–195.

Salzer-Mörling M (1998) 'As God Created the Earth...A Saga that Makes Sense?', in Grant D, Keenoy T and Oswick C (eds) (1998).

Sampson A (1973) *The Sovereign State: The Secret History of ITT*, Hodder and Stoughton: London.

Sampson A [1975] (1991) *The Seven Sisters: The Great Oil Companies and the World they Made*, Bantam Books: London.

Sampson A (1995) *Company Man: The Rise and Fall of Corporate Life*, HarperCollins: London.

Schön D (1979) 'Generative Metaphor: A Perspective on Problem-Setting in Social Policy', in Ortony A (ed) *Metaphor and Thought*, Cambridge University Press: Cambridge.

Scott A (1994) *Willing Slaves? British Workers under HRM*, Cambridge University Press: Cambridge.

Scott J C (1987) *Weapons of the Weak: Everyday Forms of Peasant Resistance*, Yale University Press: New Haven, CT.

Shotter J (2002) *Conversational Realities: Constructing Life through Language*, Sage: London.

Sillitoe A (1979) *Raw Material*, W H Allen: London.

Sims D (2003) 'Between the Millstones: A Narrative Account of the Vulnerability of Middle Managers' Storying', *Human Relations*, 56 (10): 1195–1211.

Søderberg A (2003) 'Sensegiving and Sensemaking in an Integration Process: A Narrative Approach to the Study of an International Acquisition', in Czarniawska B (ed).

Steinbeck J [1959] (1990) *Once There Was a War*, Mandarin Paperbacks: London.

Stewart M [2009] (2010) *The Modern Management Myth: Debunking Modern Business Philosophy*, Norton Paperbacks: London and New York.

Stogdill R M (1948) 'Personal Factors Associated with Leadership: A Review of the Literature, *Journal of Psychology*, 25: 35–27.

Suddaby, R. and Greenwood, R. 2001 'Colonizing Knowledge: Commodification as a Dynamic of Jurisdictional Expansion in Service Firms', *Human Relations*, 54 (7): 933–953.

Taylor D J (2019) *On Nineteen Eighty-Four: A Biography*, Abrams Press: New York.

Thompson and McHugh (1990) *Work Organizations: A Critical Introduction*, Palgrave MacMillan: London.

Tietze S, Cohen L and Musson G (2003) *Understanding Organizations through Language*, Sage: London.

Townsend R [1970] (1971) *Up the Organisation: How to Stop the Corporation from Stifling People and Strangling Profits*, Book Club Associates: London.

Tsoukas H (2005) 'Afterword: Why Language Matters in the Analysis of Organizational Change', *Journal of Organizational Change Management*, 18 (1): 96–104.

Turkina O [2014] (2015) *Soviet Space Dogs*, Fuel: London trans. Cannon I and Wasserman L.

Tyler M (2005) 'Women in Change Management: Simone De Beauvoir and the Co-optation of Women's Otherness', *Journal of Organizational Change Management*, 18 (6): 561–577.

Van der Merwe R and Pitt L (2003) 'Are Excellent Companies Ethical? Evidence from an Industrial Setting', *Corporate Reputation Review*, 5 (4): 343–355.

Van Gucht R (2015) *Hinault*, Bloomsbury: London.

Waterman R (1987) *The Renewal Factor: How to Get the Best and Keep the Competitive Edge*, Transworld Ltd: London.

Waterman R, Peters T and Phillips J (1980) 'Structure Is Not Organization', *Business Horizons*, 23 (3): 14–26.

Watson T (2001) *In Search of Management: Culture, Chaos and Control in Managerial Work*, Thomson Learning: London.

Weick K (1995) *Sensemaking in Organizations*, Sage: London.

Weick K (2004) 'A Bias for Conversation: Acting Discursively in Organizations', in Grant D, Hardy C, Oswick C and Putnam L (eds).

Whitfield D (1985) 'Peter Drucker: Guiding Light to Management', *Los Angeles Times* 14/04/1985.

Whyte W H [1956] (1961) *The Organization Man*, Penguin: Harmondsworth, Middlesex.

Williams K, Williams J and Haslam C (1987) *The Breakdown of Austin Rover: A Case-Study in the Failure of Business Strategy and Industrial Policy*, Berg: Leamington Spa.

Wright-Mills C (1978) *The Sociological Imagination*, Pelican: Harmondsworth.

INDEX

Note: **Bold** page numbers refer to tables, *Italic* page numbers refer to figures and page number followed by "n" refer to end notes.

Abernathy, W. J. 66
Acar, W. 67
Ackman, D. 82, 86
agency 143
ambiguous tales 148–151
America: business chose 25; economic decline 57; management 57; post-world war II era 57
American Bureau of Census Statistics 56
Andrew, Prince 133, 137n5
antenarrative 112, 126–129, 136
anti-mechanistic metaphors 88, 91
Aristotle 39, 127
The Art of Japanese Management (Pascale and Athos) 4, 19, 24, 25, 37, 40–41, 50
Ash, Mary Kay 213
Athos, A. G. 24–27, 29, 31, 41–44, 47, 56, 57, 190, 228, 230
Atkinson, Philip 25, 28, 29
Aupperle, K. E. 67
Austin, N. 15, 73, 75–78, 149, 171, 193, 194, 211; *A Passion for Excellence* 5, 10, 193, 211
autonomy-control duality 62, 192, 197

Banham, John Sir. 39
Bank of Boston 183
Barrett, Colleen 218
Bass, R. W. 198
Batman 130

behaviourist models 113
Beigi, M. 115, 116, 117, 137n1
belief, disavowal of 141
Bendl, R. 208
Bennett, Jim 26, 27
Berendt, John 132; *Midnight in the Garden of Good and Evil* 132–133
Black Monday 86–88
Blanchard, K. H. 79
blog posts 142
blue chip corporation 74
Boje, D. 112, 125–129, 134, 136, 151, 152
Boltanski, L. 3, 203
Booker, C. 129
'boosting' process 60
Booth, D. E. 67
Boston Consulting Group (BCG) 29
Boston Matrix 30
Brown, A. 114–116
Bunting, M. 203
Burnes, B. 89, 91
Burns, Robert 21n1
business: excellence 23, 33, 67, 94; language and practice 51; management 1, 3–6, 10, 14, 15, 17, 23, 34, 37, 51, 54, *55*, 65, 69, 80, 84, 85, 92, 102, 103, 121, 139, 151, 152, 220; mastermind 52; Peters' narratives 51; process reengineering 13, 19, 99; recession 56
Business Horizons 31

Business Process Reengineering (BPR) 99
Business Week 64, 66, 81, 82

Callahan, J. 115, 116
Carpenter, Donna 141
Carroll, D. T. 66, 67, 69, 71, 85
Carter, P. 14, 15
causal connections 143
change management 95
Chaos theory 88–89
'chaotic' nature 84
Chiapello, E. 3, 203
A Christmas Carol (Dickens) 222n1
The Circle of Innovation (Peters) 100–102, 142, 145, 185, 216, 217, 220
clan system 100
Clark, T. 15–17, 22n11, 22n12
classified tales 199; control 199, 200; equality 201–202; security 202–204
cognitivist models 113, 121
Cohen, Paul 141
collectivism 38
Collins, D. 10, 12, 14, 22n7, 140, 154, 205; *Narrating the Management Guru* 12, 135; *Sloane Rangers* 112
comic story-form 145, 152
Commerce Bank 187
committee-led decision-making 65
common sense 74, 94
communication strategy 27, 28, 86, 116, 141
competitive imperatives 138
complexity theory 4, 75, 88, 89; non-linear dynamic processes 89
conceptual critique: guilty pleasures 71–72; talk and action 70–71
conceptual sophistication 27
contrarians 92
control, classified tales 199, 200
Cornuelle, R. C. 38
corporate: research project 26; scud missiles 91, 93; sponsorship 35–36, 37
correction 87
counter-factual history 24
counternarrative approaches 114
Crainer, S. 9, 10, 11, 12, 24, 29, 30, 31, 52, 86, 94, 97, 98; excellence project genesis 29; McKinsey 7-S model 29; summary position 24
Creech, Bill 171
Critical Perspectives on International Business journal 53
criticisms 33, 53, 64, 69, 84–86, 95, 163
The Crown 133

'crypto-evangelist' project 163
culture 16, 22n7, 32, 47, 57, 60, 61, 75, 83, 174, 187, 190, 192, 219, 228
customer 62, 172, 174; intelligence 172; service issue 167, 183

Dana 168, 169
Daniel, Ron 31, 41
Dart Industries in Los Angeles 26
decision-making powers 35, 37, 40, 64
DeLamarter, R. T. 68
Deloitte 218–219
Delta Airlines 145
Denning, S. 122–124, 134; *The Springboard* 122
design problems 67
Disney 147, 206
Domino's 171, 174, 176
Drucker Day 35
Drucker, Peter 22n7, 65–66

Eastwood, Clint 133
economic crisis 56, 75
The Economist 52, 154
effective organizations 30
The Emerging Japanese Superstate (Kahn) 56
emotion 78, 122, 143, 218
empowerment 171, 176
enactment 117, 120
enigma machines 162
entrepreneurship 62
epic tales 144–145, 151–152
epiphany 227
Epstein, Jeffrey 137n5
equality-inequality duality 201–202
Esler, G. 121, 122, 124
evangelical mission 16
The Excellence Dividend (Peters) 84, 107–109, 142, 154, 158–159, 187, 195, 216, 219
excellence project 2–4, 6, 111, 112, 181, 191, 198–200, 204, 222; aims and scope 26; competitive context 29–31; corporate sponsorship 35–36; enigma machines 162; exemplars of 162–163; internal machinations 31–38; Japanese management 40–46; Latourian appreciation 29; liberal democracies 163; McKinsey effect 35; McKinsey 7-S framework 25–29; methodology of 67; nationalist trope 36; organization man 38–40; representing excellence 165–188; storytelling 37–38, 164–165; system

is to blame! 36–37; word-of-mouth
marketing 37
excellent organizations 26, 223
The Experience Curve 30

fading process 132
'failed culture of excellence' 64, 65
FedEx 183
Fiedler, F. E. 79
filtering process 131
financial performance 58, 59
The Financial Post 73
Fiorina, Carly 219
fitting process 133
fixed qualities 143
Fleck, Arthur 130, 131
focusing process 131
Forbes 42
'forensic reading' 134
Fortune 42
Fortune 500 98
framing process 130–131
Frank, T. 3
fusing process 132

Gabriel, Y. 125–131, 130, 134, 135, 139,
143–144, 145, 148, 150, 151, 152, 153
Gallie, W. B. 129
Gates, B. 73
Geneen, H. S. 42, 44, 66
General Motors 169; *Toyota* collaboration 46
generic attributions 143
Ghostbusters 132
Gibbs, A. 190n1
GNP growth rate 57
Goldblum, Jeff 88
Google 2
gotcha moment 64
Graham, Billy 16
Greatbatch, D. 15–17, 22n12
Greenwood, R. 18
Grint, K. 20, 79, 88, 89, 90
Guest, David 66, 67, 69, 70, 71
Gulf War 91, 92
gurudom 142
guru theory 17–20, 93, 95, 108, 203, 208,
209, 222, 230

Handy, Charles 82
happy atom 25, 29, 50, 51, 57
'hard s' factors 27, 57, 63
Harvard Business Review (Magazine) 14, 17,
126, 151, 219
Hayes, R. H. 66

Heller, R. 12, 35, 52, 53, 64, 68, 69;
Management Today 12
Henzler, Herb 32
Herbert, Gavin 193
Hersey, P. 79
Hewlett-Packard (HP) 30, 169, 170,
171, 219
Hindle, T. 18
Honda Motor Company 42
Höpfl, H. 207, 208, 222
Huczynski, A. A. 17–19, 86, 95
Human Relations School 39
Hyatt, J. 56, 198, 199

IBM 169, 187; customer service issue
167–168
If Not Now, When? (Levi) 131–132
implementation 31, 32
individualism 38
Ingersoll-Rand 178
innovation/responsiveness 60
In Search of Excellence (Peters and Waterman)
1–3, 5–7, 9–10, 12, 14, 19, 24, 25, 32, 33,
38, 46, 50, 55, 57, 60, 63, 65–67, 70–72,
75, 111, 140, *140,* 144, 148, 156–158,
162, 197–199, 208, 209, 223, 224, 225;
foundations of 162; narrative processes
163; storyworld 165–166
internal machinations, McKinsey:
excellence project success 35–38;
management knowledge market 34–35;
Organization Man 38–40
interpretation 117, 119
intuition 191, 224
Iraqi military 91

Jackson, N. 14, 15
Jaedicke, Robert 8
Japanese: business success 57; economic
mission 56; economic success 56;
management practices 56
Joker 130, 131
Jones, James 16
Jones, R. V. 93
Jurassic Park film 88

Kahn, H. 56; *The Emerging Japanese
Superstate* 56
Kamata, S. 43
Kaplan Thaler Advertising Agency 195
Kaplan Thaler, Linda 195
Kelleher, Herb 217
Kiechel, W. 1, 7, 37, 50, 71, 82, 83
Kieser, A. 86

Kissinger, Henry 10
the Kool-Aid test 16–17
Kraus, Max 194

Latour, B. 4, 23, 46, 91, 92, 111–114
laughter 144, 145, 148
'laws of fiction' 130
leadership 39, 75; elusive qualities of 87; emotional intelligence 78; leadership difference 78–80; religious metaphor and allusion 76–77; 'situational' appreciation 79; soft and hard factors 77–78
Lennon, John 22n6
Leonard, Carole 53
Leonard, Stew 171, 173
Letiche, H. 88, 90, 91
Levi, Primo 131, 132; *If Not Now, When?* 131–132
Lewis, J. 87
Liberation Management (Peters) 50, 53, 91–97, 143, 178, 181, 193, 201, 211
lifetime employment 43
Lischinsky, A. 20
The Little BIG Things (Peters) 106–107, 142, 154–156, 187, 194, 216, 219
Llewellyn, S. 114
The Los Angeles Times 65
Lutz, B. 64, 65

3M 170
Maidique, M. A. 69, 151, 198
management 111, 112; American system 42; anxiety and hierarchy in 191–204; appreciation of 25; balanced approach to 58; Boston Matrix 30; as common sense 74–75; 'conventional' account 66; dualistic vision 84; Experience Curve 30; Japanese approach to 49n13; knowledge 50, 53; 'loose' system 63; and organization studies 85; permanent revolution 85; Peters' books on *11*; texts/narratives 3, 14, 121, 142, 153; theatre 52, 53; women in 205–222
Management by Wandering Around (MBWA) 76, 149, 228
management guru 7, 8, 13–16, 17, 18, 20, 52, 53, 72, 82, 111, 136, 140, 163, 223–224
Management Gurus: A Research Overview (Collins) 7
management stories: anxiety and hierarchy in 191–204; women in 205–222
management theory 65

Management Today (Heller) 12
managerial control 90, 199, 200
managerial leaders 58, 76, 78, 87, 91, 99, 124
managers 5, 7, 15, 17, 18, 19, 29, 37, 39, 42, 44–46, 57, 63, 70, 71, 76, 78, 79, 84–86, 88, 90, 94, 95, 98, 112, 113, 121, 124, 150, 153, 169, 180, 198, 200, 210, 217, 228
market developments 30
Martin, J. 6, 191–193, *193,* 197, 199, 200, 202, 204
McBeth, M. 139
McConkie, M. L. 198
McCracken, Douglas 218, 219
McDonald, D. 197
McHugh, David 2, 21n2
McKinsey and Co. 7–9, 26, 27, 31, 32, 37, 47, 55, 111, 224
McKinsey 7-S framework 4, 19, 21, 24–29, *29,* 35, 50, 224; internal machinations 31–38; Peters' narratives of business 51; philosophical rationalization 51
McNamara, Robert 66
McPherson, Rene 168, 200
Michaelson, C. 115, 116
Middlebrook, M. 117, 118
middle-managers 153
Midnight in the Garden of Good and Evil (Berendt) 132–133
Milken, Michael 72
Milliken 171, 172
Mitchell, Gerald 200, 202
Mitchell, Liz 141
Mitchell, T. R. 71, 203, 204
Monsanto, Steve 182
Morgan, Peter 133
Moriguchi, C. 43
motive 143

Narrating the Management Guru (Collins) 12, 135
narrative approach 112–115, 126, 134–135, 137n1, 192, 199
narratology 113, 114, 125, 134, 191, 226
nationalist trope 36
'normal accidents' 195

The Observer 56
Ono, H. 43
operations 30, 31
opinions 129–130
opportunity 24
order generating rules 90

orderly disorder 89–90
organization 30; American experience 39;
   capability 27; as cultural manifestations
   192; dualistic vision 84, 199, *199*;
   effectiveness 9, 25, 26, 30, 31; enactment
   117; as focus for inquiry 112–116;
   interpretation 117; narrative studies of
   115; nature of 116–117; opinions 129–
   130; paradox 6; poetic tales 130–134;
   as polyphony 124–126; proto-stories
   130; reports 129; rhetoric 207–208;
   sensegiving 121; sensemaking 121–124;
   Wright, Lauren 117, 118–121
organizational stories: as cultural
   manifestations 192; enactment 117; as
   focus for inquiry 112–116; interpretation
   117; nature of 116–117; opinions 129–
   130; poetic tales 130–134; as polyphony
   124–126; proto-stories 130; reports 129;
   sensegiving 121; sensemaking 121–124;
   Wright, Lauren 117, 118–121
organizational storytelling 113–137, 138,
   139–140, *140*, 153; core concerns 225;
   decline in Peters' storytelling 140–142;
   introduction of 111–112; mapping of
   151–154; power of 226; resurgence of
   143
Organization Man 39
Organization Practice 30, 32, 40, 47, 123
organization theory 89
orthodox narratives 77, 100, 113, 114, 134,
   163, 198, 225
Orwell, George 97
outline analysis 31

Panasonic 42, 46
Pascale, R. T. 24–27, 29, 31, 41–44, 47, 56,
   57, 190, 228, 230
A Passion for Excellence (Peters and Austin)
   5, 10, 50, 54, 73, 84, 140, *140*, 146, 149,
   150, 171, 193, 211
paternalism 45
Patnode, Randy 141
Pattison, S. 15, 76
"people stuff" 31, 32
PepsiCo 61
permanent revolution 85
Perrow, C. 195
Peters, Tom 25, 28–33, 36, 37; *The Circle
   of Innovation* 100–102, 142, 145, 185,
   216, 217, 220; *The Excellence Dividend*
   84, 107–109, 142, 154, 158–159, 187,
   195, 216, 219; *Fortune 500* 98; *Liberation
   Management* 50, 53, 91–97, 143, 178, 181,

193, 201, 211; *The Little BIG Things* 106–
   107; *TheLittle BIG Things* 106–107, 142,
   154–156, 187, 194, 216, 219; *A Passion
   for Excellence* 5, 10, 50, 54, 73, 84, 140,
   140, 146, 149, 150, 193, 211; *The Pursuit
   of Wow* 54, 97–100, 141, 182, 183, 216;
   Re-imagine 8, 102–106, 142, 152, 154,
   159, 161, 186, 216, 218–220, 219, 220; *In
   Search of Excellence* 1–3, 5–7, 9–10, 12, 14,
   19, 24, 25, 32, 33, 38, 46, 50, 55, 57, 60,
   63, 65–67, 70–72, 75, 84, 111, 140, *140,*
   144, 148, 156–158, 162, 197–199, 208,
   209, 223, 224, 225; *Thriving on Chaos* 50,
   53, 83, 84–86, 151, 176, 177, 211, 216;
   The Tom Peters Seminar 97–100, 141, 142,
   152, 182; *see alsoindividual entries*
Pettigrew, A. M. 95
Phillips, Julian 27
Pio, E. 15
Pitt, L. 69
plurality 114
poetic modes 144; ambiguous tales 148–
   151; comic story-form 145; epic form
   144–145; romantic tale 147–148; tragi-
   comic tales 148; tragic tale 146–147
poetic tales 130–134, 139, 143–144
poetic tropes 143–144
poetry 207–208
policy-makers 47, 56
political machinations 31
polyphony: organizational stories as
   124–126
popular management 1, 3, 15, 17–18, 89,
   111, 112, 116, 117, 121, 134, 136, 162,
   199, 203, 205, 209, 222
Price, R. 139
Private Eye 133
problem identification 109, 119
pro-business evangelism 225
Proctor & Gamble 211
productivity 62
'professional biographies' 11–12
professional service firm 203
project excellence 226–227, 228, 229
Protestantism 38
proto-stories 130
providential significance 143
pseudo-scientific label 67
The Pursuit of Wow (Peters) 54, 97–100, 141,
   182, 183, 216

quality 154–159
quantity 154–159
quotations 142

'ready-made' science 24; *versus* science-in-the-making 4–7
reflexivity 114–115
Reich, Robert 143, 218
Re-imagine (Peters) 8, 102–106, 142, 152, 154, 159, 161, 186, 216, 218–220, 219, 220
The Renewal Factor (Waterman) 36
reports 129, 143
responsibility 143
rhetoric 207–208
Rhodes, C. 114–116
Richman, Tom 141
Roberts, Joanne 53–54
romantic tale 147–148, 152–153
Royal Dutch Shell 25, 48n4
Roy, Kenneth 16
Ryan, Leo 16

Sampson, A. 39, 46, 54
Sargent, Susan 217
Schaefer, Don 212
Schaefer, William Donald 174–175
Schlumberger 59
Schultz, Howard 155
Schwartz, Laurie 212
science-in-the-making: ready-made science *versus* 4–7
'scissors crisis' 203
Scottish mission 16
Scott, Walter Sir. 100
Scrooge, Ebenezer 211, 222n1
security-insecurity duality 202–204
self-aggrandizement 85
self-organization 90
sensegiving 112, 116, 121, 122, 124, 125, 128, 134–136, 141, 154, 191, 197, 198, 200, 204, 207, 208
sensemaking 116, 117, 120, 121–124, 128, 136, 191
Shea Schultz, Heather 206
signalling 141
Sillitoe, A. 129, 130
Simmons, Charlie 141
Sims, David 153
'six-s' framework 27
Sloane Rangers (Collins) 112
Smith, Wayne 181
'9-S' model 28
social-technical totality 24, 25, 28
The Sociological Imagination (Wright-Mills) 137n3
soft-s factors 27, 51, 58, 63
soft stuff 31, 32, 48n5

Southwest Airlines 185, 187
The Springboard (Denning) 122
springboard stories 122, 124
Stayer, Ralph 181
Steinbeck, John 189
Stewart, M. 22n9, 162–163, 184
Stewart, Willie 21
stories 37–38, 127; definition of 129; as narratives 139, 143; Peters' major works 139–140, *140*; practices and preferences 143; proto-stories 130; re-told 139; storyworld curation 134–136; *see also* management stories; organizational stories
storytelling 5, 113–137, 123, 125, 127–129, 138, 139–140, *140,* 153, 199; core concerns 225; decline in Peters' storytelling 140–142; introduction of 111–112; mapping of 151–154; power of 226; practices 4, 6, 112, 136, 163, 188, 189, 200, 204, 220, 221, 225–227, 229; resurgence of 143
strategy 30, 31
structure 30
structured interview process 58
subjectivity 115
Suddaby, R. 18
superordinate goals 27
system is to blame! 36–37

Taylor, D. J. 39
temporality 114
Tennant Company 176
terse tales 112, 126–129
Thatcher, Mark 133
'the Other' 207
Thompson, Paul 2, 21n2
Thriving on Chaos (Peters) 50, 53, 83, 84–86, 151, 176, 177, 211, 216
The Times 53
The Tom Peters Seminar (Peters) 97–100, 141, 142, 152, 182
Total Quality Management (TQM) 28
Townsend, R. 33
tragi-comic tales 146–147, 148, 151
truths 163, 169
Tsoukas, H. 113, 121
Tuchman, Barbara 85, 87
Turkina, O. 125, 137n4
Twitter 2, 12, 106, 132
Tyler, M. 208, 218

unclassified tales 197–199
Union Pacific 178, 179
uniqueness paradox 192–196, *193*

United States (US) 25, 39, 56; automobile industry 64; business excellence 41; business practice 163; car industry 64; economic decline 66; economy 66, 75; management systems 36, 41; prison system 181
unity 143
University of Auckland Business School 142
unsettling world 90–91

Van der Merwe, R. 69
Verifone 183

Wang Corporation 82
Waterman, R. 1, 4, 7, 9, 24, 25, 27–30, 33, 36, 37, 41, 47, 48n4, 55–71, 60, 68, 82, 85, 123, 144–145, 197, 198, 200, 202, 209, 210, 223, 224; *In Search of Excellence* 1–3, 5–7, 9–10, 12, 14, 19, 111, 197–199, 208, 209
Watson, T. J. 48–49n7, 48n7, 68, 70
Wayne, Bruce 130
Weick, K. 70, 119, 120, 121, 126
The Western Electric Company 45, 46
Whitfield, D. 65
Whyte, W. H. 38, 39, 44
Williams, K. 95
WL Gore 211
women: in 1982–1996 209–216; in excellence project 6; in management stories 205–222; in post 1996 216–220; tales of 208–220, **209**; in Tom Peters' storyworld 208–220, **209**
women's thing 205, 206–207, 216, 221, 222; rhetoric and poetry 207–208

word-of-mouth marketing 37
work intensification 140
workplace: moral economy 138; Peters' separation 141
works, Peters 1982–1985: autonomy and entrepreneurship 62; bias for action 61–62; close to the customer 62; conceptual critique 67–70; disappointing search 66; early 1980s recession 56; excellence, passion for 72–76; guilty pleasures 71–72; hands-on, value driven 62; Japanese economic success 56–61; leadership practice 76–80; loose-tight properties 63–64; methodological critique 66–67; Peters' biographers 52–55; productivity through people 62; *In Search of Excellence* 55; simple form, lean staff 63; stick to the knitting 62–63; talk and action 70–71
works, Peters 1987–2018: Black Monday 86–88; Chaos theory 88–89; *The Circle of Innovation* 100–102; *The Excellence Dividend* 107–109; liberation management 91–97; *The Little BIG Things* 106–107; orderly disorder 89–90; *The Pursuit of Wow* 97–100; *Re-imagine* 102–106; *Thriving on Chaos* 84–86; *The Tom Peters Seminar* 97–100; unsettling world 90–91
Wright, Lauren 117, 118–121
Wright-Mills, C. 22n7, 137n3; *The Sociological Imagination* 137n3

Young, John 30

Printed in the United States
by Baker & Taylor Publisher Services